The Amazing Love of Paul's Model Church

How the Thessalonians became disciples and reached their region with the Gospel

Edward N. Gross

David Russell Tulloch

Parson's Porch. & Book Publishing Company

Turning words into books & Turning books into bread

The Amazing Love of Paul's Model Church: How the Thessalonians became disciples and reached their region with the Gospel

ISBN: Softcover 978-1-949888-31-7
Copyright © 2017 by Edward N. Gross

All scripture quotations are from the New International Version (NIV) published by HarperCollins Christian Publishers.

To order additional copies of this book, contact:

Parson's Porch Books
1-423-475-7308
www.parsonsporch.com

Parson's Porch Books is an imprint of **Parson's Porch & Book Publishers** in Cleveland, Tennessee, which has double focus. We focus on the needs of creative writers who need a professional publisher to get their work to market, **&** we also focus on the needs of others by sharing our profits with those who struggle in poverty to meet their basic needs of food, clothing, shelter and safety.

Endorsements

In The Amazing Love of Paul's Model Church, *Ed Gross blends his burning passion for discipleship, his educational expertise and his on-the-ground experience of actually discipling people into an equipping resource. This book helps readers explore Paul's ministry to the Thessalonians while also expounding upon our ministry today. Few people I know are as passionate about Jesus-oriented discipleship – and who live it out – as faithfully as Ed. If you're serious about discipleship and formation in the Church today, you'll find this book to be enriching, challenging and beneficial to your life and ministry."*

Rev. J.R. Briggs
Pastor, The Renew Community
Founder, Kairos Partnerships
Author, *Ministry Mantras*

Paul, one of the greatest Christians and most successful church planters, called just ONE of his church plants his "model church," the Thessalonians, who both opened their homes and their hearts to a man hunted and persecuted. This book reveals the power of love to help disciples not only survive, but become one of the greatest testimonies in all of church history. Its message is especially relevant in our day of growing anti-Christian sentiments. Author Ed Gross does a wonderful job outlining the Thessalonians story, detailing everything they represented and offering a wonderful in-depth look at the Thessalonians

From *The Red River City Review*

This book on the church of Thessalonica confronts us as Bible-believing Christians with the strategic and visionary way early followers of Christ understood the good news of the Gospel, internalized it and lived accordingly--with great impact. Rev. Dr. Ed Gross succeeds in confronting Christian readers with the amazing love of God in and through the life and witness of the Thessalonians. Through reading, reflection and discussion the reader will feel the pressure early Christians and those still persecuted faced, as well as the glorious hope they embraced in the midst of harsh conditions - and through it may experience growth in understanding discipleship and being true witnesses of the risen Christ.

Rev. Dr. Henk Stoker.
Professor in Apologetics and Ethics,
North-West University, Potchefstroom, South Africa;
and Vice-Rector of the Theological School of the Reformed Churches of South Africa

In The Amazing Love of Paul's Model Church Ed Gross challenges us to see beyond a gospel of sin management to the adventure of surrender to the King of Kings. Ed not only guides us thru Paul's relationship with the Thessalonians but after each short chapter, he invites us to get our fingerprints on this message and knead it into our lives.

Rev. Roy Moran, author Spent Matches, igniting a signal fire for the spiritually dissatisfied.

This is truly a labor of love. Well-crafted by incorporating the text of I Thessalonians along with scores of other passages, it is a full treatment of the biblical understanding of love which is the ground of all fruitful discipleship. Designed to be studied and shared, it is composed of brief chapters with engaging questions for reflection and responsive action. However, this is no doctrinaire "how-to" book of techniques and tricks for building up your church or outreach program. Rather, it is a mature, thoughtful, and deeply spiritual guide which seeks to honor the diversity of the Christian faith community while challenging us all to be centered on the love of Jesus Christ as the motivating force to spread the Gospel of his kingdom. Not unmindful of the long-standing differences of interpretation and denominational preferences among Evangelicals, Ed Gross has been able to respectfully challenge all faithful Christians to place their beliefs about the necessity of conversion into the context of loving people into the kingdom just as Christ himself has done.

Rev. Lin Crowe – The Navigators and Kingdom Care Reentry Network

Without any exaggeration, I can say that I have seen more of God's love through Ed Gross than anyone else I've ever known. In the way that he preaches, in the way that he prays, and in the way he's discipled me. He has been gripped deeply by God's love for us through Christ. In a way that most of know we're 'supposed' to be, but often aren't. That shows through in everything he does. Including this book, which clearly reflects his passion for Christ, careful attention to Scripture, and how they connect with our real, everyday lives. The reflection questions also challenge us to slow down and respond practically, in faith, to God's love.

Rev Bryan Stoudt – the Christian Medical and Dental Association

Dr. Gross continues to enlighten and challenge his readers on Biblical discipleship. In "Are You a Christian or a Disciple" and Disciples Obey," readers are ejected out of their comfort zones to ask "can I be a Christian and not a Disciple?" What were Jesus' expectations when He said "Follow Me?" "Can I become a Christian, go to heaven, and not follow Jesus?"

In The Amazing Love of Paul's Model Church, *Dr. Gross reveals how the Apostle Paul discipled the young Thessalonian church to obediently follow Jesus, in very difficult times and faithfully spread the Gospel from a faith that worked through steadfast love. This timely book is a must-read for anyone desiring to be a true disciple of Jesus. It is my prayer that the Holy Spirit open our hearts, empowering obedient disciples to live out and share the truth of the whole gospel in Christ's love.*

Bruce Cobb – Retired Master Chief Petty Officer US Navy
Former Missionary - International Mission Board

Dedication

As Jesus blessed all who are persecuted for His sake, I dedicate this book to all the followers of Jesus who are being persecuted for their love and obedience to our Lord Jesus Christ and to their families, churches and nations together with all people and organizations devoted to the caring and praying for Christ's persecuted followers.

Then Jesus said, If any one will come after Me, he must deny himself, take up his cross daily and follow Me. (Luke 9:23)

Table of Content

Preface

Which model is the best to follow today?

Who's the best Christian you know? Or the church that you think is really impressive? The present model you wish everyone had a chance to experience. Is it your local congregation? Or someone in it? I hope so. But maybe your Christian life and church experience have not been all that special, leaving you without a strong opinion. I hope what you are reading will change that. And us all. This book is about the love of Jesus. How His love, at one time, so characterized a church that its growth and impact were legendary. I'll show you how God took a group of very diverse people and made them one, infusing in them a love of such power that they became the subject of everyone's conversation. With the outcome of the Lord Jesus being lifted up as the living Savior personally involved in and through them. He was amazingly "building His church, and the gates of hell could not overcome it" (Matt 16:18).

We know this is what actually happened because Paul and others witnessed and wrote about the Thessalonians. Paul, guided by the Holy Spirit, wrote: **"The Lord's message rang out from you not only in Macedonia and Achaia (modern day Greece)—your faith in God has become known everywhere. Therefore we do not need to say anything about it"** (1 Thes 1:8). Every Christian who takes the Great Commission and holy living seriously should be challenged and encouraged by this fresh, long look at the Thessalonians. It's written for all of you who know something is missing. For you who belong to small churches. And this look is needed by many of you in large churches because you still feel that something very basic is missing in your life. This is written for Christians who have never been discipled in the way Jesus, the apostles and the early church made disciples.[1]

We will see that Paul presents the Thessalonian believers as special. As believers who really understood the Christian life. So, he promoted the Thessalonian Church as the **"model"** church in many ways. Did you know that 1 Thessalonians was very likely Paul's first biblical letter? Comparing him to Moses, it was his "Genesis" for Christian living and church growth. Even though Paul mentioned them as a rare and exemplary church, few evangelical Christians or churches today understand what the model was. And why it

---

[1] You might want to read my, *Are You a Christian or a Disciple? Rediscovering and Renewing New Testament Discipleship*. Written in 2014, it carefully shows how much of western Christianity has lost the meaning and power of 1st century discipleship and how a global renewal of biblical discipleship is happening, with amazing fruit in the most astonishing places.

succeeded in the face of nearly impossible odds. As one Evangelical leader noted,

> "If Paul sat down to write a letter to the average church–to your church–how would he begin the letter? What would he thank God for? ...Paul paid these Christians the ultimate compliment, 'And so,' he wrote, 'you became a model to all the believers in Macedonia and Achaia.' (I Thes 1:7). Leon Morris calls this tribute 'high praise.' Why? Because Paul gave this distinction to no other church."[2]

So what was the big deal? Here it is–the Thessalonians were discipled by Paul to reach their region and beyond by a lifestyle of sacrificial acts of love combined with a quiet but relentless gospel witness that was expressed with absolute hope in Jesus Christ's return and ultimate victory. And according to the inspired Word of God—that is exactly what they did!

This book isn't about the Christian life as many of us have lived it. Nor of evangelism, missions, or church planting as most of us have been taught to do them. The Thessalonian model is like nothing many of us have ever seen. But we have all deeply longed for it. So, following their example will take most of us on a new journey. Not brand new, of course. All Christians know that "love works." But many of us have not made love the center of our lives and mission. As the Thessalonians did by the Spirit's power through the Christ-like discipling of Paul and his mission team. I will lead you through four phases as we explore the superpower that these early disciples were for Christ. We'll look first at "Love Being Challenged," noting the incredible opposition faced by the Thessalonians. This will prove to be a real encouragement and model for the many followers of Jesus who are persecuted for their faith today. Then we will examine "Love Taking Root," and carefully analyze the strategic first steps that were taken by Paul through the Spirit in developing God's own love in the lives of those he was discipling. Thirdly, we'll settle into investigating "Love's Amazing Look." This lengthiest part of the book will describe the lives of the Thessalonians and the impact they had on the region and world as they sought to fulfill the Great Commission. Finally, we will see "Love Working Today" in a short section that applies what we have learned from the Thessalonians to ourselves, our Western culture and our present-day churches.

Let's look forward to traveling together down this road with many a strange twist and turn. Here's a few of the surprises many of you will experience as you read. When we Western Christians look at the world of these 1st-century believers, it stuns us to see:

---

[2] G Getz, *Standing Firm When You'd Rather Retreat: Based on 1 Thessalonians* (Ventura, CA: Regal Books 1986), pp 18,36.

• That pure Christ-like love can be the most powerful thing an unbeliever has ever encountered. More powerful in its lasting effect on them than the marvel of actually seeing a miracle.

• How quickly the Thessalonians became Christ's disciples and Paul's model church (we would likely expect it would take a long time and be a slow process to become an example for all other Christian churches).

• How thoroughly they impacted their entire region by staying put and not running away or giving up under the most extreme persecution.

• How significantly God used every disciple (especially the less educated and most ordinary ones) in reaching the region.

• How lavishly they gave of themselves without complaining or expecting anything in return.

• How real the presence of Jesus was to them and how powerfully the Spirit flowed through their daily lives to interact courageously with a culture much more sexually supercharged and violently hostile to the gospel than ours today.

The Spirit of God is an inviting Spirit. "**The Spirit and the bride say, 'Come!' And let him who hears say, 'Come!' Whoever is thirsty, let him come; and whoever wishes, let him take the free gift of the water of life**" (Rev 22:17). He blesses much of what we sincerely do in inviting others to Christ. But not all we have been taught about evangelism and discipling reflects His best wisdom on how best to impact others with the gospel. This book is not an attack on others or their counsel. We thank God for them and for much of what we have learned under their guidance. There are many ways to serve God. We are to **"become all things to all men so that by all means [we] might save some"** (1 Cor. 9:22b). But there must be something fueling all those diverse efforts, if they are really following the example of Jesus. Something similar in them all. That common part would be the Spirit and love of God. Jesus promised to all that His gift to them would be the Spirit. And the Spirit's first fruit is love. As He said,

> "'Whoever believes in me, as the Scripture has said, streams of living water will flow from within him.' By this he meant the Spirit, whom those who believed in him were later to receive. Up to that time the Spirit had not been given, since Jesus had not yet been glorified" (John 7:38-39; see also Gal 5:22; Rom 5:5).

13

That experience, sadly, is not often true in many of our hearts. In our worship, witness and work. We often stop the loving flow of God's Spirit from pouring through us to others. I hope that as you read, you will *feel* what I am writing about. That the love that shocked and changed their region can do the same through you as you follow Jesus as His disciples today.

We all need each other if Christ's love is to consume us. This book will be most useful when read and applied together with other disciples. You might be surprised how rare such people are today. Even in our churches! When Paul looked at the Thessalonian Church, he saw something different about their love. It was more obvious in them than in most of the other churches he planted. And he said so. Strongly and clearly. Be ready to marvel at what God can do through loving hearts. I pray that you will learn much and be forever changed by what the Spirit inspired Paul to write about the amazing grace God poured into and through the lives of these Thessalonian disciples of Jesus.

Part One - Love Being Challenged

Chapter 1

Are many of us dangerously different from early Christians?

The short answer is, YES. You sense it and so do I. This book will help confirm that fact, I hope. Irrefutably but kindly. You see, I am your brother–I wrestle with the very temptations that have hindered many of us. Materialism. Selfishness. Wealth. Comfort. Freedom. Lust. Conformity. Fear of man. I hate these weaknesses and, like you, really want to go in a very different and more fruitful direction. But I need YOU to come with me and help me. We need one another. Let's be humbled and confess our sins together. Stimulate one another's repentance. What do you say? Do you long for a Christian faith that is truly powerful and productive–without being either scary or stupid? I do. And I am finding it through the renewal of biblical discipleship that is occurring globally and in me. I have discovered that the soil out of which 1st century Christianity grew was the soil of discipleship. **"The disciples were called Christians first at Antioch"** (Acts 11:26b). The term "Christian" would never have been coined by the pagans in Antioch unless they were observing true disciples of Christ. One of my goals for all who read this book is that every Christian will become a disciple of Jesus.[3]

In each short chapter I will ask key questions that some of us have danced around far too long. Questions arising from the biblical text. Questions that embarrass the existing norms embraced by many of us as evangelical Christians. Norms that have allowed us to settle for far less than our early Christian brothers and sisters did. I think the life most of us have chosen to live would hardly be recognized as Christian by the early followers of Christ, like the Thessalonians. But does that matter to you? Does it bother you that the same verses we hold and quote from are producing far different responses today in us than they did in them? Does that strike you as being dangerous? Frightening? It should.

I will take you into the world of the Thessalonians and of Paul through these questions. I will help you feel the pressure they faced and the glorious hope they embraced in the midst of mind boggling conditions. And I will encourage you to join me in repenting of whatever has neutralized the

---

[3] To help understand the difference between Christ's early disciples and many of today's Christians see such contemporary works as Bill Hull's Choose the Life, Jerry Trousdale's Miraculous Movements, Kyle Idleman's Not a Fan, David Platt's Radical, David Watson's Contagious Disciple Making, Juan Carlos Ortiz' Make Disciples! and my, Disciples Obey.

power of the gospel in our lives today so we can join them as being true witnesses of the risen Christ.

I love you, my brothers and sisters in Christ. I do not need to know you to love you. If we met today, we would experience His bonding love and be united by it. Together we would enjoy our brotherhood in His Family. But you won't see me today. So, I hope you will sense God's love pouring through me to you in each of the following pages. I expect that you will recognize it as a familiar love—as the Spirit's love. And I pray that it will draw us together—all of us who have the Spirit. All of us who trust in Jesus for our salvation and life. Let us let love lead us. Define us. Transform us and the world in which we live. Like the amazing Thessalonians did.

For Reflection and Discuss

1. What is the difference between Christ's command "make disciples," and our practice of making Christians?
2. Do you see how the very fulfillment of the Great Commission could be jeopardized by simply misunderstanding the word "disciple?"

Chapter 2

So how did it all begin with Paul and the Thessalonians?

"When they had passed through Amphipolis and Apollonia, they came to Thessalonica, where there was a Jewish synagogue. As his custom was, Paul went into the synagogue, and on three Sabbath days he reasoned with them from the Scriptures, explaining and proving that the Christ had to suffer and rise from the dead. 'This Jesus I am proclaiming to you is the Christ,' he said. Some of the Jews were persuaded and joined Paul and Silas, as did a large number of God-fearing Greeks and not a few prominent women. But the Jews were jealous; so they rounded up some bad characters from the marketplace, formed a mob and started a riot in the city. They rushed to Jason's house in search of Paul and Silas in order to bring them out to the crowd. But when they did not find them, they dragged Jason and some other brothers before the city officials, shouting: 'These men who have caused trouble all over the world have now come here, and Jason has welcomed them into his house. They are all defying Caesar's decrees, saying that there is another king, one called Jesus.' When they heard this, the crowd and the city officials were thrown into turmoil. Then they made Jason and the others post bond and let them go. As soon as it was night, the brothers sent Paul and Silas away to Berea." (Acts 17:1-10a).

Paul had just left Philippi, a Roman colony about 100 miles east of Thessalonica. How did things go for him there? He wrote, **"We had previously suffered and been insulted in Philippi, as you know, but with the help of our God we dared to tell you his gospel in spite of strong opposition**" (1 Thes 2:2). In fact, Paul and Silas had been **"seized and dragged into the marketplace"** (Acts 16:19) where the **"magistrates ordered them to be stripped and beaten,"** which Luke described as being **"severely flogged"** after which they were **"thrown into prison"** where the jailer **"put them in the inner cell and fastened their feet with stocks"** (Acts 16:22-24).

This took place a very short time, maybe less than a week, before Paul's team entered Thessalonica. Paul arrived with fresh wounds. But rejoicing. How would you receive such a messenger if he were sent to you today? Publicly shamed. Universally opposed. A dangerous man arriving on your doorstep in a very dangerous time with a very dangerous message. Would you have the faith to embrace him and the new day that was dawning all around him? Breaking forth with blood and suffering. Or would you continue down your own path? Safe and secure, to be sure—but missing the new way that the Holy Spirit was offering you. Too scared to be seen with him much less to listen to his message. A message that reportedly challenged the reigning Roman emperor--Claudius Caesar. How are you responding to that same message today? What would become of a person who dared to defy the decrees of a most-powerful Caesar? Who chose to follow Jesus instead? Were Jason and the others mad or sane?

Bring this home to your own life. What do you think will become of you if you do the same? It is not what you think. What you fear. What the lying spirit, Satan, subtly suggests to your mind. There is much more here than meets the eye. Instead, you will see the fact of God's faithfulness at work in and through you, His weak child. Read on and be amazed with the rest of this story. A story that I know will challenge and encourage you by considering the lives of the amazing Thessalonians.

For Reflection and Discuss

1. If you have ever been a part of a church plant or viewed a church being planted, note the differences between it and this one planted by Paul.
2. Would you join Paul's church or opt for another choice?

Chapter 3

Paul, why were you beaten in Philippi?

That would not have been a bad question to start with. There he was in the popular and prospering city of Thessalonica. The largest of all Macedonian cities. Rivaling even Philippi. He had traveled there on the Via Egnatia, the main trade route linking Rome with the Eastern world and to all its exotic wealth. Paul saw how good the Thessalonian's had it. Rome was now smiling on them again.

They hadn't been too smart a few years back when they had complained against emperor Tiberius (14-37AD) concerning taxes. That resulted in their demotion to a lower state status (imperial province) and less privileges, which Claudius (41-54AD) had recently reversed (44AD), raising them back to the status of senatorial province. But Philippi was a Roman Colony, modeled after Rome itself and enjoying special honors, so they were even more closely linked with Caesar than were the Thessalonians. The Thessalonians now knew where their bread was buttered and had to be careful. So someone got to the point and asked, "If you don't mind my asking, what happened to you in Philippi?"

Paul would have told the amazing story of the salvation of the demonized fortune teller, who, becoming a follower of Jesus, refused to serve Satan and her profiteers any longer. Luke was there and later wrote,

> **"When the owners of the slave girl realized that their hope of making money was gone, they seized Paul and Silas and dragged them into the marketplace to face the authorities. They brought them before the magistrates and said, 'These men are Jews, and are throwing our city into an uproar by advocating customs unlawful for us Romans to accept or practice.' The crowd joined in the attack against Paul and Silas, and the magistrates ordered them to be stripped and beaten. After they had been severely flogged, they were thrown into prison, and the jailer was commanded to guard them carefully. Upon receiving such orders, he put them in the inner cell and fastened their feet in the stocks."** (Acts 16:19-24).

To be beaten with rods in those days was unlike any punishment Westerners today could imagine. Shame and pain were the goal. A public example had to be made because Rome ruled by intimidation. Tarnish the

21

reputation and badly hurt the body. Getting caught in the machine that was the Roman Empire was fairly easy. And his being severely and unjustly beaten would have brought Paul sympathy with the Thessalonians. But that was not where Paul was going with this.

He did not have to be beaten. He was a Roman citizen! He could have called out and spared himself the ordeal. But the Thessalonians were now talking to someone who did not regard Roman citizenship and its rights as his most cherished possession. Paul belonged to Jesus, the King of all kings. The true Lord even of Caesar and all his Roman followers. Paul knew that the risen and ascended Jesus was in charge. His being seized, dragged and beaten were all part of a plan. A plan to astonish and to save. And that is what happened in Philippi! The jailer heard Paul and Silas singing instead of sobbing. He trembled physically during the God-sent earthquake that opened the doors and broke the chains. And then he, trembling to the core of his being, flung himself before these men wanting what he knew they had to give. **"Sirs, what must I do to be saved?"** They replied, **"Believe in the Lord Jesus Christ, and you will be saved—you and your household"** (Acts 16:30-31).

Only after the gospel reaped its harvest would Paul let it out that he and Silas were Roman citizens! Thus implying that they had been wrongly punished. Luke writes, **"The officers reported this to the magistrates, and when they heard that Paul and Silas were Roman citizens, they were alarmed. They came to appease them and escorted them from the prison, requesting them to leave the city."** (16:38-39). If Paul wanted to press the issue, these men would have been in serious trouble. But, that was not his point. He had followed the good and humble King who had taught His disciples, **"If anyone would come after me, he must deny himself and take up his cross daily and follow me. For whoever wants to save his life will lose it, but whoever loses his life for me will save it"** (Luke 9:23-24). Suffering or cross-bearing was a major part of His plan. The point is love. The goal is salvation. Even if the love leads to suffering, endure it joyfully. Sing about it. God heals jailers through the wounds of His suffering and singing saints! Many years later, in chains one final time, Paul was still believing this and wrote, **"Therefore I endure everything for the sake of God's elect, that they too may obtain the salvation that is in Christ Jesus, with eternal glory"** (2 Tim 2:10).

Would you listen to someone like Paul and Silas? Of course you would, and so did the Thessalonians and Philippians. The world wants to see a love than can be beaten unjustly and not respond in bitterness. A love that wins. A love that forgives, like Jesus did. Because people just don't always know what they are doing (Lk 23:34). The Thessalonians were amazed by that love when they came in contact with it. Sure, they were influenced by the oppressive and cruel power of Lord Caesar. Their lives had cowered in

22

his shadow. But now they were coming into contact with the transforming power of the Lord Jesus. The winds of hope began to blow over many of their souls for the first time.

For Reflection and Discuss

1. Think of a time when you had to suffer unjustly.
2. Did it end up helping or hurting your spiritual development and witness?

Chapter 4

Paul, why are you doing this? What is driving you?

Sure, the Thessalonians were impressed by Paul's willingness to be cruelly beaten in Philippi. Especially since he could have evaded the suffering. That showed no common devotion. It was obvious that he deeply believed in what he was doing and saying. But that proved nothing except his extraordinary zeal. There were always fanatics passing through the city and claiming to be spiritual insiders. Possessors of higher knowledge. And each one had his own secret motivation. So, before giving him a full hearing, Paul would have to prove to them that he was trustworthy. They would want to know: what made him so sure of himself and his message?

His first public presentation was to the Jews of Thessalonica. In their synagogue. On the Sabbath. As a renowned teacher from Jerusalem, he was invited to speak. His focus was amazing and riveted. For three weeks, he used the Old Testament Scriptures **"explaining and proving that the Messiah had to suffer and rise from the dead"** (Acts 17:2-3). There was that subject again. Suffering. It was an almost unbelievable, yet intriguing claim–a Suffering Savior. A crucified Victor.

There seemed to be many texts that linked the Messiah to suffering. And Paul apparently knew them all. Yet not in the distant and combative spirit of many rabbis. He had forsaken the famous School of Gamaliel to become a disciple of Jesus and to promote His teaching.[4] In a personal and passionate way–he would present the prophecies as one already deeply touched by them. From Eden's promise of Satan bruising Messiah's heel (Gen 3:15) to Daniel's great prophecy of **"the Anointed One who will be cut off"** (Dan. 9:26), Paul would present Jesus as the Christ. He would take them to the Passover (Ex 14) and remind them that **"Christ, our Passover Lamb, has been sacrificed** (1 Cor. 5:7). And would quote David's psalm of suffering (22), stating how verse after verse was repeated by Jesus and fulfilled in Him (as Paul's mission team colleague, Luke, would later record).[5]

It was especially when he came to Isaiah (53) that Paul spoke as few had ever heard a rabbi speak. He declared with authority that it was Jesus who was despised and rejected, a man of sorrows, familiar with suffering. It was He who was stricken by God. Crushed for our iniquities. Punished and wounded. Isaiah's words did not seem ancient when passing through Paul's lips. In fact, he applied the text to himself and declared that he was one of many who had been healed by Jesus. He didn't blink saying this, even bearing

---

4 See Acts 22:3-4; Philippians 3:4-9
5See Lk 18:31; 23:34-36, 39; 24:44.

the scabs of his recent beating, because it was obvious he was speaking of a deep inner healing. In fact his scars were a type of badge showing his authority. A link to Jesus. The Thessalonians began to understand how Messiah's suffering was designed to produce salvation. And how those who enrolled in His school as disciples could expect similar treatment. But in all of this talk of suffering they sensed the peace of Paul. Which always led him past the suffering to the texts and stories they found most amazing–those declaring the resurrection of the Messiah.

Paul reminded them how he had hated Jesus and while "**still breathing out murderous threats against the Lord's disciples**" (Acts 9:1), was forever changed. And it was here that he shocked them all. He turned away from the Psalms, where he was proving the Messiah would rise from the dead, and claimed that this had already happened! Jesus, after His crucifixion, had risen from the dead. And Paul knew this because Jesus had personally appeared to him. On a road leading to Damascus where he was heading, commissioned by the high priest, to take as prisoners any men or women who claimed that Jesus was The Way (Acts 9:2). These are Paul's own words,

> **About noon as I came near Damascus, suddenly a bright light from heaven flashed around me. I fell to the ground and heard a voice say to me, 'Saul! Saul! Why do you persecute me?' 'Who are you, Lord?' I asked. " 'I am Jesus of Nazareth, whom you are persecuting,' he replied. My companions saw the light, but they did not understand the voice of him who was speaking to me. "'What shall I do, Lord?' I asked." 'Get up,' the Lord said, 'and go into Damascus. There you will be told all that you have been assigned to do.' My companions led me by the hand into Damascus, because the brilliance of the light had blinded me. "A man named Ananias came to see me. He was a devout observer of the law and highly respected by all the Jews living there. He stood beside me and said, 'Brother Saul, receive your sight!' And at that very moment I was able to see him. "Then he said: 'The God of our fathers has chosen you to know his will and to see the Righteous One and to hear words from his mouth. You will be his witness to all men of what you have seen and heard. And now what are you waiting for? Get up, be baptized and wash your sins away, calling on his name' (Acts 22:6-16).**

Those were Paul's main credentials. And they were impressive. God had stopped him dead in his tracks. Turned him 180 degrees around. And sent him out to the world as one of the Messiah's special messengers. Jesus had chosen him and empowered him with a totally new life. **"This man is my chosen instrument to carry my name before the Gentiles and their kings and the people of Israel. I will show him how much he must suffer for my name"** (Acts 9:15-16). Of course, the Thessalonians had never heard or seen anything like that before. No one had ever come to their city with such a message! The pagan Thessalonians had seen men and women demonized. Had beheld their feats of power and heard their cryptic cries of suffering. But they were as different from Paul as darkness is from light. They were touched by two very different sources. Paul was the product of Jesus. The Jesus who had suffered horribly, died and been raised from the dead. And **"some of the Jews were persuaded and joined Paul and Silas, as did a large number of God-fearing Greeks and not a few prominent women"** (Acts 17:4). Paul had proven his point to them. His credentials were authentic enough for them to risk everything to join him and Jesus.

The day in which we live is very different. Our culture of affluence, freedom and privacy leaves us with little sense of desperate need. If we are doing so well, why change? Paul's call for a radical new life doesn't seem all that necessary today. But is there another choice? Are there verses offering another option? Can we be secret Christians rather than open disciples? Isn't it dangerous to choose the broad way? One easier than the way of Jesus, Paul and the amazing Thessalonians?

For Reflection and Discuss

1. What do you think of the following quote:

"Too often we look on Christianity as an escape from hell and a guarantee of heaven. Beyond that, we feel that we have every right to enjoy the best that this life has to offer. We know that there are those strong verses on discipleship in the Bible, but we have difficulty reconciling them with our ideas of what Christianity should be." (William McDonald, True Discipleship, p 12).

Chapter 5

What does the gospel really look like?

It is good news when someone is saved! That is what "gospel" means. Good News. Paul had been miraculously confronted by Jesus and amazingly saved by His grace. Jesus told Paul what He had in mind for him. And that is why Paul was in Thessalonica. It was to **"spread the gospel of Christ"** (1 Thes 3:2). He expressed his call this way to the Romans, **"Paul, a servant of Christ Jesus...set apart for the gospel"** (Rom 1:1). It is vital that we understand what the gospel meant to Paul. How central it was to him and what he expected it to produce in the lives of those who really believed it. A dangerous departure from Paul's understanding of the gospel has happened in our day. And I have experienced this shift first hand.

Paul used the word "gospel" six times in 1 Thessalonians.[6] That's quite a bit. Constituting something of an emphasis. John Stott notes,

> "What is of particular interest, because it applies to Christian communities in every age and place, is the interaction which the apostle portrays between the church and the gospel. He shows how the gospel creates the church and the church spreads the gospel, and how the gospel shapes the church, as the church seeks to live a life that is worthy of the gospel"[7]

While I admit the primary need of *hearing* the gospel's message in order to be saved (Rom 10:9-14), I wonder-- Does the gospel work best when standing alone as a message? Does it have a look or just a sound? Is it simply a message to be proclaimed or a life to be lived? Or both? More practically and to the point--Have you ever thought of the gospel as something you must show as well as speak?

When I was younger I would have been uncomfortable with this line of questioning. Because my circle of soul winners was mainly focused on gospel proclamation. On speaking it boldly. Which is absolutely important (cf. Acts 4:29; Eph 6:19). But boldness is not everything. I had not understood that the gospel was to be done as well as declared. So, the following words of Jesus always seemed a bit odd to me: **"You are the light of the world...In the same way, let your light shine before men, that they may see your good deeds and praise your Father in heaven"** (Matt

---

[6]See 1 Thes 1:5; 2:2,4,8,9; 3:2.
[7]J Stott *The Message of 1 & 2 Thessalonians* (Downers Grove, IL: InterVarsityPress 1991) 20.

5:14-16). I thought He would have better said, "hear your good words" instead of "see your good deeds." I had stressed the words of the gospel and neglected its works.

Even though it made us and others feel uncomfortable, we were taught to wedge the words of the gospel into every conversation. Rather than prayerfully waiting for someone to ask about our beliefs (see 1 Pet 3:15), we would go right for the jugular. I was seized by the command, **"preach the gospel to all creation"** (Mark 16:15). But I was ignorant as to how to **"make disciples"** (Matt 28:19) Texts like the following were used to buttress this imbalanced but well-intentioned approach:

> **"As the rain and the snow come down from heaven, and do not return to it without watering the earth and making it bud and flourish, so that it yields seed for the sower and bread for the eater, so is my word that goes out from my mouth: it will not return to me empty, but will accomplish what I desire and achieve the purpose for which I sent it" (Isa 55:10-11).**

This explicit statement about God speaking His words was turned into a general promise concerning our speaking biblical words. Our application of this text had God saying, You share My word and I will do the rest. It cannot return void. It will produce a crop. Get it out there. By hook or by crook. Leave it as tracts everywhere. Drop the words out of airplanes. Megaphone it in center city. Put pamphlets in doorways and ads in the paper. Corner people. It doesn't matter if they are uncomfortable. Just let them have it right between the eyes. Why? Because somewhere down the line it will influence them. To us, it was all about declaring revelation not about developing relationships.

Now—don't take me wrong. I love the distribution of the Word of God. And I have seen how the Spirit uses the Word. But an emphasis on proclamation or words ONLY is neither sound nor safe biblical evangelism. And it certainly is not what God was promising to bless in Isaiah 55! Or what Jesus taught about sowing the seed (word) in Mark 4:1-20. Or what Paul emphasized in Thessalonica.

In Isaiah's context God is speaking about His historic pronouncements of judgment and deliverance. His specific words that say, **"From the east I summon a bird of prey; from a far-off land, a man to fulfill my purpose. What I have said, that will I bring about; what I have planned, that will I do."** (Isa 40:12). Isa 55 is not a promise that all we have to do is speak the Word and then our job is done. It is a promise that when God speaks from heaven, when His divine purpose is declared—then nothing on earth can change it. When God says, **"Let there be light."** There is light! I have often evangelized and had my words mocked and rejected. The devil

28

has snatched the seed immediately with no fruit being produced then or later (Mk 4:15). My proclamation passed away with little impression being made. But, when God speaks for himself, well, that's a different case. I had misinterpreted Isaiah, justifying a brash style of witnessing.

Paul's presentation of the gospel was not totally focused on speaking the right words about Jesus. It involved more. He reminded the Thessalonians of how the gospel had come to them. **"Our gospel came to you not simply with words, but also with power, with the Holy Spirit and with deep conviction."** (1 Thes 1:5). Not just with words. But by lives that were obviously powerful and purposeful. Again, Stott states,

> "Words by themselves are seldom enough, even in secular discourse. Because they may be misunderstood or disregarded, they need somehow to be re-enforced. This is even more the case in Christian communication, since blind eyes and hard hearts do not appreciate the gospel. So words spoken in human weakness need to be confirmed with divine power. The reference is probably not to external miracles which are normally designated by the plural word 'powers' but to the internal operation of the Holy Spirit."[8]

When later in prison, Paul would write to other Macedonians and say,

> **"Whatever happens, conduct yourselves in a manner worthy of the gospel of Christ. Then whether I come and see you or only hear about you in my absence, I will know that you stand firm in one spirit, contending as one man for the faith of the gospel without being frightened in any way by those who oppose you. This is a sign to them that they will be destroyed, but that you will be saved–and that by God"** (Phil 1:27-28).

He was telling those Christians that the gospel was linked to their lives not just their lips. Their whole conduct would either support or deny its claims. And when their lives were filled with the grace of Jesus, this would strike the onlookers with the magnitude of a miracle. Like a sign from God that would warn them of their pending destruction unless they, too, repent and trust Christ. Has your life ever been so clear that it has struck someone else as being a warning from God?

Paul told the Philippians this could happen, if they lived gospel-empowered lives, because it did happen in Thessalonica. He saw it, as did all those in their region. They all knew what the gospel looked like as well as

---

[8]J Stott 1991, pp 33-34.

sounded like through the amazing Thessalonians. They had been vile pagans, but were transformed into holy and humble followers of Jesus.

They had truly learned well from Paul and his team, who said, **"We loved you so much that we were delighted to share with you not only the gospel of God, but our lives as well"** (1 Thes 2:8a). Let those words rest for a while in your heart. Paul **"delighted"** to share the gospel and his life. It was no chore that he longed to get out of the way. The Thessalonians remembered his joy. He was a genuinely happy man. His ministry was not merely a cross to bear. It was the joy of his heart! He did not punch a time card. He gave his life away with delight! And the Thessalonians, filled with the same Spirit, lived the same way. Both teacher and student spoke and showed the Good News of a new life. Even in the midst of profound persecution. One author reflected,

"Several years ago, in a church in Scotland, I heard a preacher quoting an old   poem which sums this up exactly. I don't know who wrote it, but they might have been reading 1 Thessalonians. This is exactly what Paul was talking about.

'I'd rather see a sermon than hear one, any day; I'd rather one would walk with me than merely show the way. The eye's a better pupil, more willing than the ear; Fine counsel is confusing, but example's always clear.'"[9]

We must think about the impression our lives are having on those watching us. The gospel is designed to make a lasting and deep impression. Good words can influence others, especially when thrust home by the Holy Spirit. But God knows us well. Humans do look on the outward appearance of things (1 Sam 16:7). So, when the surprising words of the gospel come from a life of love, they often strike deeper.

Today's unbelievers need to see individuals and churches truly shaped by the gospel. Not half-hearted salesmen, but saints stunning everyone by hearty works of love that lead to words of amazing grace. People consumed by the Good News of God's grace. Christians personifying what grace is: *love to the undeserving.* To rebels. Enemies. Everyone. Patiently portraying Christ's love as well as proclaiming it. The West needs to see a different type of Christian. Strikingly different from all other people. How often have we seen the gospel lived out? Even more directly, have you ever persistently loved anyone in this way? Showing grace and kindness even when they repeatedly mistreated you?

---

[9]NT Wright *Paul for Everyone: Galatians and Thessalonians* (Louisville, KY: Westminster John Knox Press 2006), 100.

I have spoken boldly to thousands, with some responding. I truly thank God for those few who have professed faith in Christ. But how much greater fruitfulness would have resulted from my life had it been fully shaped by the gospel of God's grace? Had I developed relationships of love that touched their hearts rather than simply speaking gospel words that touched their ears? Had I prayerfully waited on the Spirit to open their minds? And then, in answer to their desperately expressed cries, poured in the medicine of the priceless gospel of Christ. Had I listened in love rather than spoken in haste?

By His grace, I have turned from that one-sided witness. And seen God bless with greater fruitfulness. I remain deeply thankful for the training that urged me to call on everyone to trust in Christ before it is too late. To those who reminded me, *"Behind every face is an eternal destiny."* But I am glad that the Spirit has added to that the fuller wisdom of learning that, important as courage is, love is even more important. In fact, I have seen that the love of Christ in me creates the courage I constantly used to try to work up in order to witness to others. Because love is willing to do anything to help the one we love. It will joyfully risk everything without a worry. This is what many early disciples were famous for.[10] God used the amazing Thessalonians to help me experience this. I hope He does the same for you, too.

For Reflection and Discuss

1. Has the evangelism you have taken part in been a process of pressure and unnatural manipulation, rather than conversations of peace that naturally flowed?

2. Would you be interested in learning about the DMMs (Disciple Making Movements) globally occurring today which emphasize evangelism by peaceful means, rather than pressurized tactics? (If so, see my Are You a Christian or a Disciple? and Miraculous Movements by Jerry Trousdale).

---

[10]E Gibbons, *The History of the Decline and Fall of the Roman Empire* (London: Penguin Books, Ltd. 2000), see chap 15 - "Five Causes of the Growth of Christianity."

Chapter 6

What threats immediately pressured the Thessalonians?

As we begin to examine the opposition that immediately confronted the young Thessalonian converts, we are truly standing on holy ground. No mere human could withstand such pressure. Yet they did. And so do many throughout the world today! We will better appreciate the grace God gives to His suffering children and the marvel of their perseverance by considering the hostilities facing these Macedonians. The obstacles were so many and varied that we will take several chapters to introduce them.

The first and most repeated obstacle was Caesar, himself. The enemies of Jesus had used this trump card when Pilate showed reluctance to condemn him. John recorded, **"From then on, Pilate tried to set Jesus free, but the Jews kept shouting, "If you let this man go, you are no friend of Caesar. Anyone who claims to be a king opposes Caesar."** (John 19:12). We can imagine those words entering Pilate's heart like a cold knife. His whole future now hung in the balance. All his hopes of leaving the dust of Judea and returning to the grandeur of Rome were threatened. His dreams and desires were threatened. And he wavered. Who wouldn't? It would take a miracle not to cave in. **"Shall I crucify your king?"** Pilate asked. **"We have no king but Caesar,"** the chief priests answered." And John records Pilate's cowardly-yet-understandable acquiescence to this pressure with the sad conclusion, **"Finally Pilate handed him over to them to be crucified."** (John 19:15b-16). The Thessalonians supernaturally did exactly the opposite under similar pressure.

Macedonia was no third-rate Roman sub-province like Judea. It was a senatorial province, with both greater freedoms and responsibilities. And its main city, Thessalonica, was much closer to Rome and to the ears of the emperor than was Jerusalem. When the accusers stated their complaint against Jason and the other brothers (Paul and Silas could not be found), they didn't waste any time but went right for the jugular.

> **"These men who have caused trouble all over the world (Roman empire) have now come here, and Jason has welcomed them into his house. They are all defying Caesar's decrees, saying that there is another king, one called Jesus."** (Acts 17:6b-7).

The Thessalonians were being implicated in treason! The word produces little emotion from us, as few are accused and condemned for treason today. But since Tiberius Caesar (14BC-37AD), brutality in punishing enemies of the Roman state increased. Treason meant death. A horrible death. Slowly burned alive or being sewn in a sack with a snake or mad dog and thrown into the sea were not uncommon punishments for men from lower classes. Some of them were forced into gladiatorial conquests or battles with beasts. The directors of "the games" planned the most shocking deaths possible to please the degraded onlookers' bloodlust. If your status was high, you might simply be beheaded outside the city or exiled. But the consequences would not stop with you. Your loved ones were made a spectacle of suffering as well.

Treason would often throw one's family into economic and social ruin. Property could be confiscated and sons severely treated because it was assumed that they shared their father's views. And would likely try to avenge his death. To show mercy to a victim's family could be grounds for treason as well.

To confess Jesus as Lord at a time when Caesar was honored as Lord, meant certain suffering. The governmental heads of cities (*politarchs* in Thessalonica) officiated at public pledges of loyalty to Caesar. These were festive occasions of great importance that kept benefactions rolling into a city. These oaths were pledges of absolute loyalty, as is obvious from one taken in Paphlagonia (Asia Minor):

"I swear...that I will support Caesar Augustus, his children and descendants throughout my life in word, deed and thought...that in whatsoever concerns them I will spare neither body nor soul nor life nor children...that whenever I see or hear of anything being said, planned or done against them I will report it...and whomsoever they regard as enemies, I will attack and pursue with arms and the sword by land and sea...."[11]

Similar loyalty oaths to Tiberius and Caligula (37-41AD) have been found. Claudius (41-54AD), the emperor when Paul wrote this epistle, instituted the imperial cult in Britain at Colchester in AD43. There was a temple "to the Divine Claudius subsequently erected"[12] there. The seriousness of these oaths might well explain the zeal with which Jewish officials in Thessalonica opposed Paul and his missionary team. Claudius had opposed Jews in Rome for several years before expelling them completely (51AD) around the time of Paul's mission to Thessalonica. Jewish officials there would have had enormous pressure put on them to prove their loyalty to Rome and Claudius by opposing Paul's brash brand of Christianity.

---

[11]E.A. Judge *"The Decrees of Caesar at Thessalonica,"* RTR 30 (1971): p. 6.
[12]P Garnsey & R Saller *The Roman Empire* (Los Angeles: Univ of California Press 1987), p 166.

Moving against him quickly could help remove all accusations that they were anti-Roman. It could deflect any cause for further investigation or action against them or their synagogues. Remember, the deep insecurity of their brothers in remote Judea who moved quickly against Jesus when they were faced with similar pressures and filled with similar fears. **"If we let him go on like this, everyone will believe in him, and then the Romans will come and take away both our place and our nation"** (John 11:48).

We have great difficulty grasping the pressure of a totalitarian power pushing against our brothers in Thessalonica. Most of us live in developed democracies. How many of us have ever felt the tension of a "do this or die" ultimatum that challenged our faith? Not many, but we sense that this is not impossible in our day of increased anti-Christian persecution. We have all felt how today's "culture of tolerance" seems to tolerate everyone but Jesus and everything but biblical Christianity.

Have you ever had to suffer for taking a public stand for Jesus or His truth? How much governmental pressure would it take for you to stop following Jesus? Would your financial giving be the same if the government revoked the tax-exempt status for your church or favorite charity? Would you, like Jason, be willing to post bond for your faith in Christ? To jeopardize your family, wealth and honor? We may never have to endure this. But that does not mean that we cannot know how we would respond under such pressure. This we know–it is not likely that a person would jeopardize everything for Jesus in the future if he is not willing to suffer a little for Him now. This is true because God will not likely infuse into us the miracle of living then like we have never chosen to live now.

The amazing Thessalonians did not wait long to show their love for Jesus. They loved him from the start and showed that love day by day. Not by a miraculous infusion of grace arising during some public showdown. But by the fruit of love naturally budding and blooming before their neighbors' eyes every day. The fruit began dropping from the trees all around them. Love was winning. And no threat of suffering or even death could vanquish what they were experiencing of the power of the love of God. Don't you long to see the harvest of that love, too?

For Reflection and Discussion

1. How do you think it would affect your church if the government began to persecute Christians?

Chapter 7

Was Paul really challenging Caesar?

At this point, I want to be clear. Paul knew that Christianity was on a collision course with Caesar. And he did not try to buy time so that his fragile little church plant could grow in the safety of seclusion. Such a strategy does not appear to be wise. Paul did not dread the coming storm. He knew what the major outcome was going to be. Victory through suffering! Quite a remarkable outlook since all the political power, wealth, armies and weapons were on Caesar's side. So, let's probe the evidence that strongly indicates that Paul, like David running towards Goliath, was strangely "itching for a fight" it did not look like he could win.

As we look closely at the words Paul used when communicating with the Thessalonians, we must ask, "What would those words have meant to a 1st century Macedonian?" Should they really be interpreted as, "**defying Caesar's decrees**" (Acts 17:7)? Absolutely. Undoubtedly. The Thessalonians were astonished, I am sure, with just how defiant Paul's words seemed to be. He was clearly challenging Claudius and any other Caesar before or after him. No one spoke publicly about those rulers and Rome in that way--and lived very long. Certainly no one put into writing what Paul wrote, signing his own name and including others, too. It was like writing your own death sentence. And those who received it, too, were in great danger unless they turned the author in to the authorities. The amazing paradox was that this man spoke and wrote humbly. Lovingly. He was not inciting revolution but encouraging redemption. He hoped and prayed for everyone's salvation–even Caesar's! The fight Paul was picking was "**the good fight of the faith**" (1 Tim 6:12). Which is the most disarming of all tactics (see Rom 12:20; Pr 25:21-22).

Many scholars have concluded, with Donfried, "That Paul is intentionally engaging and challenging the political, civic and religious structures of pagan Thessalonica."[13] Our present chapter will focus on how Paul challenged the political life of Thessalonica and the empire in three specific ways.

First, Paul uses the term "*kurios*" (Lord) to constantly refer to Jesus. He is "the Lord Jesus Christ" from the outset. **"Paul, Silas and Timothy, to the church of the Thessalonians in God the Father and <u>the Lord Jesus Christ</u>"** (1 Thes 1:1a). Nearly 50 times in his two Thessalonian epistles Paul declares Jesus to be Lord. This is very likely Paul's first epistle. And he did not decrease his devotion to the Lordship of Christ in his other letters,

---

[13]K. Donfried, *Paul, Thessalonica, and Early Christianity* (Grand Rapids, MI: Wm. B. Eerdmans Publishing Co. 2002) , p. 144.

even though it cost him and his brothers dearly. For those were "fighting words" in the increasingly volatile context of the mid-late 1st century Roman empire. Caesar was to be confessed as supreme Lord. Paul "dares also to apply kurios (Lord) to Jesus Christ, the word appropriated by Claudius and other emperors in the emperor-worship...."[14] Paul even goes further, calling Jesus "the Lord," that is, "the one and only true King." Jesus was not simply "a Lord" alongside of Caesar. This tact directly challenged the absolute rule of the emperor. Those were not democratic days with citizens enjoying the freedoms of speech and religion we cherish today. Paul was leading his Thessalonian disciples on to very dangerous turf.

We know, in later trials, this issue became the actual focal point of one's innocence or guilt. If the person would curse Jesus and call Caesar, "Lord," offering sacrifices to his image, then he was not to be regarded as a Christian, and could go free. But if he refused to call Caesar, "Lord," he or she was executed.[15] In fact, some scholars believe that Paul actually did something similar when, in his years of angry unbelief, he tracked down and eliminated Christians (Acts 22:4), using torture to "**force them to blaspheme**" (Acts 26:11). Paul's (and the Spirit's) repeated choice of using the word "Lord" of Jesus would intentionally put the new religion in a perilous place, facing all Christians with a most dangerous decision. Who has your allegiance: Christ or Caesar?

Paul's next challenge to Caesar came when he wrote often of "**the coming of our Lord Jesus Christ**" (1 Thes 5:23; also 2:19; 3:13; 4:15), choosing a familiar word used of the emperor or one of his representative's officially visiting a city. "When a dignitary paid an official visit (parousia) to a city in Hellenistic times, the action of the leading citizens in going out to meet him and escort him back on the final stage of his journey was called the apantesis."[16] The citizens on those occasions would go out to meet the emperor as he arrived, with great fanfare and escort him back into "his" city. Those visits were chronicled, inscribed on monuments and remembered as highlights of the city's history. So, again, Paul was upstaging Caesar with Jesus. For not only are the living going to meet Jesus, but all dead believers will rise from the dead to join the welcoming hosts (4:16)! Though many had been killed by him, no one had yet risen from the dead to welcome Caesar. The message was clear. Don't back the loser. Follow Jesus instead!

Lastly, Paul knew that the emperors were nervous about retaining power and passing it on only to their chosen heirs. So, they did not take kindly

---

[14]A.T. Robertson, *Word Pictures in the New Testament* (Grand Rapids, MI: Baker Book House 1931), vol. 4, p. 6. And A. Deissmann, *Light from the Ancient Near East* (New York: Doran, 1922), pp. 351-8.

[15]See Pliny's letters to Emperor Trajan - 10:96-97.

[16]F.F. Bruce, *1 & 2 Thessalonians* (Waco, TX: Word, Inc. 1982) Word Biblical Commentary, Vol. 45, p. 102.

to predictions of future saviors who would come on the scene to help mankind. That was <u>the emperor's</u> role. Some had actually issued edicts forbidding such prophetic remarks. Tiberius became so paranoid that he put "astrologers and magicians and such as practiced divination in anyway whatsoever...to death."[17] It just was not a safe practice for religious leaders or their followers to predict the future. Yet Paul, repeated over and over again that Jesus is coming back. In fact, in our chapter and verse format, every single chapter in his first letter closes with a prediction of the Second Coming! And here are some of the predictions that the Lord Jesus will fulfill:

· He "**rescues us from the coming wrath**" (1:10b).

· He will be accompanied by "**all His holy ones**" (3:13b)

· "**For the Lord himself will come down from heaven, with a loud command, with the voice of the archangel and with the trumpet call of God**"(4:16a)

· "**For God did not appoint us to suffer wrath but to receive salvation through our Lord Jesus Christ**" (5:9)

· From that moment on "**we will be forever with the Lord**" (4:17)

For Paul to speak so often and so clearly about the Lord Jesus coming to transform the world in the future was, at least, clearly challenging Caesar. And at most, it was against the law. Love does not always choose to lead others down the easiest path. Jesus sent 72 disciples out **like lambs among wolves**" (Luke 10:3b). Recognizing this, the amazing Thessalonians refused to look to the West (Rome) to save them, instead they looked up, waiting for the awesome "**day of the Lord**" (5:2).

For Reflection and Discussion

1. In what ways has the concept of "the lordship of Jesus" affected your life and not only your theology?
2. How often do you think about the coming of Christ? And how does that truth impact your daily life?

---

[17]Dio Chrysostom, Nest. 57.15.8 in Donfried's *Paul, Thessalonica and Early*   *Christianity* (Grand Rapids, Mi: Wm B Eerdmans Publishing Co. 2002) pp. 32-33.

Chapter 8

Was Paul Really Challenging Caesar? - Pt 2

The previous chapter showed several ways that Paul had unmistakably pitted Christ against Caesar. Paul had made it clear. Yet he was going to make sure it was crystal clear–Caesar had met his match and it was Jesus!

Monuments were erected throughout the Roman empire describing the benefits of Rome's bringing "peace and security" to the Mediterranean world. This was the fabled Pax Romana (Peace of Rome) which was certainly an impressive accomplishment. But everyone knew the Roman peace was achieved through brutal conquest, oppression and intimidation. Was this really the peace of God? Paul was not buying it and dared to challenge it writing, **"While people are saying, 'Peace and safety,' destruction will come on them suddenly...and they will not escape"** (1 Thes 5:3). Witherington notes, "Paul must have thought, 'What foolish slogans and vain hopes when the day of the Lord is coming.' He is critiquing the slogans and propaganda about the Pax Romana."[18]

That peace was not a cheaply achieved luxury. It had been bought by the blood of many a Roman. Paul certainly was not belittling it. But to agree that Rome produced the peace every soul longed for--was unthinkable to the Apostle. As he would remind the Ephesians, **"But now in Christ Jesus you who were once far away have been brought near through the blood of Christ. For he himself is our peace"** (Eph 2:13-14a). No one else brings peace. No other price can purchase it but His blood. What any and all of the conquests of the emperors achieved are as nothing when compared to the peace Christ delivers to the believer.

Paul's next point further challenged Rome, forbidding the Thessalonians from considering it as the true kingdom of God. **"God calls you into his kingdom and glory"** (1 Thes 2:12, cf 2 Thes 1:5). *"Kingdom"* was a political word. In a hostile environment, it is best not to use buzzwords that could set oneself up for possible misunderstanding and the inevitable pain accompanying it. Be clear on this. Either Paul did not care about what happened to his readers (like some generals who have nonchalantly sacrificed their men in battle) or, the fact that Christians belonged to another kingdom was basic to their faith. A non- negotiable truth worth suffering for.

There can be absolutely no doubt that Paul cared for the Thessalonians. He wrote, **"...we were gentle among you, like a mother caring for her little children. We loved you so much that we were**

---

[18] B Witherington *1 and 2 Thessalonians* (Grand Rapids, MI: Wm B Eerdmans Pub Co., 2006), p 147

delighted to share with you not only the gospel of God, but our lives as well...You know that we dealt with each of you as a father deals with his own children" (2: 7-11). Paul did not declare "the kingdom of God" out of ambivalence to the crushing impact that phrase would have on his hearers. Rather, to whose kingdom one was primarily devoted, Christ's or Caesar's, <u>must have been an absolutely vital and central point to his message</u>. No doubt this is why, at various points, Paul's preaching was summarized as "**preaching the kingdom of God**" (Acts 20:25)[19] Jesus is our ultimate King, not Caesar. So Paul would later remind the Christians living in Caesar's shadow in Rome, "**For none of us lives to himself alone and none of us dies to himself alone. If we live, we live to the Lord; and if we die, we die to the Lord. So whether we live or die, we belong to the Lord**" (Rom. 14:7-8).

We belong to Jesus and are members of His kingdom. His Word is our supreme Law, not Caesar's decrees. We are all **"under Christ's law"** (1 Cor 9:21b). It is difficult for us who live among the nations, with all our nationalism, to even start thinking rightly of belonging <u>first</u> to the kingdom of God.[20] How can we really understand the following verse that so many of us have memorized? "**But seek first his kingdom and his righteousness, and all these things will be given to you as well**" (Matt 6:33).

Paul seemed further to tighten the noose around Christians' necks by speaking of Jesus, not Caesar, as the true **"Son from heaven"** (1 Thes 1:10). Yes, Tiberius wanted to be known as "the Son of God" because he was the son of Caesar Augustus, who was the first Roman emperor. Subsequent emperors wanted to use the term "a son of the gods" for themselves. But Paul will not allow Jesus to have a rival. He is the true, Divine Son. When we add that to the growing list of Paul's denials of Caesar's deity, we grow in wonder that any Thessalonian dared to believe.

Finally, when Paul often featured the word "gospel" (*euangelion*-good news) in his Thessalonian epistles, he was also stepping on the emperor's toes. The word "gospel" was not coined by Christians. Jesus was not the first to bring "good news" from heaven. The birth of Caesar was the supreme gospel to the Romans. An inscription found near Ephesus declared,

> "and since the Caesar through his appearance has exceeded the hopes of all former good messages (euangelion), surpassing not only the benefactors who came before him, but also leaving no hope that anyone in the future would surpass him, and since for the world the birthday of the god was the beginning of his good messages...."[20]

---

[19] See also Acts 19:8; 28:23, 31.
[20] B Witherington, 2006, p. 71.

39

Paul would rather die than deny the gospel of Christ. Or put Caesar's birth and accomplishment on a par with those of Jesus. So, "**...with the help of our God we dared to tell you his gospel in spite of strong opposition**" (2:2). It is hard to go into a city already supposed to be the recipients of a matchless message of goodness and tell them that they have it all wrong. That, in fact, they have been deceived. That their king is a fraud. An impotent imposter who ought not to be feared.

What would you have likely thought had you lived then? The Thessalonians saw the foes of Caesar crucified and their families sent into abject poverty and disgrace. Yet many of them still followed Jesus. The persecution seemed to be a side issue to them. Is it to us? The severest pressure forced against those early disciples did not succeed in stopping the spread of the true gospel. Does its mildest form now stop us? It is time for us to see the source of the difference between us and them. Because we know there is a difference. That difference made the Thessalonians arguably the most successful church Paul ever planted. And it can revive our churches today so that we become the power for God and good in our day that the amazing Thessalonians were in their day.

For Reflection and Discussion

1. Which affects your way of life more—the teachings of the Bible or the liberties and choices of being a citizen in a free country?

Chapter 9

Paul, it's okay to leave - we'll be fine

The normal response for a child in danger is to cry out for a parent. The Thessalonians were still in what many would consider a stage of spiritual infancy when they did a most remarkable thing. **"As soon as it was night, the brothers sent Paul and Silas away to Berea"** (Acts 17:10). And with that they were gone. The believers were cut loose after only a few months of ministry. Let's conclude this first section of the book imagining what this might have meant for the future of the Thessalonians.

They had utterly forsaken their old way of life. Some were probably already facing divorce proceedings. Others would have been disinherited. The pressure to renounce the renegade Paul and his crucified King would have been beyond imagination. What father would want to see his son throw away all that he had dreamed and planned for him? What brother could bear seeing his sister hounded and hunted as a criminal? What mother could think of her husband plunging the family into financial, social and domestic chaos? And added to all this--the latest news was--the leader has left town!

But not on the sly. Not with a bag full of money. Like so many charlatans had before. No. Paul's spiritual children covertly gathered and, making a family decision, bit the bullet and begged him to leave. He must go so others could hear the Good News. While there was still time. Sure, he could stay and win some to Christ in the Thessalonian prison. Like he had in Philippi. They knew he would not shrink back from that cross if he had to bear it. But his disciples did not want to see him suffer any more. The bloody strokes from Philippi were enough. How much more could he take? Maybe he and Silas argued with them. That would not surprise me when I consider his love for them. But the young believers would not relent. Out came their trump card. He could go because they would be just fine without him. They had Jesus!

Somehow these young Christians had fully matured. This book will attempt to unfold in detail just how that likely happened. And what that looked like. The fact is, they would not only survive. They would thrive. They would not only thrive. They would win. They would become Paul's model church. The church of the Thessalonians would amaze thousands in their day and millions down through history. How? They had Jesus. Who needed Paul when they had his King? Why beg him to stay and teach at Thessalonica? They would be daily guided and comforted by his Teacher, the Holy Spirit. Who could feel orphaned if Paul and Silas left? They would be as safe as they should be, for God was their Father.

It would have been with very heavy hearts that Paul and Silas eventually agreed to go. But they knew the amazing Thessalonians were right. Ultimately they would be okay. Paul showed this when he would soon write, **"Paul, Silas and Timothy, to the church of the Thessalonians <u>in God the Father, and the Lord Jesus Christ</u>"** (1 Thes 1:1). You can't be better off than that! In God. In Christ. Not just close to them. Not physically walking behind a rabbi and gathering his dust. But IN Him! Many New Testament scholars see Paul's constant use of "in Christ" (164 times!) as his description of the disciples ongoing relationship with Jesus. He liked it so much that he described them "in Christ" rather than as His "disciples" in the letters he wrote to them. He wanted them to know that they were surrounded on every side by God. Totally covered. Sheltered. That is why Paul could leave Thessalonica within weeks of planting the church. And that is why they could ask him to leave. They knew that "in Christ" they had all they needed. And they all knew it.

After a long life filled with evangelism, revival and writing, British minister Roy Hession wrote a final little book, "We Would See Jesus." In it he laments at having written on so many other topics. I think if you read it, you will find yourself returning to it again and again. The truth he and his wife Revel eventually discovered was what the Thessalonians had been taught by Paul in their first months of faith. That Jesus is the Way. Not only the Alpha and the Omega, the Beginning and the End. But everything in between. He is the means as well as the end. He is the "it" that everyone is seeking. The Way. That simple belief marked the amazing lives of early believers.[21] I hope it will be your simple faith as well. He wrote,

> "The truth is that many of us who have entered by the Door (Jesus-Jn 10:9) are not really walking (down) the Way (Jesus-Jn 14:6) at all.... We have slipped off the Highway that has been divinely provided and are painfully dragging our steps through the swamp that abounds on either side. Sometimes I have heard a Christian apply to himself the expressive word 'stuck' when he is in that condition.
>
> Basically, this difficulty is due to the fact that we are not seeing *Jesus* as the Way but are trying to make other things the way, and they just do not work. Some feel that prayer is the most important thing in the Christian life, and it becomes the way for them. Others would put Bible study in that place, others fellowship, others personal witnessing, others attendance at church and commitment to the sacraments, and yet others Christian neighborliness. It is felt that if

---

[21] See Acts 9:2; 19:9,23; 22:4; 24:14,22.

we do these things we shall then be really living the full Christian life–and so we consider them to be the way onward.

None of these things, however is the Way, and they only make the Christian life hard and barren when we try to make them such, even in a small degree.... Only the Lord Jesus Himself is the Way; to attempt to walk on any other is to fall and to despair. This does not mean that we are not to do these things, for they are to occupy a prominent place in the Christian's life. But it does mean that they are not the Way, as so often we make them. The Lord Jesus Himself is the Way. None else will suit our stumbling feet."[22]

Do we really know this? Of course, we have heard it. We might have even memorized John 14:6. But I mean do you trust in and walk through life depending on Jesus for everything? As your Way. Because you have nothing else. And want no one other. The whole world could be against you. Like it was with the Thessalonians. Yet you gladly bid your teacher farewell, because you **"know whom you have believed, and am convinced that he is able to guard what you have entrusted to him for that day"** (2 Tim 1:12). Those later words of Paul were written early on the hearts of his spiritual children. So they were no longer infants. In a few months, they had grown, as we will see, to full spiritual stature and strength. They did not cry out for Paul to stay and help them. They were already helping to save and instruct others.

Are those words of faith written on your heart and clearly read by those who observe you? Would they describe you as "in Jesus"? As one who follows Him as your Way? Please join me in humbling asking Jesus for help. We need to lay aside all the other "secrets of Christian living" and re-discover him and His love. He is still near us and will help us just as He did the amazing Thessalonians.

For Reflection and Discussion

1. Whom would you say is the leader of your local church?
2. How do you think your church would be affected without its pastor or primary leader?
3. How often do you think of the presence of Jesus?

---

[22] Roy and Revel Hession, *We Would See Jesus* (Fort Washington, PA: CLC Publications 2006), pp 103-106.

Chapter 10

The amazing love of Paul

Now that we have a better understanding of the many difficulties facing these first century disciples, let's look at how their faith could flourish. It is good to note that what we see in the Thessalonians, was first found in Paul. They followed his steps. They learned their spirituality and activity from him. Like all New Testament era disciples, the Thessalonians mastered both what the discipler taught to them and imitated how their discipler lived. They were not more loving than he. Yet it is here that Paul has really gotten a bad rap. He is often pictured as sort of a dill pickle. Mainly because he was not willing to yield an inch regarding the gospel. Not to Barnabas (Acts 15:36-41) or to Peter (Gal 2:11-21). But if you picture him as cantankerous and overbearing, you do not understand him. He was a man of incredible love. In fact, Paul probably never saw a Jew he didn't love! That was amazing given the manner in which he was opposed, hounded and persecuted by them. Yet he wrote, **"Brothers, my heart's desire and prayer to God for the Israelites is they may be saved."** (Rom 10:1).

How far was he willing to go to see his fellow countrymen saved? You can get a glimpse of Paul's love by his answer to that question.

> **"I speak the truth in Christ–I am not lying, my conscience confirms it in the Holy Spirit–I have great sorrow and unceasing anguish in my heart. For I could wish that I myself were cursed and cut off from Christ for the sake of my brothers, those of my own race, the people of Israel**." (Rom 9:1-4a).

Leon Morris, in the NIV Study Bible notes wrote,

> "The Greek for this word (curse) is anathema, and it means delivered over to the wrath of God for eternal destruction_(see 1Cor 12:3; 16:22; Gal 1:8-9). Such was Paul's great love for his fellow Jews."[23]

Love willing to die for another is great love. Love willing to be eternally punished for another is divine. It is born and bred by God. This was the spirit in which Paul served God and man. He was filled with the Spirit of God as he served. And that Spirit was and always is a Spirit of love.

---

[23] L Morris in *NIV Study Bible* (Grand Rapids, MI: Zondervan Publishing House 1995), p 1721.

The Thessalonians knew they were loved by God as they were loved by this extraordinary man. Because Jews did not love Gentiles the way Paul loved the Thessalonians. To love is to cherish another person. To really want to be with him or her. To listen, soaking in the words of the beloved one. To want to respond in whatever way possible to help the situation of the one loved. Listen to Paul and let his love for the Thessalonians move you.

> **"As apostles of Christ we could have been a burden to you, but we were gentle among you, like a mother caring for her little children. We loved you so much that <u>we were delighted</u> to share with you not only the gospel of God but our lives as well, because you had become so dear to us....**
>
> **You are witnesses, and so is God, of how holy, righteous and blameless we were among you who believed. For you know that we dealt <u>with each of you </u>as a father deals with his own children, encouraging, comforting and urging you to live lives worthy of God, who calls you into his kingdom and glory"** (1 Thes 2:6b-12).

You can just feel the love there because the love of God is tangible. Even when reading about it from a piece of paper. Paul's love was gentle, like a mother's. Wow! No matter who gives up on you, you can usually return to mom. Paul's love, like a mother's, delights in sacrificing for others. Service out of duty is something totally different than service out of love. Paul laid his life aside for the Thessalonians. They knew it. They saw it. They felt it. And they were formed by it. They then imitated it, sharing God's love with each other and their neighbors.

Paul loved like a father. He was the total package of love. Encouraging and comforting. You can hear fatherly words like these pouring daily out of his heart, "You can do it. That was a great try. You cannot fail. I am so proud of you. Look at how Jesus is using you. I love you so much." And Paul loved them <u>all</u> this way. He **"dealt with each one"** with love. Converted slave. Patrician. Temple prostitute. Leather worker. It did not matter to Paul. He loved them all.

And when he had to leave them, how did he describe it? Was it, "Anchors away! Full speed ahead"? Was he that kind of professional missionary who bonded with the job rather than with the people? He wrote,

> **"But brothers, when we were torn away from you for a short time (in person, not in thought), out of our intense longing–we made every effort to see you. For we wanted to come to you– certainly I Paul did, again and again–but Satan stopped us. For**

45

what is our hope, our joy or the crown in which we will glory in the presence of our Lord Jesus when he comes? Is it not you? Indeed, you are our glory and joy" (1 Thes 2:17-20).

Paul had to be torn away from them. Why? Because love doesn't leave the beloved ones easily. Only Satanic opposition, working through his Roman emissaries, could keep Paul away. Many think Paul was officially banished from the city for a while. That was like torture to this man of love. But while away, in body not in spirit, he would **"night and day pray most earnestly that we may see you again"** (1 Thes 3:10a). That sounds like a mother's prayer for a son who is in danger. Or like a father's prayer for a daughter who is ill. But these were Paul's spiritual children. The bond of Christian love extended to his fellow disciples as if they were his naturally born siblings or children.

You can't fake that type of love. So Paul wrote, **"You know, brothers, that our visit to you was not a failure...For the appeal we make does not spring from error or impure motives, nor are we trying to trick you"** (1 Thes 2:1-3). When the Thessalonians received this letter, they were not rolling their eyes, saying, "Who's he trying to kid?" They were weeping their eyes out. Because that is what love does when it remembers one's true lover. Especially when he or she has been forced to leave the beloved quickly.

One big goal of this book is to acquaint you with an amazing group of people. But what made that group great was found in their teacher. Their seeker. Their disciple maker. Their lover, Paul. And, Paul always said that the only reason it was in him to love was that God had saved him. Changed him. Filled him with love instead of hate. Paul loved the Thessalonians to Jesus. And Jesus loved the Thessalonians through Paul.

Paul bonded with all his churches through love. It is just that the Thessalonians swallowed it hook, line and sinker. And realized that they were to imitate the love of God to everyone. Everywhere. All the time. I hope you swallow it, too.

The one prayer that Paul wrote here to the Thessalonians begins, **"May the Lord make your love increase and overflow for each other and for everyone else, just as ours does for you"** (1 Thes 3:12). There it is. He wanted them to love one another and everyone else just as he loved them. He knew that God was the source of this love, so he prayed that God the Spirit would keep pumping it into them. And through them to one another and then to all others. We will see just how amazingly God kept answering this prayer over and over in the Thessalonians. May He do the same for you all.

For Reflection and Discussion

1. Is there someone outside of your biological family whom you love the way Paul loved the Thessalonians? Why do you think those relationships are so rare today?

Part Two – Love Taking Root

Chapter 11

Paul shocks his audience–by working

We will never understand how the Thessalonians impacted their world unless we grasp their view of occupational work. And being good disciples, as in all areas of life, they took their cue from Paul. The apple did not fall far from the tree. Why was Paul so hyped about the work ethic of his converts? Was it an old-school thing? Or could it have really been connected with his understanding of the gospel? Right now just take note of the way this subject of work kind of consumed Paul. We will later explore why it was such a big issue to him.

> **"You know we never used flattery, nor did we put on a mask to cover up greed–God is our witness.... As apostles of Christ we could have been a burden to you.... Surely you remember, brothers, our toil and hardship; we worked night and day in order not to be a burden to anyone while we preached the gospel to you."**(1 Thes. 2:5-9).

You need to appreciate just how unique this approach of Paul was. How it set him apart from everyone else.

"Perhaps the most remarkable thing about Paul's missionary work is that when he arrived in a new town the people there had quite literally never seen anything of the sort before...none of them behaved as Paul did. They had no idea that this sort of lifestyle was possible, let alone desirable...To teach them by example what sort of a life would bring glory to the living God he was telling them about...The first thing was about money...if he accepted money where he was working , people might accuse him of working only for pay...He has settled it as his own practice that he will work with his own hands to earn what he needs while he engages in primary evangelism and teaching"[24]

This point about work was the major thing that some of the Thessalonians did not get. It was the most obvious flaw of some. Hey, nobody's perfect. Later you will better understand the problem in Thessalonian culture and how some of them could despise manual labor. But for now, just note how firmly Paul was convinced he had to speak about this

---

[24] NT Wright Paul for Everyone: Galatians and Thessalonians (Louisville, KY: Westminster John Knox Press 2004) pp 97-98.

problem. Even though it related to only a small number among them. And ask yourself, "What's the big deal? Why was this so serious an issue to Paul?" His second letter included this lengthy and strongly stated warning:

> "**In the name of the Lord Jesus Christ,** we command you brothers to keep away from every brother who is idle and does not live according to the teaching you received from us. For you yourselves know how you ought to follow our example. We were not idle when we were with you, nor did we eat anyone's food without paying for it. On the contrary, we worked night and day, laboring and toiling so that we would not be a burden to any of you. We did this not because we do not have the right to such help, but in order to make ourselves a model for you to follow. For even when we were with you, we gave you this rule: 'If a man will not work, he shall not eat.'

> "We hear that some among you are idle. They are not busy; they are busybodies. Such people we command and urge <u>in the Lord Jesus Christ</u> to settle down and earn the bread they eat. And as for you, brothers, never tire of doing what is right.

> "If anyone does not obey our instruction in this letter, take special note of him. Do not associate with him, in order that he may feel ashamed. Yet do not regard him as an enemy, but warn him as a brother." (2 Thes 3:6-15).

When Paul invoked the name of Jesus, as he does twice in this warning, he was pulling out his biggest guns. As amazing as the Thessalonians were, the way that some approached work was potentially lethal. And we will see that it likely had nothing to do with believing Jesus was coming soon. A few were holding on to a privileged way of life that, to Paul and the Spirit, was potentially cancerous to the whole group. And to their witness in the world. Deadly in its gospel implications, as we shall see! Paul was nearly rabid about how his disciples approached work because there was nothing that would prove the gospel's supernatural origin as powerfully as that. Talk is always pretty cheap. But love works!

Paul's concern about work arose, partly, from the clear teaching of the Lord Jesus. Paul made a big deal out of money and possessions because Jesus did. In his farewell to the Ephesians elders, Paul said,

"I have not coveted anyone's silver or gold or clothing. You yourselves know that these hands of mine have suppled my own needs and the needs of my companions. In everything I did, I showed you that by this kind of hard work we must help the weak, remembering the words the Lord Jesus himself said: 'It is more blessed to give than to receive'" (Acts 20:33-35).

Jesus had taught His disciples about the dangers of money, greed and covetousness. Luke, Paul's missionary companion, relentlessly quoted Jesus' lessons on money. Here's a few of them. **"Watch out! Be on your guard against all kinds of greed; a man's life does not consist in the abundance of his possessions"** (Lk. 12:15 also 16-21). The Savior said that His followers should not be like pagans, filled with worry concerning food and clothing (Lk 12:22ff). Instead they are commanded, **"Sell your possessions and give to the poor. Provide purses for yourselves that will not wear out, a treasure in heaven that will not be exhausted, where no thief comes near and no moth destroys"** (Lk 12:33).

Paul, the former Pharisee, knew how enslaved to covetousness he had been (see Rom. 7:7-8). And how money mattered to him and to his Jewish colleagues. Probably reflecting Paul's influence, Luke noted this tendency in the Pharisees, **"The Pharisees, who loved money, heard all this and were sneering at Jesus."** (Lk 16:14). What were they sneering at? It was when Jesus said, **"No servant can serve two masters. Either he will hate the one and love the other, or he will be devoted to the one and despise the other. You cannot serve God and Money"** (Lk 16:13). Jesus seemed to go too far for everyone when He warned, **"Indeed, it is easier for a camel to go through the eye of a needle than for a rich man to enter the kingdom of God"** (Lk 18:25). Is that too far for you?

Peter asked, **"We have left all we had to follow you!"** And Jesus responded, **"No one who has left home or wife or brothers or parents or children for the sake of the kingdom of God will fail to receive many times as much *in this age* and, in the age to come, eternal life"** (Lk 18:28-29). A simple question here. Where does all the gain promised by Jesus come from "in this life?" From the government? From a rich sugar daddy relative? No--from the church! The kingdom of God. Our new family in Christ. Paul had forsaken the old, tightfisted Phariseeism for the new openhanded liberality of the Spirit of Christ. And he taught all his disciples, **"Follow my example, as I follow the example of Christ"** (1 Cor 11:1). Most of the Thessalonians did! Some did not at first. With which group are you standing?

When Paul began his letter to the Thessalonians, he immediately noted their devotion to strenuous work. Instead of separating the physical realm and spiritual realms, Paul linked them. He wrote, **"We continually remember before our God and Father your *work* produced by faith, your *labor* prompted by love, and your *endurance* inspired by hope in our Lord Jesus Christ"** (1 Thes 1:3). From the outset of his writing, Paul emphasized both the outward, visible aspects of a believer's life (work, labor and endurance) together with the inward, unseen beauty (faith, love and hope). Stott captures Paul's balance well.

> "What Paul and his companions especially remembered about the Thessalonians was the three most eminent Christian graces (faith, love and hope), which characterized their lives.... Each is productive. It is this that Paul emphasizes. Faith, hope and love sound rather abstract qualities, but they have concrete, practical results. Faith works, love labors and hope endures. A true *faith* in God leads to good works, and without works faith is dead. Here Paul and James are seen to agree, even if Paul usually stresses the faith which issues in works and James the works which issue from faith. A true *love* for people leads to labor for them; otherwise it degenerates into mere sentimentality. Moreover this 'labor' is *kopos*, which denotes 'either the fatiguing nature of what is done or the magnitude of the exertion required'. And a true *hope*, which looks expectantly for the Lord's return, leads to endurance which is patient fortitude in the face of opposition"[25]

This uniting of hand and heart clearly sets Paul against some pagan and pseudo Christian philosophers who gloried in their mystical abstractions. They would most often emphasize the mind at the expense of the body. So, they had no problem indulging the flesh. They taught that it was the spirit that mattered most. Paul, on the other hand, was practical--a real meat-and-potatoes Christian. He continually remembered the blood, sweat and tears of the believers. And this was especially true of the Thessalonians, his model church. He wanted to see love. Not only hear about it.

NT Wright notes, "Love—which, as Paul will show later in the letter (4:9-12), is a very practical thing—also requires the kind of effort we associate with hard physical work"[26] This was Thessalonian love. Not a love of "words" rather than "actions" (1 Jn 3:18). Nor the Cain-like love that can coldly ask, "Am I my brother's keeper?" Such a love, the apostle John

---

[25] Stott 1&2 Thessalonians (Downer's Grove, IL: InterVarsity Press 1991) pp 29-30.
[26] NT Wright, 2004, p 90.

reminds us, comes from "the evil one" (1 Jn 3:12). Let us marvel at the love that the risen and reigning Jesus was pouring out on the Roman empire through these early disciples. Through John, Paul and their followers, like the amazing Thessalonians. The true love of God that works for others. **"This is how we know what love is: Jesus Christ laid down his life for us. And we ought to lay down our lives for our brothers."** (1 Jn 3:16).

For Reflection and Discussion

1. What is your attitude towards work in general?
2. How often do you freely work for others, because you love them?
3. Does it really bother you when you do something for someone and they do not thank you for it? Discuss why that may be the case for us.

Chapter 12

What was the Thessalonians' bottom line?

In the Western world, 'the bottom line" has come to mean money. How much is it going to cost? How much profit will I make? Can we afford it? Those questions, ultimately, determine what many of us decide to do. In every culture, one's values produce his behavior. Today, a value system based on increasing one's personal wealth seems to reign in the USA. Before Paul arrived in the city, the Thessalonians shared a belief and value system with their neighbors. It was either paganism or Judaism. But, after he lived there for only a few months, at the longest, the bottom line had shifted. Totally. Jesus' disciples in Thessalonica became radically different from what they had been before. What caused the seismic shift? We cannot understand the obvious differences between them and us without getting this point.

In this chapter, we will begin considering the supernatural source of their worldview change. In a few chapters, we will then probe the human Love Taking Root. Paul described the difference between what they were and what they became: "**...we know, brothers loved by God, that he has chosen you, because our gospel came to you...with power, with the Holy Spirit, and with deep conviction.... In spite of severe suffering, you welcomed the message with the joy given by the Holy Spirit**" (1:4-6).

God was the difference. He had personally come into contact with them in new ways. Therefore, their lives had been changed. That which was ungodly in their behavior was challenged by God. The Thessalonians responded to His work. But, it was He who started it. And what God starts is really started. When we start something, it may last for a while or quickly sputter out and die. But when God determines to do something, it will be done. Paul saw this same God-start in their fellow Macedonians at Philippi and wrote, "**...being confident of this, that he who began a good work in you will carry it on to completion until the day of Christ Jesus**" (Phil 1:6).

Paul described God's special work in three ways: by first highlighting His love, then His election and lastly, the work of His Spirit. The difference between many of us and them, starts here.

God loved the Thessalonians. They were in bad shape and did not thoroughly know it. There were a lot worse places to live than Thessalonica in their opinion. But not to God. They were lost and needed to be found. So God sent His finders to them. Paul and his missionary team, who wanted to go elsewhere (Asia), and had even tried, but **"the Spirit of Jesus would not allow them to"** (Acts 16:7). Instead, **"during the night Paul had a vision of a man of Macedonia standing and begging him, 'Come over to Macedonia and help us.'"** (Acts 16:8b-9). That was all it took. Luke, joining them for the first time at that place, wrote, **"we got ready at once to leave for Macedonia, concluding that God had called us to preach the gospel to them"** (16:10).

Why did Paul's team not go to Asia? For this simple reason--the Thessalonians were destined by God to be the next ones to be shown His saving love. Don't miss the point. Yes, God loves the world. BUT, He shows special love wherever He sends His servants to share the gospel. And that includes you, today!

Have you ever really gotten the significance of that truth? God really loves you. Yes, you. Not everyone has heard. Not every messenger has gone, as we will see. But someone came to you. And you heard what some others have not heard. Don't stumble over asking WHY you heard and others did not. Just marvel at it. Let it sink in. This is what happened at Thessalonica.

The Christians there were amazed at God's love for them through Jesus. They had never imagined such persistent and gracious love. Oh, they had heard the stories for centuries. You see, great Mt Olympus (9,793 feet high) was about 50 miles south of the city. Within view. This is where Zeus and the gods were supposed to live. It was in his honor that the Olympic Games originally began. But nowhere in Greek mythology had they ever heard that Zeus loved them all so much that he would send his son to live and die for them. And to be raised from the dead, thereby assuring that all who put their faith in him would also physically be raised to eternal life. That was Paul's gospel. And he so believed in its primacy that he was willing to face repeated threats of persecution and death just to share it with others. The Thessalonians were deeply impressed with Paul's commitment to that gospel and its message of unbelievable love.

Are you amazed at God's love for you today? How would you rate your love for Jesus? Are you "madly in love" with Him? Or just subtly flirting? The Thessalonians were head-over-heels in love and that is why they were willing to do what appeared crazy to others. Like trust in Jesus and His kingdom instead of Rome's. Even at risk of death. When a young man has the chance to marry the girl of his dreams, he either drops everything and goes for it. Or he regrets it forever! When love becomes his bottom line, his life is changed forever. What is your bottom line with Jesus?

Has it ever really grabbed you--that you are truly loved by God. That you are, so to speak, "the one of His dreams." That He left heaven to pursue you, willing to wash away your sins and wanting to share with you His amazing glory! The Thessalonians were gifted to grasp this in the deepest way. And they were never the same again. Jesus had once tried to teach a

57

Pharisee the same lesson, when he was horrified at the prostitute who washed Jesus' feet with her tears. Listen carefully to his words,

> "Two men owed money to a certain moneylender. One owed him 500 denarii, and the other 50. Neither of them had the money to pay him back, so he canceled the debts of both. Now which of them will love him more?" Simon replied, "I suppose the one who had the bigger debt canceled." "You have judged correctly," Jesus said. Then he turned toward the woman and said to Simon, "Do you see this woman? I came into your house. You did not give me any water for my feet, but she wet my feet with her tears and wiped them with her hair. You did not give me a kiss, but this woman, from the time I entered, has not stopped kissing my feet. You did not put oil on my head, but she has poured perfume on my feet. Therefore, I tell you, her many sins have been forgiven—for she loved much. But he who has been forgiven little loves little." (Lk 7:41-47).

Maybe that is the first big difference between the amazing Thessalonians and many of us today. We have forgotten how much we have been forgiven and how much we are loved. They were not loved MORE than we. It is just that they did not forget the love of God. The message and reality of His love was not replaced by anything else. It displaced all previous loves and conquered their souls. Or as Paul would write, "**The love of Christ compels us**" (2 Cor. 5:14a).

Be honest with me. Aren't many of us today really like the Ephesians, to whom Jesus would later send the message: "**Yet I hold this against you: You have forsaken your first love. Remember the height from which you have fallen! Repent and do the things you did at first. If you do not repent, I will come to you and remove your lampstand (local church) from its place**" (Rev. 2:4-5). Is this why so many churches down through the ages have died? Why an estimated 3,750 churches close in the USA each year? God's love eventually lost its luster to them? Something replaced the love of Jesus in their hearts. How many of our churches today would have already died had not someone's financial legacy kept them alive? What is keeping your church alive? Is it still the old, old story of Jesus and His love? Or something far less beautiful and compelling? Did you awake this morning amazed by His love for you? If not, you probably did not show much love for Him throughout the day. One big way they differ from most of us is that the Thessalonian disciples were amazed at God's love for them and, in turn, became amazing in their life of love for His Son. Is your love for Jesus growing? He can help you with that. Why not ask Him to?

For Reflection and Discussion

1. How often do you pause and think about the amazing love of God for you?
2. How could you help cause the love of God to be focused upon more in your home and church?

Chapter 13

How high did you go in God's draft?

The dream of many athletes is to go pro. The higher you go in the draft the greater you are valued and the more you get paid. To be a 1st round draft pick is a huge honor as it says you are among the most esteemed players available. It must be quite an experience to be recruited and drafted as a pro. Something not easily forgotten.

Paul introduces us to God's "draft" by writing that he knew the Thessalonians were God's chosen ones - or as theologians would call them - His elect ones. **"For we know, brothers, loved by God, that he has chosen you"** (1 Thes 1:4b). This Greek word for "chosen" is used only 6 other times in the NT and always of God's selection of certain humans. Jesus assured Ananias that Paul (Saul) was **"his chosen instrument to carry my name to the Gentiles and their kings and before the people of Israel"** (Acts 9:15). The one time Peter used this word was as a warning for his readers to **"be all the more eager to make your...election sure"** (1 Pet 1:10). Peter was writing to a large group of professing believers, not all of whom were living like they belonged to "the Lord's team." Some were hardly living like those who had been taken in "God's draft." Peter's readers were like many today who forget how special it is to be chosen by God.

The Bible speaks of **"elect angels"** (1 Tim 5:21) and fallen angels (Jude 6). There are those God takes and those He leaves to themselves. Paul does not here say why God chose the Thessalonians instead of others. He just says that they were specially loved and selected by God. And that this made an obvious difference right from the start. The drafted player acts differently than the one passed over. The one celebrates and is thankful. His life is enriched and forever changed. The other just goes on with life, trying to make ends meet.

I am not trying to upset anyone unnecessarily with these statements. The debate over predestination is centuries old and unfortunately continues to divide Christians. The reason I mention it here is that Paul brings it up right at the beginning and makes quite a point of it. It is the second big way that many Christians today differ from the Thessalonians. We are afraid to talk about this subject. Paul wasn't. We view it as impractical. The Thessalonians didn't. The fact of their election incredibly motivated them. They realized the one amazing fact about God's draft– No one wanted to be drafted on to His team. It was all by surprise. All of grace. There is no room on God's team for self-exalting pride. We are a humble team of misfits transformed into His All-Pros through Jesus, alone!

Loved and chosen. Never lose that link. Not like the flea-ridden cat that crept into your yard when your neighbor died. What else could you do when your child looked up at you with those eyes full of tears and declared, "You can't take Fluffy down to the SPCA. You know what will happen to him there!" The cat became an object of your pity. And out of some warped sense of obligation you graciously allowed it into your home–but you let it be known from the outset, "I am not going to take care of it!" Your choosing (electing) the cat would not have been motivated by true love. God's was!

The Thessalonian disciples were His beloved and cherished possession! So, Paul immediately introduced them to the high mysteries of God's predestination without a worry. He could do that because it was not a matter merely of mind–it was a matter of the heart! His choosing them was a matter of divine love NOT a matter of a divine logic! Some things deeply impact and change us that we can hardly grasp, intellectually. This is huge for us to get. We need no arguments to defend God's election when we begin to grasp that it was an act of pure love. And when we understand that God has, in love, marked out our destiny–then we'll go wherever that love takes us. Even if it means a showdown with Caesar. It is the nature of discipleship for the disciple will follow the Master wherever the Master goes. "**They follow the Lamb wherever he goes**" (Rev. 14:4). What will be true of the 144,000 disciples in the last days, was true of the first followers of Jesus (see John 4:4-9) and of these disciples at Thessalonica.

This is another difference, in my opinion, between many of us and the Thessalonians. Many see this discussion about God's election as an unnecessary and divisive point of doctrine. Obscure and irrelevant. As something that really doesn't matter. Paul, inspired by God, saw it as vital. And he wanted to make sure that everyone who read that letter knew God had done something very special to them. He had chosen them. He would repeat the same truth again in his second letter saying, "**But we ought always to thank God for you, brothers loved by the Lord, because from the beginning God chose you to be saved through the sanctifying work of the Spirit and through belief in the truth**" (2 Thes 2:13). They were loved by God and they were chosen by God. Slaves, businessmen, home keepers, politicians and street cleaners. These were God's elect. And they were all first round picks!

Paul did not need to see any other evidence than what he had seen demonstrated already by this fledgling congregation. They were only months old and Paul knew they were the real deal. God's All Stars. He wanted to make sure the Thessalonians realized that their ship had come in. The signing bonus was sure. Eternal benefits were theirs. There was great excitement and high expectations in Thessalonica. Is there today with us? Do we act like first round picks?

Soon we will examine the evidence that made Paul certain of the

Thessalonians' high status as the Lord's chosen ones. We must pause and wonder, if he were looking at us, would he likely say the same thing about us? Do we see ourselves as the blessed ones? Honored beyond words to be on God's "team?" Joyfully wearing His uniform wherever we go?

Or might Paul's assessment of our lives and churches run parallel to what he wrote to the more worldly Corinthians, **"Examine yourselves to see whether you are in the faith; test yourselves."** (2 Cor 13:5). The Spirit did not inspire him to give the same level of assurance to them because they did not warrant it. In fact, he warned them, **"So, if you think you are standing firm, be careful that you don't fall!"** (1 Cor 10:12).

Paul was sure of the Thessalonians' election and so were they. They knew that they had been selected and were living like the Lord's draft picks. When you think about it, that is really important. It is no small thing. There is no good reason why a child of God should live with his head down in constant defeat. He is on the winning team! Yes, it is a great honor to be drafted first round by men. It is unspeakably higher and more special to be selected by God.

It is one thing to say of others, "Sure, I think they are Christians." It is quite another thing to say, "They are definitely God's chosen ones." All true believers *are* God's elect. How special is that to you? Do we really appreciate how unworthy we all are as God's first round draft picks? He did not choose us because we would improve His team. Quite the opposite. We often test and weaken and drag the team down. Yet we all remain equally loved by God. What an owner! We are all carried by the superstar, Jesus. What a Savior!

Teams often trade their draft picks because professional sports is a business. Nothing personal, they say. But God never trades one of us because our relationship with Him is NOT a business deal. It is totally personal. It is a matter of love.

Unlike pro athletes, our being selected is never jeopardized by our performance! He has loved us with an everlasting love. There is a no-trade clause in all of the contracts signed by God. He paid a great price for us because He loved us. When the honor of being one of His first rounders is constantly remembered, and cherished in our hearts, we will be changed. We will then see what the amazing Thessalonians saw and joyfully serve Him with amazing love every day of our lives!

For Reflection and Discussion

1. Has this chapter made you think differently of the importance of the doctrine of election? How so?

Chapter 15

What form does God's power take in YOUR life?

So, what was the source of the Thessalonians' amazing resolve to follow Christ even when opposed by Caesar and his empire? We have seen that, right from the start, they realized two things: they were (1) loved by God and (2) chosen by God. That set them off from many of us who wrongly look at ourselves and our fellow Christians as being "nothing special."

Now we can add a third amazing difference – they were empowered by God. **"For we know, brothers loved by God, that he has chosen you, because our gospel came to you not simply with words, but also with power, with the Holy Spirit and with deep conviction"** (1 Thes 1:4-5a). The Thessalonians were empowered by none other than God, Himself. But their story does not take the turn we might expect, with tales of signs, wonders and mighty deeds regularly proving God's presence. Miracles likely happened, but they were not, with the Thessalonians, the most prominent proofs of the Spirit's power. Love was. And we will see that love did what no miracle could do. As they patiently and sacrificially opened their hearts up to the world around them, that special love opened the door of the world up to these disciples like few others. God's love is still pouring through His disciples and amazing the world. Get a copy of "Miraculous Movements" (by Jerry Trousdale), and read how the love of former Muslims (now Jesus followers) is leading hundreds of thousands of other Muslims (even Jihadists) to fall in love with Jesus!

Paul was likely writing this first letter when he started his church plant in Corinth (see Acts 17:16-18:28). He had fled from Berea to Athens and then went to Corinth. Miracles, we know, flourished among the Corinthians. But love did not. Paul, when later writing to the Corinthians, reminded them to eagerly desire the greater gifts and then showed them "**the most excellent way**" (1 Cor 12:31). The way of love. The agape of God. Love is so powerful and essential a part of how God works, that without it even miracles prove meaningless! Tongues (13:1), prophecy (13:2), miraculous knowledge (13:2), social sacrifice and martyrdom (13:3) *without love* are proclaimed "**nothing**." Read again of the love of God in 1 Cor 13 and make it your quest to be filled with it and to have it overflow from you to all around you. Then you will know how the Thessalonians were super-empowered by the Spirit.

In 1st century worship, demon-empowered cults were often combined with the more formal emperor worship in city temples around the empire. The emperor-cult priests would also become devotees of a mystery religion. These imports would supercharge the worship with examples of supernatural (though demonic) manifestations. The chief religious cult that was joined with emperor worship at Thessalonica was most likely "worship of the Cabiri, the mystic deities of Samothrace, and so here the emperor was deified as Kabeiros, as the coins show. Kabeiros is described as 'the ancestral and most holy of all gods'...."[27] Donfried notes, "As with some of the other cults in Thessalonica, so the mysteries of Samothrace are 'subject to Bacchic frenzy'".[22] [28]And the following description of Bacchic frenzy should suffice to show that the Thessalonians were very familiar with demonic influence in their lives, even with its expressions of tremendous power.

"This predominantly emotional experience...marked for the [Bacchic leaders] the beginning of a new life. In a very real sense it was a new birth for the individual who experienced it. Hitherto he had been a man merely. Now he was something more; he was man plus god, a divinized human. Certain aspects of his new divine life deserve to be noted in order to emphasize the contrast with life as it was lived at the ordinary levels of human experience.

"In its temporary emotional aspect, it was characterized by excessive indulgence as contrasted with the reasoned moderation that was typical of Greek life generally. For Greeks, self-control was one of the four cardinal virtues and "nothing in excess" was a fundamental Hellenic principle of life. The Bacchic experience, however, cut sheer across this principle....

"More than all this it was a life of miraculous power; for by the very fact of divine possession the [Bacchic disciple] believed himself to have acquired the power of the god. Hence, he could heal diseases, control the forces of nature, and even prophesy. Plato reflected the popular conviction that the Bacchae could work miracles in his famous comparison of the lyric poets to the maenads.... The Bacchae of Euripides literally teems with miracles....

"The life of the [Bacchic disciple] was, therefore, a dynamic life in which the peculiar power of the deity operated to perform wonderful deeds through men. Most important of   all, the new Bacchic life in

---

[27] B. Witherington, 1 and 2 Thessalonians (Grand Rapids, MI: Wm B Eerdmans Publishing, Co., 2006) p. 5.

[28] K. Donfried, *Paul, Thessalonica, and Early Christianity* (Grand Rapids, MI: Wm B   Eerdmans Publishing Co. 2002) p. 29.

its emotional and dynamic aspects was viewed as but the foretaste of a happy existence in the future.... So the unusual emotional experiences fostered by the Dionysian rites: the intoxication of wine or of the dance, the frenzy of the orgy, the divine gift of foresight or miracle-working power--these were more than merely proofs of divine possession. They were a definite foretaste and assurance of a blessed future life. In the crude physical emotionalism of Bacchic ecstasy, therefore, the devotees of the wine-god found a new birth experience which guaranteed them a happy immortality."[29]

I have included this rather lengthy quote so you can better understand that the Thessalonians, like many other pagans, had a background of spiritual power. But it had all been demonic. Paul was speaking familiarly to them when he warned of the coming lawless one. The Antichrist's satanic-empowered work would include **"all kinds of counterfeit miracles, signs and wonders"** (2 Thes 2:9). The power that filled the Thessalonians, though, was obviously from a different source. It was from the Holy Spirit of God. And the power of the Spirit in the amazing Thessalonians looked unlike the power displayed in any other religious devotees of their day. It looked like love. Unbelievable, sacrificial, humbling-yet-joyful love. What power do you have flowing into and from you as a Christian? If it does not look like love, it is not worthy of the King of Love and His Kingdom of love. The Kingdom that the Spirit is now spreading all over this earth.

For Reflection and Discussion

1. Discuss the power you have felt when someone showed you an act of incredible love.
2. Why do you think love impacts others more permanently than seeing a miracle?

---

[29] H. Willoughby, *Pagan Regeneration* (Chicago: Univ of Chicago Press, 1929) chap. 3 sect. 2.

Chapter 16

Is your commitment to Jesus "a done deal"?

As we consider Paul's description of how the Thessalonians were brought to faith, note that the gospel came **"with the Holy Spirit and with deep conviction."** This was another reason why the Thessalonians were who they were and did the amazing things that they did. They were quickly convinced by the Spirit. Christ's reality as Lord, and the life that was available only through Him, went from the realm of possibility to certainty in their hearts. Their faith was a grounded, **"deep conviction."** Anchored and unmovable. "When used of persons in the NT, the meaning [of this word] is to be convinced or fully persuaded...When used of things, it has the notion of completing or finishing."[30] When the Spirit seals the deal in this way, it is a done deal. Do you live like life's meaning is a closed case to you? Like Jesus has delivered to you all you need to know. Does your life reveal you as satisfied and sure? Or are you still dabbling with the notion that sin might actually be rewarding? Not quite sure if Christ's call to follow Him will actually lead to a satisfying life here and beyond. If you are still testing the waters, in that way you differ greatly from the Thessalonians and from all true 1st century disciples.

Paul wanted every believer he had not seen to live with the certainty of the amazing Thessalonians. He said so, when he wrote to the Colossians, **"I want you to know how much I am struggling for you and... for all who have not met me personally. My purpose is that they may be encouraged in heart and united in love, so that they may have the full riches of <u>complete</u> understanding"** (Col 2:1-2a). He used the same word again. He struggled to see an understanding of Christ that was complete or fully assured. A deeply convicted understanding in all believers. Not wishy washy. Not changing with each pressure that culture or Caesar would throw their way.

Is your mind settled on Christ? No matter what, you will follow Him. Your life is "signed, sealed and delivered" to Him and His kingdom. His love has won your heart. No one arrives there without the Holy Spirit being His Teacher. Such a conclusion is supernatural. And amazing works will follow such a life of deep and unmoving conviction. But little or no fruit is produced in the lives of the wavering and unconvinced.

Jesus spoke of those who **"believe for a while, but in the time of testing they fall away"** (Lk 8:13b). They possess a momentary and passing

---

[30] A.T. Robertson, *Word Pictures in the NT* (Grand Rapids, MI: Baker Book House 1931), vol 2, p 4.

faith, rather than the concrete convictions of Thessalonian-like disciples. When we recognize the pressures the Thessalonians faced, we are astonished at the Spirit's mighty work of producing such deep and unchanging conviction. The obstacles were so many and varied that their very endurance proved the presence and power of God. But they did so much more than just persevere, as we will see. Pray with me that the Spirit will seal Christ's work in our hearts with similar resolve. That we will live like the deal has been done and our worldview is settled. No longer up for grabs to the highest bidder. That you will follow Jesus today as they followed Jesus through the tribulation of their times.

Pray with me the famous words (author unknown) we often sang at summer camp and in youth group. Words that capture the work of God in the hearts of the amazing Thessalonians and of every committed disciple of Jesus:

"I have decided to follow Jesus, I have decided to follow Jesus, I have decided to follow Jesus. Not turning back, no turning back.

The world behind me, the cross before me; the world behind me, the cross before me; the world behind me, the cross before me. No turning back, no turning back.

Tho' none go with me, still I will follow; Tho' none go with me, still I will follow; Tho' none go with me, still I will follow. No turning back, no turning back.

Will you decide now to follow Jesus? Will you decide now to follow Jesus? Will you decide now to follow Jesus? No turning back, no turning back."

For Reflection and Discussion

1. By what means do you think we can measure the depth of someone's commitment to Jesus?

Chapter 17

What does it mean "to receive" Jesus?

The essence of this chapter has radically changed my life and ministry. Because of the nature of this book, I will only be able to share the essential points with you. But, to get the full picture, you will likely need to read a bit further in books like those listed below.[31]

Many of us were taught that Christian conversion involved "asking Jesus into our hearts." Or receiving Jesus as our personal Savior. Studying the evangelism of Jesus and the apostles has shown me just how different our definitions can be from those intended by biblical words. The simple truth is this—what I meant by "receive Jesus" is not what that phrase meant in the New Testament.

There is a reason why Paul described the saving work of the Holy Spirit and the faith of the Thessalonians with these important first words,

"The Lord's message rang out from you not only in Macedonia and Achaia—your faith in God has been made known everywhere. Therefore, we do not need to say anything about it, for they themselves report <u>what kind of reception you gave us</u>. They tell how you turned to God from idols to serve the living and true God, and to wait for his Son from heaven, whom he raised from the dead—Jesus, who rescues us from the coming wrath" (1 Thes 1:8-10).

I understood everything in this passage except his first point. Why would Paul highlight the manner in which the Thessalonians received him? Does it really matter what kind of reception they gave to Paul and his mission team? Isn't it enough that they turned from idols to serve God? I could not understand Paul's need to emphasize the manner in which he was received, mentioning it first in his list of remarkable proofs of the Spirit's work and the Thessalonians' faith. Until I studied New Testament discipleship. Then everything became clear.

When Jesus trained His disciples to become "fishers of men," He had them listen to and watch Him evangelize. Then He sent them out to do the same. There are several texts describing the several times He did this (see

---

[31] Miraculous Movements by Jerry Trousdale; Father Glorified by P Robertson and David Watson; Contagious Disciple Making by David and Paul Watson; Are You a Christian or a Disciple? by Edward Gross, Not a Fan by Kyle Idleman, etc.

Matt 10:1-15; Mark 6:6-13; Luke 9:1-6, 51-56; 10:1-24). These were training missions, before His crucifixion, which preceded the Great Commission after His resurrection (Matt 28:16-20; Mark 16:14-20; Luke 24:44-49; John 20:19-23). The early missions helped to prepare the disciples for the Great Commission.

Notice how important the reception of His disciples was when Jesus sent them out on their early training missions. Here are some of the explicit instructions He gave to them. And until I studied just how carefully 1st century disciples obeyed their rabbis, these details did not matter much to me. Each detail would have been memorized and carefully followed by the disciples as they went on these missions. Here are some of Jesus' commands regarding reception:

- The harvest is plentiful but the workers are few. Ask the Lord of the harvest, therefore, to send out workers into his harvest field. (Luke 10:2; also in Matt 9::37)
- Whatever town or village you enter, search for some worthy person there and stay at his house until you leave. (Matt 10:11)
- As you enter a home give it your greeting. If the home is deserving, let your peace rest on it; if it is not, let your peace return to you. (Matt 10:12-13)
- When you enter a house, first say, "Peace to this house." If a man of peace is there, your peace will rest on him; if not, it will return to you. (Luke 10:5-6)
- When you enter a town, and are welcomed, eat what is set before you… But when you enter a town and are not welcomed, go into its streets and say, "Even the dust of your town that sticks to our feet we wipe off against you…. (Luke 10:8-11)
- And if any place will not welcome you or listen to you, shake the dust off your feet when you leave as a testimony against them. (Mark 6:11)

Prior to this, when teaching His disciples, Jesus warned them, **"Do not give dogs what is sacred; do not throw your pearls to pigs. If you do, they may trample them under their feet, and then turn and tear you to pieces"** (Matt 7:6). After one of the training missions, Jesus warned of their future mission work and said,

> **"I am sending you out like sheep among wolves. Therefore, be as shrewd as snakes and as harmless as doves. Be on your guard against men; they will hand you over to the local councils and flog you in their synagogues. On my account, you will be**

brought before governors and kings as witnesses to them and to the Gentiles" (Matt 10:16-18)

Did you realize that Paul followed a similar model when he and his team planted their mission churches? If a region rejected them, **"they shook off the dust from their feet in protest against them and went to the next region"** (Acts 13:50). When the synagogue rejected his message in Corinth, **"he shook out his clothes in protest and said to them, Your blood be on your own heads! I am clear of my responsibility. From now on I will go to the Gentiles"** (Acts 18:6b).

Now, we return to the question of "asking Jesus into our hearts." The reasoning goes like this. If Jesus is on the outside, you are lost. He stands at the door and knocks. If anyone opens the door He will come in and save them (See Rev. 3:20). Like John said, **"He came to that which was his own, but his own did not receive him. Yet to all who received him, who believed in his name, he gave the right to become children of God'** (John 1:11-12).

The problem with how many of us were taught to unpack these verses is that we did NOT understand that receiving Jesus or welcoming Jesus meant to take Him home with us. To open your entire life to Him. It most certainly does NOT mean, with every head bowed and every eye closed to slip up one's hand. Or to receive Jesus into your "heart" and tuck Him away somewhere safely. The main issue, of course, is ON WHOSE TERMS is this relationship with Jesus established? On ours or on His?

Please do not rush here. New Testament discipleship is the model Jesus employed and sanctioned for the spread of His Faith throughout the world. The command is, **"Go and make disciples."** Many of us, instead, have gone and made Christians (See Appendix One). God has given us two ways to reach the world. Preach the gospel. Make disciples. Paul always did both, as Luke records, **"They preached the good news in that city and won a large number of disciples"** (Acts 14:23). When Paul had a respondent to the gospel, what did he do? Lead him or her in prayer to close the deal and make sure they would not go to hell? No, Paul made disciples of those who wanted to be saved from his gospel preaching.

There has been an emergence of incredible fruitfulness in the last ten years, all over the world, by missionaries who have begun to follow Jesus' model more carefully. Disciples are making disciples who make disciples. Churches are multiplying. Exactly what Paul said happened at Thessalonica is happening again all over the world!

People of peace are being identified by the thousands. Their lives have been readied by the Lord of the harvest. And prayerful disciple makers have gone out in love to find them. When peace is spoken, the readied soul responds and fruitful gospel engagement begins. Many of today's witnesses

70

are using the Discovery Bible Study method, which is so simple that absolutely everyone can make disciples. So what we are seeing today is, just like in the 1st century, every disciple can become a disciple maker.

And it all begins with a prayerful providential preparation of one of God's chosen ones, the person of peace. As Jesus said, **"No one can come to me unless the father who sent me draws him… It is written in the Prophets, 'They will all be taught by God.' Everyone who listens to the Father and learns from him comes to me"** (John 6:44-45). David Watson, a missionary powerfully used by God to see hundreds of thousands of disciples made by following Jesus' model, wrote,

> "Making disciples and planting churches is easier if you're working with God and the people He has prepared rather than trying to force the Gospel on people who aren't ready. Engage a community, and then find the Person of Peace. Actually, if we do things right, the Person of Peace finds us. Learning how to be found is key."[32]

In 2012, Jerry Trousdale, wrote, "Our experience in Africa now counts approximately 18,000 different people of peace who have opened the doors of their communities for disciple makers."[33]

The Prince of Peace has sent out His disciples in peace. **"Peace be with you! As the Father has sent me, I am sending you."** (John 20:19-20). You will be astonished as you read how peacefully, how quietly, how carefully and prayerfully the Thessalonians went out to make disciples of all the nations. And none other of Paul's church plants were so successful. He had found them at just the right time. And this incredible group of people of peace, fueled by the love of Christ, reached their entire region with the gospel of Christ.

For Reflection and Discussion

1. What does receptivity to the Gospel prove about the hearers?
2. Discuss how different one's evangelistic strategy will be if we focus on the receptive rather than on everyone.

---

[32] David Watson, Contagious Disciple Making, p 123 – see the whole chapter 14, Finding a Person of Peace.
[33] Jerry Trousdale, *Miraculous Movements*, p 91.

Chapter 18

Is it stupid to ask, "Can demons repent and be saved?"

What was your conversion like? What form, if any, did it follow? What changes in your life have taken place since that time? Questions like these mattered enormously to Paul, who described the Thessalonians' conversion: "**...you turned to God from idols to serve the living and true God and to wait for his Son from heaven, whom he raised from the dead–Jesus, who rescues us from the coming wrath**" (1 Thes 1:9).

It is important that we look for a moment at what the Thessalonians were before they turned to God. And what that turnaround looked like. Because this change had an amazing impact on those who observed them. Though they all had their favorite deities, the idols and religious devotion they turned from were many and varied. NT Wright graphically captures their setting:

> "The remarkable thing was the instant effect the gospel had. At the heart of it...was the call to worship the true God rather than idols. That was simply unheard of in Paul's world. It would be like asking people in a modern city to give up using motor cars, computers and telephones. The gods of the Greek and Roman paganism were everywhere. If you were going to plant a tree, you would pray to the relevant god. If you were going on a business trip, a quick visit to the appropriate shrine was in order. If you or your son or daughter was getting married, serious and costly worship of the relevant deity was expected. At every turn in the road the gods were there: unpredictable, possibly malevolent, sometimes at war among themselves, so that you could never do too much in the way of placating them, making sure you'd got them on your side."[34]

Someone who had turned from all idols to one God was truly odd. Not only because it would set you apart and adrift socially–and it would almost certainly do that. But to forsake the gods was to remove yourself from a definite source of supernatural power. It was important to have a god on your side given the uncertainty of weather, crops and health. Even if these

---

[34] Tom Wright, *Paul for Everyone: Galatians and Thessalonians* (Louisville, KY: Westminster John Knox Press 2004) p 91.

gods were demons, as Paul taught, "...**the sacrifices of pagans are offered to demons, not to God, and I do not want you to be participants with demons**" (1 Cor 10:20, cf. Gal 4:8).

So, to turn from idols was no small thing. It was a total change. 180 degrees. To turn from a demonic being of power, who manifested itself through its idol's worship, would be both dangerous and stupid unless the power source turned to was greater and better. In open defiance to sacred traditions and political pronouncements, the Thessalonians began claiming that Jesus was replacing them all. He became their one-size-fits-all-situations God! Unheard of in Thessalonica. And far too little seen in America!

We will concentrate on application later (in Part Four--Love Working Today). However, let me ask you—what idolatry did you reject when you received Christ? I know there were no wood and stone forms you bowed to. But did you forsake the idols of materialism, consumerism and individualism when you chose Christ? Or did you just turn from "sin" generally? Were there no specific idols named and repented of in your conversion? Paul mentions greed as idolatry (Col. 2:5; Eph 4:22). And the dictionary defines greed as "desire for more than one needs or deserves." Is not greed one of the idols enshrined in many of our hearts and homes?

Maybe you are not quite sure what you turned from, but you are much more certain who you "turned to." Let me explore your turning. By the way, turning from idols and turning to God involve more than just words. True repentance is not proven merely from what is said. It flows from the heart and takes hold of one's life. In discipleship language, repentance has two sides—a sound and a look. The sound of repentance is heartfelt confession of sin. The look of repentance is following Jesus. A sound without a look is a counterfeit. But, since American conversions so often focus mainly on saying the right thing, let me ask you. What did you say when you became a Christian? Did it involve:

- worshiping and confessing Jesus as the Son of God
- boldly declaring His unique holiness
- crying out to God in a worship service
- acknowledging Jesus as the Messiah
- glorifying Christ as the sole Judge of all
- lifting up Jesus as the way of salvation

Let me tip you off. The above expressions may all sound good to you; but, some who said those things were *not* disciples. In fact, the list is actually taken from the statements made by seriously demonized people! The demons were doing the "confessing."[26] We know that no demon will be saved. Yet they professed a degree of faith in Christ. As James warns, **"You believe that there is one God. Good! Even demons believe that—and shudder"** (James 2:19). Our profession of faith better involve more than just "the right words." Like the Thessalonians, we need a life change that shows a total makeover.[27]

Two questions emerge from Paul's letter and now beg to be asked. Whom are you serving? What are you waiting for? The Thessalonians served **"the living and true God,"** while they **"waited for his Son from heaven."** The word "serve" means to be devoted to someone as a slave. John Stott wrote,

> "To claim to have turned to God from idols is manifestly bogus if it does not result in serving the God to whom we have turned. We must not think of conversion only in negative terms as a turning away from the old life, but also positively as the beginning of a new life of service. We could say that it is the exchange of one slavery for another, so long as we add that the new slavery is the real freedom. In this way authentic conversion involves a double liberation, both *from* the thralldom of the idols whose slaves we were and into the service of God whose children we become"[28]

What marks of ownership does Jesus have over your life? Does His reign extend to your thoughts, speech, feelings and actions? If so, which ones is He really Lord over? Is He Master of our time? Of our disposable income? Our social relationships? Our work? I am not sure Paul would recognize many of us today who profess to be Christians as true Christ-followers. Simply because we do not live like the slaves of Jesus (or, that is, as the servants of God).

The amazing Thessalonians proved their new birth also by waiting for Jesus. Anticipating a divine Person. Because they loved Him. Not merely because they anticipated some reward or accomplishment. Or some painless existence. Certainly, not for revenge on their opponents and persecutors. They loved the One who had shown such amazing grace as to save them from the darkness and stranglehold of demonic paganism. They waited, longingly, for Him—doing whatever they could to acknowledge Him and advance His kingdom until He returned. Do we wait for Jesus in this way? I

---

[26]See Mk 5:6,7; Lk 4:33-34; Acts 16:16-18.
[27]See E Gross, Miracles, *Demons & Spiritual Warfare: An Urgent Call for Discernment* (Grand Rapids, MI: Baker Book House 1990), ch 12 - Saving Faith or the Experience of   Demons, pp 124-134.
[28]J Stott, *The Message of 1 & 2 Thessalonians* (Doners Grove, IL: IVPress 1991) p 41.

doubt it. We aren't "waiting only" for Jesus if we hardly ever think about Him. You often think about the ones you love. How often do you think about Jesus each day?

The Thessalonians' conversion revealed a dramatic and amazing change of worldview. It was a repentance that showed. The kind of fruit that John the Baptist would approve of when he warned Pharisees and Sadducees, **"You brood of vipers! Who warned you to flee from the coming wrath? Produce fruit in keeping with repentance...The ax is already at the root of the trees, and every tree that does not produce good fruit will be cut down and thrown into the fire"** (Matt 3:7-10). John wanted the "religious ones" to know that being baptized was not enough. Jesus, Paul and James want us to know that the words we say may be no consequential than the professions made by demons.

If we, by His power, prove our profession by turning from our idols, serving God and waiting for Jesus, then we have begun to show similarities to the amazing Thessalonians. But if we try to belong to Christ on lower terms of commitment, with none of these fruits marking our lives, then, we are in danger. Whom do we think we are kidding?

Of course we know that demons will not be saved. But it is not a stupid question to ask today, as many are risking their souls on having merely spoken a few right words during a time of spiritual struggle. Words not greatly different from those spoken by demons under duress. Let us never forget - **"Faith without deeds is dead"** (James 2:26b). A faith that is "dead" is both unproductive and unconvincing. But "a faith that works through love" (Gal 5:6) is the real thing. And that was obviously the faith of the amazing Thessalonians! Is it ours?

For Reflection and Discussion

1. How dangerous do you now think it is to have a profession of faith without the fruits of following Jesus?
2. What idols do those in your culture need to "turn from" in order to truly follow Jesus?

Chapter 19

Amazing Faith

The seed of salvation had now taken root in Thessalonica. And Paul described the fruits of its harvest. They were specimens like no one had ever seen! Like sure winners at any country fair. Lives, like trees, bowed over with large and luscious fruit. What fruit? The beautiful fruits of faith, love and hope. In several places, Paul highlights the Christian's life by noting the characteristics of faith, hope and love.[29] This triad, made famous in 1 Cor 13, first appeared in his letter to the Thessalonians when he wrote, **"We continually remember...your work produced by faith, your labor produced by love, and your endurance inspired by hope in our Lord Jesus Christ"** (1 Thes 1:3). And he mentions them again later in this first letter. **"But since we belong to the day, let us be self-controlled, putting on faith and love as a breastplate, and the hope of salvation as a helmet"** (1 Thes 5:8). Why does he summarize their lives by using these three virtues? The great Reformer, John Calvin, sees these three as "a brief definition of true Christianity."[30] We will examine the strength of each of these characteristics as they were exhibited in the Thessalonians. But first, John Stott writes concerning all three of them,

> "Each is outgoing...Every Christian without exception is a believer, a lover and a hoper. Faith, hope and love are thus sure evidences of regeneration by the Holy Spirit. Together they completely reorientate our lives, as we find ourselves being drawn up towards God in faith, out towards others in love and on towards the Parousia in hope. The new birth means little or nothing if it does not pull us out of our fallen introversion and redirect us towards God, Christ and our fellow human beings."[31]

What does it look like to have one's religious convictions completely change or reorientate his life? With all phases of life being touched by the living Christ. It's not like a new hair style or color, which can make us look twice at someone. No, it is something much more radical. A letting Jesus in on everything. This is what happened to the Thessalonians. They didn't simply put on some different colored togas. **"The old has gone, the new**

---

[29]See 1 Cor 13:13; Rom. 5:2-5; Gal 5:5-6; Col 1:4-5.
[30]J Calvin, *First Epistle to the Thessalonians* (Grand Rapids, MI: Baker Book House, 1984), vol. 21 p. 239.
[31]J Stott *The Message of 1 & 2 Thessalonians (Downers Grove, IL: InterVarsity Press* 1991), pp 29-30.

has come!" (2 Cor 5:17). Pause for a moment and ask yourself–How much of my life has been reshaped by Jesus and His truth? Have I experienced a shocking total makeover?

A few minutes considering "our fallen introversion" would serve us well. What does our fallen introversion look like? Maybe all you have to do is look around you! In your own family and church. Into your own heart. God made us to be outward focused. Adam's Fall caved-in our souls, crushing us with concerns for ourselves. Which is it with you: inward gaze or outward gaze? Your house, your job, your kids, your education, your car, your vacation, your retirement? Or your neighbor's needs, your fellow-Christian's struggles, the closed-down plant's workers, the family across town who lost everything in a house fire? Be sure of this–the Thessalonians lives were rescued from their awful introversion. Their love was turned inside out.

The first great change that took place was at the core of their belief system. They had faith and, thereby, became "believers." 22 different times in 1 & 2 Thessalonians we run into the fact of faith expressed by its nouns (13 times) and verbs (9 times). The Thessalonians were saved by faith, that is by "**belief in <u>the truth</u>**" (2 Thes 2:13). The truth about Jesus. THAT became <u>the</u> truth not merely <u>a</u> truth. His gospel was the central and guiding fact of their lives. As so many have sung: "Christ has died. Christ is risen. Christ will come again." Do our lives see all truth connected to this reality about Jesus?

From the beginning, Satan has assaulted faith. As when he asked Eve, "**Did God really say, 'You must not eat from any tree in the garden?'**" (Gen 3:1). So, he did the same with the Thessalonians. He tried to create doubt. Paul wrote of this conflict in 3:1-10 where he mentioned faith no less than five times. "**For this reason, when I could stand it no longer, I sent to find out about your faith. I was afraid that in some way the tempter might have tempted you and our efforts might have been useless**" (1 Thes 3:5). This sounds serious because it was (and is) serious. Paul knew that everything is lost when faith is lost. We cannot do well without a strong faith. How strong is your faith? Is it growing by your use of it? Are you tenderly caring for the condition of your brother's faith?

NT Wright again captures the original context so well:

> Paul's basic fear is that they may have been swept off track, like a ship blown away from its proper course, or like someone lured away from their proper path by enticing words. Paul may mean that their sufferings themselves are the force that could distract them; or perhaps that, in the midst of these sufferings people near and dear to them will begin to suggest that, if only they compromised a bit on their extraordinary allegiance to Jesus, they wouldn't have to undergo such things...What Paul is afraid of is compromise, of them abandoning their firm hold on the gospel, their unswerving loyalty

to their new-found king."[32]

Today, it may not be the threats of a cruel dictator that spark compromise. Rather it more likely is **"life's worries, riches and pleasures"** that choke the little seeds of faith so that **"they do not mature"** (Lk 8:14). Whatever it is—resist it. Use your faith and watch it grow. Determine today, right now, to do something by faith. To speak, to pray, to act out of your belief in God's presence and power. Once you do a little you are on your way to doing a lot. You will be on the same track as the amazing Thessalonians.

Paul's second letter to them begins with great thanks to God noting, **"your faith is growing more and more"** (2 Thes 1:3). My friends, guard your faith. If it is not growing it is diminishing. It does not stay at a level place. And it does not grow without your acting on it. Paul spoke of that and said, **"...we constantly pray for you, that our God may...by his power...fulfill every good purpose of yours and every act prompted by your faith"** (2 Thes 1:11). How many of your acts today will be **"prompted by your faith"**? How many prompted by your flesh? Ask God to help you to die a little to your sinful desires so that you can live a little more for His Son. And soon enough, in this way, you will begin to join Paul and all disciples who literally **"live by faith, not by sight"** (2 Cor 5:7). You won't likely see big changes all at once. But steps become a path. And a path, by His grace, becomes a pattern for life. And before you know it, by exercising your faith in Christ, your testimony will look more and more like the amazing life of faith lived by the amazing Thessalonians.

For Reflection and Discussion

1. Are Christians whom you know more known by the sound or the look of their faith? Why is this an important issue?

---

[32]NT Wright *Paul for Everyone: Galatians and Thessalonians* (Louisville, KY: Westminster John Knox Press 2002), p 109.

Chapter 20

Amazing Love

True faith never exists alone. It always has a twin. Her name is love. The faith of the Thessalonians was a **"faith expressing itself through love"** (Gal 5:6b). Several times he mentioned their love in its deep connection with their faith. **"Your <u>faith</u> is growing more and more, and the <u>love</u> every one of you has for each other is increasing"** (2 Thes 1:3). **"But Timothy has just now come to us from you and has brought good news about your <u>faith and love</u>"** (1 Thes 3:6). And again, **"But since we belong to the day, let us be self-controlled, putting on <u>faith and love as a breastplate</u>"** (1 Thes 5:8). When our lives are devoid of a strong faith linked with love, it is like exposing our chest and its vital organs to the arrows of the enemy. It was suicidal to go into battle without a breastplate. Today, we need faith and love like a warrior needed his armor in the day of battle.

The chief purpose of this book is to show you what happened when the love of Christ flowed through the Thessalonians. When they followed Jesus like He followed His Father. And to encourage you to desire and experience the same for yourselves. So you can glorify Jesus and impact your area similarly through His power. In the way the Thessalonians reached their region.

Paul used the noun and verb forms of "love" (agape) twelve times in 1 & 2 Thessalonians. We will carefully break those verses apart so you can enjoy their fruit. For now, you will have to be satisfied with just an appetizer. Later I hope you will be filled with the fruitful love of the amazing Thessalonians.

When commenting on their love, NT Wright wrote,

> "In particular, he is delighted to hear...about ...their love. This love was truly one of the astonishing things in the early church. Imagine, within that world, a new community where people from different social, cultural and racial backgrounds treated each other   with the love appropriate within a family! This was a sign, which Paul regularly celebrated, of God's dramatic work, starting something quite new, the like of which the world had not seen before."[33]

---

[33] NT Wright *Paul for Everyone* (Louisville, KY: Westminster John Knox Press 2004), p 112.

Paul had many heart-wrenching memories in mind when he mentioned their **"labor prompted by love"** (1 Thes 1:3). He was recalling specific uncalled-for-acts of astonishing love that naturally flowed from their born-again hearts. In this chapter we will quote several scholars who, comparing the Thessalonians' love to their own contexts, have come away in awe of that early work of the Spirit. As one writes,

> "When he speaks of their *labor prompted by love* Paul means more than small deeds of kindness done without hope of reward. The word *kopos* denotes laborious toil, unceasing hardship borne for love's sake.
>
> *Love* is our translation of *agape*, a word not used much before the Christians took it up and made it their characteristic word for love. They had not only a new word but a new idea, an idea we see in the love shown in Christ's death for sinners.... *Agape*... is not a love of the worthy.... On the contrary, it is love that seeks to give. God loves, not because people are worthy of that love, but because he is that kind of God; it is his nature to love, he *is* love.
>
> When his love comes to us we are faced with a challenge we cannot ignore.... Either we yield to the divine *agape* to be transformed by it, to be re-made in the divine image, to see people in measure as God sees them, or we do not. And if we do not, in that lies our condemnation. We have shut ourselves up to lovelessness. But those who yield themselves to God are transformed by the power of the divine *agape*, so that they rejoice to give themselves in the service of others. Paul thanks God that this is what the Thessalonians have done. "[34]

Think for a moment what love **"for each other and for everyone else"** (1 Thes 3:12) would have demanded of them. A love **"every one of you has for each other"** (2 Thes 1:3). A **"brotherly love"** they shared as those **"who had been taught by God to love each other"** (1 Thes 4:9). A love that encompassed **"all the brothers throughout Macedonia."** (1 Thes 4:10). We will spend many chapters unpacking the specifics implied in these phrases. But, for a moment, just ask yourself. Have I seen or known such love? A single person who has loved each one as he does all others? And treated them all as friends?

The great Church Father, Chrysostom (347-407AD), lamented the loss of such love and such friends in the church of his day as he preached

---

[34]L Morris *1 & 2 Thessalonians*. Pp 42-43.

from the Thessalonian epistles,

"He who loves ought so to love (like Paul loved the Thessalonians), that if he were asked even for his own life...he would not refuse it. I do not say 'if he were asked,' but so that he would even run to present him with the gift. For nothing, nothing can be sweeter than such love... For what will not a genuine friend perform? ...Though you should name infinite treasures, none of them is comparable to a genuine friend...A friend rejoices at seeing his friend, He is knit to him with an union of soul that affords unspeakable pleasure....

I speak of genuine friends, men of one soul, who would even die for each other, who love fervently...If anyone has a friend such as I speak of, he will acknowledge the truth of my words. He, though he sees his friend every day, is not filled. He prays for him for the same things as for himself.

And where is it possible, somebody asks, that such an one should be found? (It isn't) because we have not the will; for it is possible. If it were not possible, neither would Christ have commanded it; he would not have discoursed so much concerning love. A great thing is friendship, and how great, no one can learn, and no discourse can represent, but (only) experience itself. It is this, the lack of love, that has caused the heresies...He who loves does not wish to command, nor to rule, but is obliged when he is ruled and commanded. He wishes rather to bestow a favor than to receive one, for he loves...
He is not so much gratified when good is done to him, as when he is doing good...I think that many of you do not understand what has been said.

I know that the greater part do not understand what is said... A friend is sweeter than the present life. Many therefore after the death of their friends have not wished to live any longer. With a friend one would bear even banishment; but without a friend, they would not choose to inhabit even his own country. With a friend even poverty is tolerable, but without him both health and riches are intolerable.[35]

And in our days, another great preacher, when commenting on the contagious Christianity of the Thessalonians wrote,

---

[35] J Chrysostom *Homilies on Thessalonians* (Grand Rapids. MI: Calvin College Ethereal Library 2009), pp 953-957.

The Thessalonian Christians not only knew that they were supposed to love fellow believers, but they made their knowledge come alive in their relationships with other Christians. They were not simply hearers of the truth but were doers as well.... The Thessalonians were called to do that which was best for fellow believers to the highest degree attainable. Their love was to be modeled after the sacrificial love Christ manifested toward them when He willingly died on the cross in man's behalf. When Christians display this kind of love toward one another, it attracts the attention of the unsaved. Why? Because non-Christians are used to a love they must be earned. So when they are confronted with unconditional love–a love that accepts others regardless of who they are rather than for what they can achieve–they see something that they want. That desire generally opens a natural door for sharing the good news about Jesus Christ. The Lord was well aware that the exercise of genuine Christian love among His people would have this effect. That's why He instructed His disciples with these words: 'A new commandment I give to you, that you love one another, even as I have loved you.... By this all men will know that you are My disciples. If you have love for one another.'[36]

The world does not know what to do with such love. You see, the love of Jesus is even greater than the Golden Rule. The latter teaches us **"to do to others what you would have them do to you"** (Matt 7:12). Treat others the way you want to be treated. That would be great to experience. But the love of Christ is a new commandment. Higher, holier and infinitely more powerful than the Golden Rule, for it makes Jesus the standard not ourselves. **"As I have loved you, so you must love one another"** (Jn 13:34). And His love is very unlike ours. His love is infinite grace. He loves all because it is His nature to love. Because love is good all the time--even when it is spat on, hated and killed. This is the love of Christ. And the Spirit of God delights in flooding our souls with it and flowing it through us–if we will but cherish and desire it. Like the amazing Thessalonians did.

They had been taught this new love by Paul. He confessed that it was the actual love of Christ that was compelling him (2 Cor 5:14). Not his own love. Jesus' love. One of my favorite authors, Charles Hodge (1797-1872), when preaching to his seminary students in 1850 spoke on this verse and said,

"The word (constraineth) means to restrain, to have in one's power.

---

[36] C Swindoll *Contagious Christianity - A Study of First Thessalonians* (Fullerton, CA: Insight for Living, 1985), pp 40-41.

This is the sense here. The love of Christ takes possession of us, of all our faculties, of our thoughts, affections and powers. It masters and controls us. How inconceivable the blessedness of those thus possessed. It elevates them; it fills them with courage, patience and power. If we have this we need naught else for our happiness or usefulness"[37]

Paul had learned what Jesus meant when he said, "**As the Father has loved me, so have I loved you. Now <u>remain in my love</u>**" (Jn 15:9). He had shown the Thessalonians what it looked like to rest or remain in Christ's love. To see nothing and no one untouched by His love. To filter everything in life through this question: How does the love of Christ relate to this? John, the Beloved Apostle, spoke of the same powerful filling of God's love, "**God is love. Whoever <u>lives in love</u> lives in God, and God in him**" (1 Jn 4:16b). To live in love is to have the love of Christ control you by the power of the Spirit. To be compelled or consumed by His love.

It is obvious that the Thessalonians were filled with the love of Christ. Nothing else could explain why they did what they did. This alone explains the impact that they had on their region. The promise made by Jesus was fulfilled in the Thessalonians. All knew they were His disciples because they loved one another with His persistent, undying love. Even paganism taught that the work of God was distinguished from demons by its long lasting impact of goodness and love.[38] We should pray that the love of Christ will fill and compel us, too, using the prayer of Paul for the Ephesians and all other Christians:

> "**I pray that you, being rooted and established in love, may have power, *together with all the saints*, to grasp how wide and long and high and deep is <u>the love of Christ,</u> and <u>to know this love</u> that surpasses knowledge–that you may be filled to the measure of all the fullness of God**" (Eph 3:17b-19).

The love of Christ is said to be greater than knowledge. Yet which do we so often choose? Where do we spend most of our time–studying Jesus facts or practicing Jesus love? How can anything surpass knowledge? Isn't knowledge power? Sure, but it is not the greatest power. Love is greater, as NT Wright asserts,

> "Jesus calls his followers to a new mode of *knowing*. I have written

---

[37]C Hodge *Princeton Sermons* (Edinburgh: Banner of Truth Trust 1979)219-220.
[38]R Mac Mullen, *Paganism in the Roman Empire* (New Haven: Yale University Press, 1981), pp 95-97.

elsewhere about what I call an epistemology of love. We have traditionally thought of knowing in terms of subject and object and have struggled to attain objectivity by detaching our subjectivity. It can't be done, and one of the achievements of postmodernity is to demonstrate that. What we are called to and what in the resurrection we are equipped for, is a knowing in which we are involved as subjects *but as self-giving. Not self-seeking, subjects*: in other words, a knowing that is a form of love.'[39]

Put in another way, Wright insists that the aging scientific method is being

"overcome by the epistemology of love, which is called into being as the necessary mode of knowing for those who will live in the new... world launched at Easter, the world in which Jesus is Lord and Caesar isn't.

"...We must take the risk and open the curtains to the rising sun. When we do so, we won't rely on the candles anymore, not because we don't believe in evidence and   argument but because they will have been overtaken by the larger reality from which they borrow, to which they point and in which they will find a new and larger home. All knowing is a gift from God, historical and scientific knowing, no less than that of faith, hope and love; but the greatest of these is love."[40]

Is it not time for your life to be challenged and amazed by the power of Christ's love? And, then, with it flowing through you, to reach your region for him? Speaking the one language of love that everyone is waiting to hear and to see. The same language of the Spirit spoken so eloquently and shown so clearly by the amazing Thessalonians.

For Reflection and Discussion

1. How contagious is the love expressed by your life and your church?

---

[39]NT Wright *Surprised by Hope* (NY: HarperCollins Publishers 2008), p 239.
[40]Ibid., p 74.

Chapter 21

Amazing Hope

It is always inspiring to hear a story of someone who did not give up against all odds. And ended up winning. I pray that this chapter will inspire you as you look at the amazing hope of the believers at Thessalonica. Of the big three--faith, hope and love--it is obvious that hope is the little sister. The one which is often overshadowed by the others. But this is dangerous because, as important as love and faith are, the Thessalonians would never have been amazing without their hope. **"We have this hope as an anchor for the soul, firm and secure"** (Heb 6:19a). Without hope we can drift with every strong current of opposition, making no headway for our Lord and His kingdom.

Hope is not as prominent in 1 & 2 Thessalonians as faith and love, being mentioned four times in the first letter and once in the second.[41] It is hope that inspires endurance or "patient fortitude in the face of opposition."[42] So, hope is described as a helmet that secures our salvation during the opposition we all face in this world. Hope was for them (and is to us) a very special gift from **"our Lord Jesus Christ himself and God our Father"** (2 Thes 2:16).

The hope of the Thessalonians was specifically **"hope in our Lord Jesus Christ"** (1Thess 1:3). It was grounded in His death and resurrection. And was primarily directed towards His Second Coming and their future life together with Him. As Paul would later write to Titus, his helper in Corinth and Crete.[43] **"It teaches us to...live...godly lives in this present age while we wait for <u>the blessed hope–the glorious appearing of our great God and Savior, Jesus Christ</u>"** (Titus 2:12-13). Why do we need so little hope today? When did pessimism become an acceptable Christian outlook? Hope encourages. Despair discourages. We are not as alarmed as we should be by today's lack of hope.

> "The Thessalonian church was eminently a HOPEFUL church. The difference between the religion of fear and that of hope is immense. One gathers blackness to the soul even at noon-day, and uses light and sunshine to make shadows with, and the other sees in all sorrows some grounds for joy.... Fear depresses, hope elevates. Fear crushes, hope expands.... The energy of despair or the fitful rage of fear is no

---

[41]See 1 Thes 1:3; 2:19; 4:13; 5:8; 2 Thes 2:16 .
[42]J Stott, *1 & 2 Thessalonians* (Downers Grove, IL: InterVarsity Press, 1991), p 30.
[43]See also 2 Cor 7:5-6; Titus 1:5.

match for the steady, joyous buoyancy of hope.

Hence God has given to his people a *hope*...a hope like an anchor to the soul; a hope that maketh not ashamed. And this hope the church at Thessalonica had taken as their heritage and great consolation.... For this great, grand glorious thought–that all will come right at last, that the weary shall find rest and the fainting refreshment, in the kingdom of God–that tears shall be dried, pains removed, sorrows banished and death destroyed– is an incentive of unparalleled power, to urge us onward in the heavenly way.

This the Thessalonians had...Their hope rested not in fogs, myths, and mysticism, but in Jesus and the resurrection."[44]

When you take away a Christian's hope, he is left only with the shell of Christianity. With words and songs and worship that move no one. A Christianity that serious challenges no one. A social phenomenon that one can take or leave. How hopeful is your heart? Your hope can be measured by what you are willing to do for Christ at a cost. That is why Paul spoke of "**the hope of salvation as a helmet**" (1 Thes 5:8). Our salvation draws enemy fire. And it cannot endure without clearly focusing on Jesus' present reign and future return. How well-protected is your salvation? It is hope that keeps us strong when everything else in us would cave in.

> "The most vulnerable part of a person in a life-threatening situation is the head.... Here the helmet is the hope of salvation. What protects the believer against a mortal blow to his faith is to some degree the hope of salvation. If one has no hope or trust that God will one day make things right, then one's faith is fragile and can be overwhelmed by the problems and injustices of the present. But this hope not only protects in the present, it gives courage in the face of the coming judgment of God, knowing that the one will be saved or rescued from that maelstrom."[45]

Another renowned scholar added,

> "Hope is the 'helmet of salvation' because it protects the believer's most vital part from the assaults of his enemies. In the hand-to-hand conflicts of old, the head was the worst exposed. Its protection was of the first importance. Hence the helmet was as necessary as the shield. No soldier could venture into battle without it. So with the Christian, the hope of salvation is necessary to prepare him for the

---

[44]H Hastings *Thessalonica or The Model Church* (New York: Rudd & Carleton, 1861), pp 77-78.
[45]B Witherington, *1 and 2 Thessalonians* (Grand Rapids, MI: Wm B Eerdmans Publishing 2006) p. 150.

battle on which he enters."[46]

Let's be honest with one another. The reason hope today is rarely mentioned is because few of us see it as being necessary. Hope implies something that is not yet fully experienced. Something yet to be. But many Evangelicals are living like they have it all. We are quite comfortable with the status quo. How many Christians that you know really have a strong urge for Jesus to return? How godly we live in this life does not *really* seem to matter to many of us Evangelicals. We are saved by faith not works, right? Salvation is all of grace. True enough. But can true grace in us be held in secret? As something not all that special to us? As a gift that we do not need to share with others? Listen to a contemporary critic,

> "Many of us have misplaced our hope. We've settled in. Our sense of security is in what we have—our freedom, our material possessions, our jobs, our families and so on. But this was not true of the Thessalonian believers. They lived in the midst of persecution. They never knew when they might be jailed—or even killed. At any moment, they could have lost everything they owned. That's why the second coming of Christ meant so much to them. Their hope was in Christ—in Christ alone. And this hope gave them a sense of security no matter what happened to them personally or to the things they had accumulated. So it should be with us! Our hope should be in the Lord—not in our American society and all of its earthly blessings."[47]

The battle may not be as evident to us who live in present day America. But, that is because many today don't see Satan's strategy. We might clearly see his opposition in an emperor's demanding to be worshiped. But we do not see it as clearly in a society that demands an endless consumption of new products. Or in so worrying about our kids and their future that we hunker down in fear and isolation, forgetting that Jesus said, **"Go into all the world and make disciples."** Getz is right. Many have misplaced their hope. We need a renewal of hope! Of something that will carry us above the lure of wealth and possessions. We need something to rescue us from the subtle but strong pull of pleasing everyone but God. We need a cause that demands risk because our hope is for something greater than anything we can risk! It promises more than we can ever lose. As NT Wright brilliantly writes,

---

[46]C Hodge, *Princeton Sermons* (Edinburgh: The Banner of Truth Trust 1979), p 230.
[47]G Getz , *Standing Firm when you'd rather Retreat: Based in 1 Thessalonians* (Ventura, CA: Regal Books 1986), p 16.

87

"Who, after all, was it who didn't want the dead to be raised?....It was, and is, those in power, the social and intellectual tyrants and bullies; the Caesars who would be threatened by a Lord of the world who had defeated the tyrant's last weapon, death itself....And this is the point where believing in the resurrection of Jesus suddenly ceases to be a matter of inquiring about an odd event in the first century and becomes a matter of rediscovering hope in the twenty-first century. Hope is what you get when you suddenly realize that a different worldview is possible, a worldview in which the rich, the powerful, and the unscrupulous do not after all have the last word. The same worldview shift that is demanded by the resurrection of Jesus is the shift that will enable us to transform the world."[48]

What matters most to you? "Christ has died. Christ is risen. Christ will come again." Those biblical truths should live at the center of our worldview. Impacting how we really view ourselves, our world and our future. If the imperishable Jesus is our hope, then what can we really lose? If He who gave Christ for us will be giving us all things through Him (Rom 8:32), what do we really need now other than Him? Is He not in control? Does Jesus not care about us? Will He not keep his promises today?

If you find yourself wavering in how you answer those questions, then your worldview is not as stable as it should be. You are not living a life of Christian hope. You might be losing your way. You need a new way of thinking. As Paul would call it, a **"renewing of your mind"** (Rom 12:2). Based on the amazing fact that death has been defeated. That redemption has begun. What used to cause men to fear, need not concern them now. The night of sin's reign is over. The new day has dawned. Or as NT Wright would again say,

"The reality that is the resurrection cannot simply be 'known' from within the old world of decay and denial, or tyrants and torture, of disobedience and death. But that's the point. To repeat: the resurrection is not, as it were, a highly peculiar event within the *present* world (though it is that as well); it is, principally, the defining event of the *new* creation, the world that is being born with Jesus. If we are even to glimpse this new world, let alone enter it, we will need a different kind of knowing, a knowing that involves us in new ways, an epistemology that draws out from us not just the cool appraisal of detached quasi-scientific research but also that whole-person engagement and involvement for which the best shorthand is 'love,'

---

[48]NT Wright, *Surprised by Hope* (New York: HarperCollins 2008), p 75.

in the full...sense of *agape*."[49]

Our hope in Christ helps us now to live in love. To obey like true disciples. To love our enemies. To turn our other cheek. To give away our shirts as well as our coats. We speak a new language in the certain hope of a new and changing world. That language is love. Recognized by all with eyes to see. Felt by all who have grabbed the love of the world and been disappointed with what it delivered.

> "(Love)is the language Jesus spoke, and we are called to speak it so that we can converse with him. It is the food they eat in God's new world, and we must acquire the taste for it here and now. It is the music God has written for all his creatures to sing, and we are called to learn it and practice it now so as to be ready when the conductor brings down his baton. It is the resurrection life, and the resurrected Jesus calls us to begin living it with him and for him right now. Love is at the very heart of the surprise of hope: people who truly hope as the resurrection encourages us to hope will be people enabled to love in a new way. Conversely, people who are living by this rule of love will be people who are learning more deeply how to hope"[50]

With this we end Part Two and our look at the amazing way that the seed of the gospel was planted in Thessalonica. The salvation of God was rooted in amazing faith. It grew by amazing love. And was watered by amazing hope. May God prepare you for what now follows. For we will see an amazing harvest that occurred through very normal people. And that harvest can happen again. Through you and your church, if you will desire Christ's amazing love to flow through you to all those He has placed in your life.

May you hear Jesus calling you, "Follow Me." For, as you do, you will join the millions globally being renewed by the Spirit to keep their eyes on Jesus. All power has been given to Him. And He has promised to be powerfully present in the lives of every disciple who goes out into the world with the goal of making disciples of love everywhere. **"and I am with you always, to the very end of the age"** (Matt. 28:20).

For Reflection and Discussion

1. How significant a role has hope played in your life?
2. How has this chapter helped to show you how hope should mark your life? Will it?

---

[49]NT Wright 2008, p 78.
[50]NT Wright, 2008, p 288.

Chapter 22

If love is the greatest thing–why replace it?

We are finally there. The reason this book had to be written. Somehow. Inexplicably. The love of God has been lost. For whatever reasons, large segments of Western Evangelicalism have replaced what God called "most important" with other things. Sure many of those things are important. But when we displace God's often-stated priority, we actually become harmful. And that is happening all around us. And maybe within us. Before we can "keep first things first," though, let's prove that love is the first thing. Then we will marvel at our departing from it.

Who could hate love? Yet Jesus, God-in-flesh, perfect Love, was hated by many. And still is. His detractors wanted to trap Him in some condemnable error. So they could embarrass and eliminate Him. Like many of us, they desperately wanted to stay in control. To be followed. One legal expert tested Him by asking, **"Teacher, which is the greatest commandment in the Law?"** Instead of being defensive, Jesus just answered him. And we should be eternally grateful that He did. For what is more important than to have God tell us which of His commands matters most? Cherish His answer. Never forget it or allow it to be placed second to anything else. Because this is God's "first thing."

> **"Jesus replied: "Love the Lord your God with all your heart and with all your soul and with all your mind. This is the first and greatest commandment. And the second is like it: Love your neighbor as yourself. All the Law and the Prophets hang on these two commandments"** (Matt 22:37-39).

Go over to the most valuable picture in your house. Your favorite. The one in the beautiful frame. Take your left hand and support it while you remove the nail from the wall behind it. The nail on which the picture is hung. Now, with the picture up against the wall in its normal place, without the nail behind it, quickly take your supporting hand away from the picture. Just let go.

What will happen? Your masterpiece will crash to the ground. Its glass will shatter and its frame will break or bend. The picture will be damaged. Maybe ruined. Why? Because you did something foolish. You removed the supporting nail from the wall and tried to hang it on nothing. Now that's not very smart. Do you get my point? This is what you and I do every time we choose not to love! Because God said, love is the nail.

That is what Jesus meant when he said, **"All the Law and the Prophets hang on these two commandments."** Everything God has revealed is elevated by love. Without love, all His words and ways ends up in a crumbled, wasted mass on the ground. Useless and ugly. A mere shell of their glory. So is God's Word whenever it is preached or read or practiced without love. It becomes a fraction of what it could be. And so is every effort to please God or to help our neighbor without love. Love makes a huge difference in everything. It does make "the world go 'round." And the earth would quickly become an awful, frozen mess if it stopped revolving. So does our life when we stop loving.

Jesus was asked for the greatest commandment. He gave the top two and linked them together. Randy Frazee represented this important response as follows:[51]

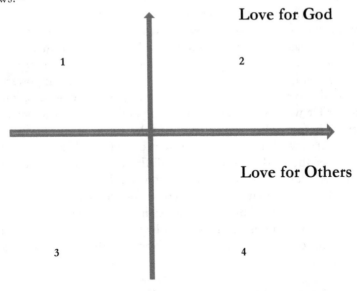

Frazee explains,

"Put simply, Jesus tells us that the first and foremost law of life is to

[51]R Frazee *The Connecting Church* (Grand Rapids, MI: Zondervan 2001), p 71

love God. Flowing out of and motivated by our love for God is love for others. There is a vertical dimension to our life (that is, loving God) and a horizontal dimension to our life (that is, loving our neighbor). A helpful way to understand Jesus' construction of the fulfilled life is to draw these two components to form a quadrant graph. The objective of the Christian life is to reside in Quadrant 2, which entails that a person must both love God and love others"[52]

We desperately need both lines of love, not just the vertical line. Otherwise we can and will do some very strange things. All in the name of love for God. We will pretend to be close to God while we stay far away from others. Jesus warned, **"in fact a time is coming when anyone who kills you will think he is offering a service to God"** (John 16:2).

When our church studied Frazee's book, we repented of choosing Quadrant-1-living over Quadrant- 2-living. Many of us were self- deceived, thinking we could be close to God while being detached from others. Have you thought that, too? We are too good at playing games with God and ourselves. We need the outward acts of love to our neighbors to keep us honest.

My life has never been the same since that time, many years ago, when I turned my back on my own love and asked the Spirit to fill me with the love of Jesus. I began to truly follow Jesus. Up until that time, I often called the shots, deciding when, where and how I would "serve" Him. My love often said, "NO!" to the Spirit. But true repentance empowered me to go in another direction—and to truly follow Jesus. The new direction became wherever He was leading me. And love empowered me to go where I could never go before. That is why true disciples must be filled with His love. Because Jesus will lead us where only love can take us. His love is now taking me all over the world and into some difficult and dangerous places. But I have never felt safer, because I really know that He is with me.

Jesus purposely put the two commands to love together. Because we prove our love for God by loving our neighbors. By loving those whom God loves. This vital truth is further proven by the following verses. In them the first commandment (love for God) is replaced by the second commandment (love for neighbor).

> **"Let no debt remain outstanding, except the continuing debt to love one another, for he who loves his fellowman has fulfilled the law. The commandments, 'Do not commit adultery,' 'Do not murder,' 'Do not steal,' 'Do not covet,' and whatever other commandment there may be, are summed up in this one rule:**

---

[52]R Frazee, 2004, pp 71-72.

'Love your neighbor as yourself.' Love does no harm to its neighbor. Therefore love is the fulfillment of the law" (Romans 13:8-10).

"**The entire law is summed up in** *a single command*: '**Love your neighbor as yourself**'" (Gal. 5:14)

"**If you really keep the royal law found in Scripture, 'Love your neighbor as yourself' you are doing right**" (James 2:8).

Love for our neighbors is, according to these texts, the one rule. The single command. The king of all laws or the royal law. Love for neighbors is the summary or fulfillment of God's will. What God most desires from us. How important is love for others to you?

God knows we operate best when love controls us. When we love with all our heart, soul, mind and strength, there is no room left for anything else. Something full can't have more of anything crammed into it. It is full. Have you ever sought to be filled with God's love?

Love, to Jesus, was the ultimate test of a church's worth (Rev 2:4-5). Without it, He said, the church must go! Concerning love, the gospel and the last days, He warned, "**Because of the increase of wickedness, the love of most will grow cold, but he who stands firm to the end will be saved. And this gospel of the kingdom will be preached in the whole world as a testimony to all nations, and then the end will come**" (Matt 24:12-14). Could this passage really be saying that only those who persevere in love will be saved? That unless we are standing in love, we are not standing on firm ground? That the preaching of the gospel of the kingdom should be combined with a lifestyle of love? Don't be deceived. Love matters most. In all your relationships. And in every act of Christian service and worship.

The Corinthians were the southern counterparts of the Thessalonians. They lived in Achaia. We have seen how the Thessalonians "**became a model to all the believers in Macedonia and Achaia**" (1 Thes 1:7). The Thessalonians were famous for their "**labor prompted by love**" (1 Thes 1:3). In regard to love, the Corinthians were drastically lacking. That is important to note. Two churches planted not long after one another, in the same general area, by the same Apostle—could be very different. One very strong, though young and persecuted. The other very weak, though enjoying Paul's ministry for 1.5 years (maybe 6 times longer than his time spent with the Thessalonians-Acts 18:11). Reflect for a minute on the difference love makes between any two churches. This should encourage you. Because your life and church can be different from all others around you, with God's help. Your love can move others to love.

The Corinthians were spared the severe persecution that the

Thessalonians suffered. The ruling of Gallio, proconsul of Achaia, allowed the Christians in Corinth similar religious freedom as Jews were given (see Acts 18:12-17). The city was huge, with half a million Romans and slaves living there. The infamous temple of Aphrodite (so-called Goddess of Love) was served by 1,000 priestess/prostitutes. They scoured the city seducing as many as they could into a combination of worship and prostitution. Corinth was so infamous for sexual immorality that the Greek language created a verb from the word "Corinth" which meant "to practice sexual immorality."

When Christianity was planted in this "city of love," the lifestyle of love that controlled the Thessalonians was not as evident there. Instead the Corinthians allowed both unholiness and selfish pride to thrive[53]. The spirit of self-promotion fueled many of their desires concerning spiritual gifts. The more outwardly remarkable (miraculous) gifts were wanted. And this grieved Paul, their spiritual father. The Corinthians were not models. Their profession of faith, though accompanied by miraculous power, was questioned. Paul knew the Thessalonians belonged to God. But he told the Corinthians, "**Examine yourselves to see whether you are in the faith; test yourselves**" (2 Cor 13:5a). What would Paul think of us, today?

We must realize that Christian churches and individuals choose to go in many directions. But there is just one model to follow. And Paul reminded the Corinthians and us of it– "the most excellent way" (1 Cor 12:31) in these unforgettable words:

> "**If I speak in the tongues of men and of angels, but have not love, I am only a resounding gong or a clanging cymbal. If I have the gift of prophecy and can fathom all mysteries and all knowledge, and if I have a faith that can move mountains, but have not love, I am nothing. If I give all I possess to the poor and surrender my body to the flames, but have not love, I gain nothing.**

> "**Love is patient, love is kind. It does not envy, it does not boast, it is not proud. It is not rude, it is not self-seeking, it is not easily angered, it keeps no record of wrongs. Love does not delight in evil but rejoices with the truth. It always protects, always trusts, always hopes, always perseveres.**

> "**Love never fails. But where there are prophecies, they will cease; where there are tongues, they will be stilled; where there is knowledge, it will pass away. For we know in part and we prophesy in part, but when perfection comes, the imperfect**

---

[53]See 1 Cor. 5:1-5, 9-11; 6:13-20; 3:21; 4:7, 18; 5:6.

disappears. When I was a child, I talked like a child, I thought like a child, I reasoned like a child. When I became a man, I put childish ways behind me. Now we see but a poor reflection as in a mirror; then we shall see face to face. Now I know in part; then I shall know fully, even as I am fully known.

"And now these three remain: faith, hope and love. But the greatest of these is love" (1 Cor 13).

Listen carefully to NT Wright,

> "Think of the wonderful poem we call 1 Corinthians 13, which looks forward to the exposition of the resurrection in 1 Corinthians 15. The poem itself is complete, and exquisite. But it speaks of something that is incomplete...: Our knowledge is incomplete; our prophecy is incomplete; but when completeness arrives the incomplete is done away....

> "The poem...yearns over the fact that our experience of love, as of everything that matters, is decidedly incomplete.... But Paul is urging that *we should live in the present as people who are to be made complete in the future.* And the sign of that completeness, that future wholeness, the bridge from one reality to the other is love....

> "The last stanza of the poem, insisting on the incompleteness of our present experience, points on to the final great discussion of the letter, namely chapter 15, in which Paul gives the fullest exposition in all early Christian writing of Jesus' resurrection and what it means. It means that a new world order has opened up in the midst of the present one....

> "The point of 1 Corinthians 13 is that love is not our duty, it is our *destiny.* It is the language Jesus spoke, and we are called to speak it so that we can converse with him.... It is the resurrection life, and the resurrected Jesus calls us to begin living it with him and for him now.[54]

Jesus lived 1 Cor 13 every hour of every day. In every relationship. Read 1 Cor 13 again. Right now. And replace "love" by "Jesus," for God is love. Make His love for you real to you. He died to break the chains of selfishness and allow love to flow through you. To give you the power to

---

[54] NT Wright *Surprised By Hope* (New York: HarperCollins 2008), pp285-288.

love. He rose from the dead as Victor. And ascending, poured out the Holy Spirit, on us who believe. The Spirit of love.

We need to be filled with the Spirit. To let love in. Again. Let it flow through you. Repent of rejecting it. Of replacing it with your walls and your works. With your control. Take the chance. Sure you will be hurt at times. His love pouring through you will be rejected. Just as it was when it flowed perfectly through the Son of God. But be assured of this: love will always leave its mark. Everyone wants it. Everyone needs it. Open your hearts to love again. Like the amazing Thessalonians did.

For Reflection and Discussion

1. What steps will you take to help love fill the center of your being?
2. What is the best way to share what you have learned with others and convince them of its importance?

Part 3 – Love's Amazing Look

Chapter 23

Are you an imitation or an original?

We are at the very heart of this book. And in it our goal is to let you see Paul, his team and the Thessalonians in action. How did they feed off of each other? How much independence did they enjoy? What level of accountability did they experience? How much did they need each other? What was their concept of following Jesus? Of discipleship? How did they show their love to Jesus, each other and the pagans around them? What did that all look like?

Let's start with an amazing statement of the apostle. "You became imitators of us and of the Lord...." (1 Thes 1:6). Many of us have a problem right there. A difficulty so great that some of you may really struggle to get over it. This could be, for you, a real deal breaker. You might be tempted right here to say, "That's it. Not me." And all because of one word. Imitator.

Deep within the human heart there is a desire to create. We were made in the image of the Creator. But that impulse to be creative and original can quickly go bad. Because of pride. Like the men of Babel who, forsaking God, wanted to make a name for themselves (Gen. 11:4). To be original.

We have copyrights to prove originality because people will steal others ideas and inventions. There are laws concerning plagiarism to keep us from claiming originality at someone else's expense. The very fact that we as humans are tempted to plagiarize shows our broken desire for recognition. We want to impress others with our words. So if someone else said it better or wrote it better, we will go so far as to jeopardize our credibility and even job—just to appear original. Creative. Brilliant.

The Thessalonians were imitators not originators. The word Paul used was from the Greek word, "mimos" (mimic or actor). Does it bother you to follow another so closely that you are accused of being a sheep? That was no problem for either Paul or the Thessalonians. Or to the Psalmists of old. Paul claimed that he imitated Jesus. To be original as a Christian can be dangerous. We were saved to follow Jesus. And as long as our spiritual leaders follow him, we are encouraged to follow them. "Remember your leaders, who spoke the word of God to you. Consider the outcome of their way of life and imitate their faith" (Heb 13:7; see also 1 The 5:12-13). Is anyone in the context of your life really imitating Jesus? Would you like to follow them as they follow Jesus? Is there any chance that you can? These questions are really asking—do you have a real opportunity to be discipled? Few Christians do! Because few have ever been discipled. We cannot do for others what we have not experienced ourselves. You cannot make disciples if you are not a disciple. If you have never been discipled.

The Corinthians were much more "open minded" than the Thessalonians in their choice of models to copy or guides to follow. So Paul wrote, "Even though you have 10,000 guardians in Christ, you do not have many fathers, for in Christ Jesus I became your father through the gospel. Therefore, I urge you to imitate me" (1 Cor 4:15-16). And later, he commanded them, "Follow my example, as I follow the example of Christ" (1 Cor 11:1). This is the same word and it indicates more than merely to follow. It is a command to copy. And that just does not sit very well with us, does it? Have you ever heard the words "copy cat" used in a favorable light? It was not different in Paul's day.

Paul knew what mimics were thought of in the Roman Empire. In a recent book, Prof. LL Welborn shows that this was a major problem in Corinth. When Paul speaks of himself as a "fool" and of his preaching as "foolishness," and when he calls on them to "mimic" his life as he mimics Jesus, he is using words of their contemporary theatric culture. The mimes were the actors. And their status was certainly nothing like Hollywood today. Just the opposite! And this proved too much for many of the Corinthians. I hope that you will follow the example of the Thessalonians here and not the Corinthians. That's what Paul wanted, too. And that is why he called them the model church and not Corinth.

Wellborn, in speaking of the context of 1 Corinthians 1-4, wrote,

"Paul describes the apostles' social status: the apostles are the lowest, the meanest, the basest of people. Mime actors, together with gladiators and prostitutes, belonged to a group of persons considered degraded, that is they had lost the status of respectable citizens, in the court of public opinion and even in the provisions of the law.

"...The mimes were repeatedly banished from the cities of the Empire. The mime's life was a precarious one, most were slaves, and those who were not eked out a dubious living, greatly dependent on the largess and indulgence of patrons....As members   of   the lower class, mime actors were frequently publicly beaten."[35]

The Thessalonians did not see it as degrading to closely imitate both Paul and Jesus. So, Paul wrote that they "became imitators." Past tense. Their commitment to imitating was established right at the start of their Christian experience. However, to the Ephesians, Paul later wrote, "Be imitators (mimics) of God, therefore, as dearly loved children and live a life of love,

---

[55] L L Wellborn, Paul, the Fool of Christ (London: T&T Clark Publishers 2006), pp54-68.

just as Christ loved us and gave himself up for us as a fragrant offering and sacrifice to God" (Eph. 5:1-2). What the Ephesians were encouraged to become, the Thessalonians had already become. Even though Paul was writing to the Ephesians following a ministry of several years among them. Maturity, you see, does not necessarily come with age. Nor does it take long to develop, with the help of the Spirit. We need faith to act. To step out and obey. Right now! Obedience leads to maturity. Disobedience, especially in being passive and doing nothing, keeps us immature.

So, concluding our thoughts on this description of the Thessalonians as mimics, I must ask a few questions. In what way do you mimic Jesus? I am not speaking of a faint similarity. But a true replica. Could it be that our lack of growth and fruitfulness is partially caused by our lack of simple obedience? Just doing as we have been told? This will be explored in detail later. For now ask yourself: am I an imitation or an original? You might find it very helpful to read one of my recent books, which reveals in detail just what it meant in the New Testament era to be the disciple of a rabbi. What were their unique marks? How did Jews follow their rabbis and how did Christ's disciples follow Him? If the Great Commission is "make disciples," how do you know you have ever done that if you do not know what a New Testament era disciple was? The books I am referring to: Are You a Christian or a Disciple? Rediscovering and Renewing New Testament Discipleship and Disciples Obey: How many Christians rebel against Jesus.

The Thessalonians were not imitating a dead Legend, but a risen and reigning Lord. One who was coming back. And would, upon His return, judge the lives of those He left to carry on for Him while He was away. The living Christ was leading Paul and them by His Spirit. Step by step. People who imitate others try to walk in their footsteps. Are you following their tracks? Does the following verse mean more now? "Since we live by the Spirit, let us keep in step with the Spirit" (Gal 5:25). In step with the Spirit of Jesus. The Spirit of love. Pray for faith and courage to join the amazing Thessalonians in a life devoted to imitating the main Actor. The Headliner. The only Star who never can dim, grow old and wrinkled, and forget his lines–Jesus. Above all else, to imitate Jesus, Paul and the Thessalonians, we must devote ourselves to lives of gracious and joyous love! Because love matters most.

For Reflection and Discussion

1. How closely have you wanted to follow or imitate the life of Christ?
2. You might profit greatly, as I have, in reading the ancient classic, The Imitation of Christ, by Thomas a Kempis.

Chapter 24

If they are God's model church - which model are YOU following?

Love looks like Jesus. He, alone, is perfect love personified. "**This is how we know what love is: Jesus Christ laid down his life for us**" (1 John 3:16a). The giving of His life for us in death became the summary of His life of love. But everything He ever did before that supreme act of love was also love. Whatever He said or did not say was the perfection of love at that moment. To live a life of little love is to turn away from Jesus. The Thessalonians imitated Him. They did not only perform random acts of kindness. They lived in love. As did Paul. And this was shocking to behold, as we will see.

The Thessalonians became model Christians in all those ways that they imitated Jesus. The Lord sanctioned this church as our example when Paul wrote, "**You became imitators of us and of the Lord...And so you became a model to all the believers in Macedonia and Achaia**" (1 Thes 1:6-7). Architects use models or blue prints to build exactly what they want. By using the word "model", God has also implicitly said something. *"Follow the Thessalonians' lives of love."* And this carries with it His implied warning, "Beware of other models of Christian life, worship and witness that are not similar to theirs."

The word that Paul uses for "model" is found 15 times in the New Testament where it is usually translated in the NIV as "example", "pattern", "model" or "form." It refers to someone or something that should be exactly copied or followed. The word is used in this way of several Christian leaders whose faith and life were to be emulated. Paul urged others to carefully imitate his life (Phil 3:17; 2 Thes 3:9). This was not because Paul was on a super ego trip. It was a kindness to those who needed guidance. You would hardly be offended if you were lost in a treacherous and narrow cave and someone came along with a flashlight, offering to help you out by taking your hand and leading the way. That's what Christian leaders are called to do. Paul urged both Timothy (1 Tim 4:12) and Titus (Titus 2:7) to live as models. Peter did the same to all church elders (1 Pet 5:3). So, this word "model" is used of many Christian leaders. But it is never used of any entire, local church-- *except the Thessalonians.*

To call any church a "model" group is extraordinary. Much more so when it is a very young church. Stott writes,

"It is truly remarkable to read Paul's comprehensive portrayal of the Thessalonian church. It is only a few months old. Its members are newborn Christians. Freshly converted from either Judaism or paganism. Their Christian convictions have been newly acquired. Their Christian moral standards have been recently adopted. And they are being   sorely tested by persecution. You would expect it to be a very wobbly church in a very precarious condition. But no. Paul is confident about it, because he knows it is God's church, and because he has confidence in God"[56]

The declaration by Paul of this church's "model" status is a statement of fact not feeling. It is factual because Paul wrote this truth by the inspired guidance of the Holy Spirit. The words he chose to write were just those which God wanted written because they expressed the truth as God wanted Paul to express it. This young, struggling, persecuted group of Christians, alone, were to have the unique honor of being called "a model" among all the churches written to in the New Testament.

What others were needing yet to learn and to put into practice–these Thessalonian disciples--by God's amazing grace and Spirit, had learned and were putting into practice. In fact they had already perfected the simple basics of the Christian life and witness in such a way that the Spirit of the living God led the apostle Paul to make, as it were, a startling announcement--**the mold is ready**! The pattern is developed to adequate specifications. No more time and testing are needed. The model is ready. Let this likeness be produced everywhere!

A 19th century Christian magazine editor, H.L Hastings was also impressed by the Thessalonians and wrote,

"If we should consult the epistles of Paul at length upon this point, we might gain a very full and accurate idea of the character of each individual church, from the words of instruction, rebuke, admonition, and encouragement which his quick understanding and parental affection, under the guidance of inspiration, enabled him to give to each, according to their needs. Judging by this criterion, it is worthy of remark that among all the churches to which Paul addressed epistles, the church at Thessalonica must be regarded as emphatically the MODEL CHURCH"[57]

---

[56] J Stott, *The Message of 1 & 2 Thessalonians* (Downers Grove, IL: InterVarsity Press 1991) pp 26-27
[57] HL Hastings, *Thessalonica - The Model Church: Sketch of Primitive Christianity* (New York: Rudd & Carleton, 1861) p. 11.

Since it is a major goal of this book, let this point sink in. To Paul, arguably the wisest of church planters, a young church (like the Thessalonian) can actually attain to all that is essential. It can become a model to all others! Effective Christian life and witness aren't as complicated as we have chosen to make them. We've gummed up the works of the Kingdom by a host of practices, demands and hoops that we make young converts go through before encouraging them to **"go and make disciples."** Many of these restrictions are well-intentioned. But the fact that the Thessalonians were so young and, still, a model should give us reason to reflect on what we call maturity. And how long we think it takes to get there.

Long ago, Roland Allen wrestled with this and criticized some of the missionary strategies of his day because they did not seem to allow for the spontaneous expansion of the church under the guidance and power of the Holy Spirit. He wondered, why should we disapprove of what Paul approved of in the Thessalonians? Allen wrote,

> "By spontaneous expansion I mean something which we cannot control. And if we cannot control it, we ought, I think, to rejoice that we cannot control it. For if we cannot control it, it is because it is too great, not because it is too small for us. The great things of God are beyond our control. Therein lies a vast hope. Spontaneous expansion could fill the continents with the knowledge of Christ: our control cannot...."[58]

My point here is simply that the Thessalonians had not followed a long process. They had not been given a certificate after years of study. Yet they were certified. They had not grown wiser only through years and experience (which I have nothing against). Yet they were the example. They were in the midst of their first love and zeal. Yet they were the model. Paul did not fear that they would recklessly head into error and get off track unless they were tutored for a year or two under his guidance. He trusted that the best Teacher, the Spirit of God, would do his work in them (1 John 2:20,27). Listen to Roland Allen again.

> "The Church of that day was apparently quite fearless of any danger that the influx of large numbers of what we should call illiterate converts might lower the standard of church doctrine. She held the tradition handed down by the apostles, and expected the new converts to grow up into it, to maintain it and to propagate it...The Church of those ages was afraid of the human speculation of learned men; we are afraid of the ignorance of unlearned men."[59]

---

[58]R Allen, The *Spontaneous Expansion of the Church* (Grand Rapids, MI: Wm B Eerdmans Publishing Co., 1962), p 13.
[59]R Allen, 1962, p 48

I heartily recommend you read his entire book. It is filled with helpful insights that compare New Testament principles with the accepted evangelical practices of his day. Going backwards into church history for helpful insights might seem un-progressive to some of you. Listen, though, to CS Lewis on that point,

> "We all want progress. But progress means getting nearer to the place where you want to be. And if you have taken a wrong turning, then to go forward does not get you any nearer. If you are on the wrong road, progress means doing an about-turn and walking back to the right road: and in that case the man who turns back soonest is the most progressive"[60]

If we accept from Paul that the Thessalonians were models, then we will benefit greatly by carefully analyzing what that model was. And following its shape. But here we must beware. For the model of the amazing Thessalonians will challenge a good deal of contemporary Christian thought and practice in the West. Good models are made to be followed. Especially when God says so! May we all be willing to compare our present practice with that of His model. Comparing the present with the past. The alleged with the authentic. And may we repent wherever we are convinced that the present form has become a distortion of the simple authorized model. Let us proceed carefully, prayerfully and humbly as we look further at the amazing Thessalonians.

For Reflection and Discussion

1. How closely do you think your church follows the model of the Thessalonian church?
2. If it has never considered the Thessalonian model, what model is it following and why?

---

[60]CS Lewis, *Mere Christianity* (New York: MacMillan Publishing Co., Inc 1978), p 36

Chapter 25

Paul's boast

Paul already had quite a lot of church planting experience before meeting the Thessalonians on his second missionary journey. He had led outreach ministries for several years and established churches. His travels had taken him to Cyprus, Pamphilia, Pisidian Antioch, Iconium, Lystra, Derbe, Perga and Philippi before arriving at Thessalonica. And though he took personal care of all the churches (2 Cor.11:28), he was not led by the Spirit to write to them all. His first letter, inspired by God for the ongoing edification of the Church, was reserved for the amazing Thessalonians.

We have seen that the Thessalonian church alone is called a model for other churches. There are some other ways that Paul showed how the Thessalonians were set apart from other churches. He wrote, **"For what is our hope, our joy or the crown in which we will glory in the presence of the Lord Jesus when he comes? Is it not you? Indeed, you are our glory and joy"** (1 Thes 2:19). Paul had just spoken of how Satan had kept him from returning to see the Thessalonians (2:18). Some see in "Satan" a veiled reference to the political leaders' possible banning of Paul from the city. He wrote elsewhere of people being Satan's pawns (2 Cor 11:3). Here, he first used the word for an official "coming" (parousia). Not of Caesar coming on an official visit. The one that the politarchs are trying to impress by opposing Paul and the gospel. No, Satan can hinder Paul, but he cannot thwart the coming of the real King. Jesus.

When the Lord comes, he will not give crowns like Caesar did to the Olympic champions. Paul used the word laurel wreath (*stephanos*) for crown, which Olympians received with great glory. No, Paul's crown would be the Thessalonians themselves. "Paul shows how much he treasures his converts by lavishing on them eschatological significance. They are Paul's hope and joy, but more to the point they are the crown or crowning achievement of his ministry which he hopes to lay at Jesus' feet and boast in when the Lord Jesus returns."[61] Paul does not frequently use the word for "boast" (glory) of his church plants, as he does here. He does not use it of the Ephesians or the Philippians. And he states to the churches of Galatia, **"Not even those who are circumcised obey the law, yet they want you to be circumcised that they may boast in your flesh. May I never boast except in the cross of our Lord Jesus Christ"** (Gal 6:13-14).

---

[61]B Witherington *1 & 2 Thessalonians* (Grand Rapids, MI: Wm B Eerdmans Pub2006), pp *90*-91.

When he writes his second epistle, he goes even further in his boasting of the Thessalonians. He states, **"We ought always to thank God for you, brothers, and rightly so, because your faith is growing more and more, and the love every one of you has for each other is increasing. Therefore, among God's churches we boast about your perseverance and faith in all the persecutions and trials you are enduring"** (2 Thes 1:4). Leon Morris noted,

> "The result of the increase of faith and love was that Paul and his companions boasted of the Thessalonians to other Christians....Instead of the simple *we*, Paul has the emphatic 'we ourselves', while the verb translated boast (a compound here only in the New Testament) is not the simple verb Paul generally uses. The meaning appears to be that it was not the habit of the preachers to boast of their converts; but in this case the merits are so outstanding that even the founders of the church are constrained to sing its praises."[62]

The reason for such boasting by Paul? That even in persecution their faith was growing. And that **"the love every one of you has for each other is increasing"** (2 Thes 1:3). They applied Paul's instruction and followed his model with unusual thoroughness.

I have just wanted to show that Paul had a special place in his heart for these amazing Thessalonians. A church where everyone was filled with the love of God for each other. If he were to observe us and our churches today, would we have a special place in his heart?

For Reflection and Discussion

1. Think of how amazing it is that Paul, the Jewish disciple of Gamaliel turned disciple of Christ Jesus, portrayed a largely Gentile church as his model. His pride and joy. Think of how far away the synagogue system he was raised in had strayed and that he never saw a single synagogue totally discipled and become followers of Christ! He started with them, but ended up being kicked out of several. Would he look at your church and want to leave it or stick with it?

---

[62]L. Morris *1 & 2 Thessalonians* (Downers Grove, IL: InterVarsity Press 1984) pp.117-118.

Chapter 26

When the Good News gets contagious

It is so important that you *feel* this chapter. Deeply. That you remember the love you have felt for God. To remember what it was like when you first believed. How you had to tell someone. The relief that dawned on your soul was too big to contain. The good news of the gospel likely felt "too good to be true" to you. But when you realized it was true and life was yours, then love opened your lips. You had to share it with someone. Like the picture of your firstborn. This is how the Thessalonians heard Paul. And, in turn, it was the way the Thessalonians were being heard throughout their part of the Roman world. Paul described the amazing scene saying,

> "**You became imitators of us and of the Lord in spite of suffering, you welcomed the message with the joy given by the Holy Spirit...The Lord's message rang out from you not only in Macedonia and Achaia–your faith in God has become known everywhere. Therefore, we do not need to say anything about it, for they themselves report what kind of reception you gave us. They tell how you turned to God from idols to serve the living and true God**" (1 Thes 1:6-9).

NT Wright captures how the Good News passed from Paul to the Thessalonians:

> "There are some experiences which are so remarkable that you just have to talk to   someone about them. Sometimes you hear a piece of music, read a book, watch a movie, or witness a scene which is so striking that you can't help yourself. As soon as you meet someone you can tell, you say, 'I must tell you about...

> "What happened when Paul and his companions arrived in Thessalonica made that sort of impression, not only on the people who heard and believed the gospel, but on people of all sorts, all around Greece and the neighboring countries.[63]

The Thessalonians embraced Paul's message. The importance of the gospel

---

[63]NT Wright *Paul for Everyone: Galatians and Thessalonians* (Louisville, KY: Westminster John Know Press 2004), 90-91.

outweighed the reality of the suffering imposed on them for receiving it. The news was too good to lose. How good does the Good News look on you today as others observe your life? The Thessalonians became a sounding board for Paul's gospel about Jesus. They echoed its message in word and deed. This is what the verb "rang out" means. A kind of ceaseless echo repeating itself around the region. Like a shout through the Alps. Roland Allen realized how the Good News traveled through regions like Macedonia. He wrote,

> "If we seek for the cause which produces rapid expansion when a new faith seizes hold of men who feel able and free to propagate it spontaneously..., we find its roots in a certain natural instinct. This instinct is admirably expressed...in Cicero: "If a man ascended to Heaven...his feeling of wonder...would lose its sweetness if he had not someone to whom he could tell it." This is the instinctive force which drives men even at the risk of their life itself to impart to others a new-found joy. That is why it is proverbially difficult to keep a secret... The Spirit of Christ is a Spirit who longs for, and strives after, the salvation of the souls of men, and that Spirit dwells in them. That Spirit converts the natural instinct into a longing for the conversion of others which is indeed divine in its source and character."[64]

Stott reminds us,

> "There is an important lesson to learn here. We are a very media-conscious generation...we want to use the media in evangelism.... Nevertheless, there is another way, which (if we must compare them) is still more effective. It requires no complicated electronic gadgetry; it is very simply. It is neither organized nor computerized; it is spontaneous. And it is not expensive; it costs precisely nothing. We might call it "holy gossip" It is the excited transmission from mouth to mouth of the impact which the good news is making on people. 'Have you heard what has happened to so and so? Did you know that he has come to believe in God and has been totally transformed? Something extraordinary is going on in Thessalonica: a new society is coming into being, with new values and standards, characterized by faith, love and hope.'" [65]

---

[64]R Allen *The Spontaneous Expansion of the Church* (Grand Rapids, MI: Wm B Eerdmans Pub Co., 1962), 9.
[65]J Stott *The Message of 1 & 2 Thessalonians* (Downers Grove, IL: IVP 1991), 37-38.

How quickly and extensively did the message grow? NT Wright notes,

> "...Everybody who had heard about them was telling someone else without being asked. That's the meaning of what Paul says here: the message was echoing around north and south Greece (Macedonia in the north, Achaia in the south), and everywhere else as well—presumably Asia and Bithynia (modern Turkey) to the east and Illyricum, Moesia and the other small Balkan countries to the north."[66]

Have you ever lived in an experience like this? I have. I was converted as a young man in a small town in which hundreds were eventually saved. Much in the same way as in Thessalonica. By people who were despairing of life. Seeing and hearing the Good News in and from others. And they believed. Many in our own home. I was so excited I could not stop telling the Good News. My parents modeled the life of sacrificial love in many ways. It was truly amazing.

One of the reasons the faith spread like wildfire was that our leaders encouraged us to speak of Christ and to share our testimonies everywhere possible. So we did. Sure there was mild persecution. Nothing like Thessalonica, of course. Were you encouraged to share your testimony when you first believed? Or did you believe Satan's lie that "religion and politics are two subjects not to talk about." That silence often stops monumental growth from immediately occurring in the young believer's life.

Recently in South Africa, there was an amazing movement of the Spirit of God sweeping through the land. Central to that amazing movement of the Spirit is the man, Angus Buchan. You can read his story in "Faith Like Potatoes: The Story of a Farmer who Risked everything for God."[67] The day he was converted, he was given a challenge that would make him a different type of Christian, a Thessalonian-like Christian. Angus wrote,

> "That afternoon a couple from the church came to visit us. Eustace and Trish van Rooyen were believers, and they had something special to say. 'We saw you respond to the altar call in church. Did you mean it?' I did, with all my heart, and so did Jill. We told them so. 'Then I have a challenge for you,' said Eustace. 'If you mean business with Jesus, then tell the first three people you meet tomorrow morning what has happened to you.'

---

[66]NT Wright, 2004, p 91.
[67]Published by Monarch Books in Oxford, England and Grand Rapids, MI, 2006

"It was some challenge. On Friday night, I had been in the pub with the boys, and on Sunday morning I had given my life to Christ. My friends were mostly rough characters like me, and they would be pretty surprised by all this. I wondered if I could do it."[68]

Well, he did. Two years later the man he first told gave his life to Christ, too. Angus wrote,

"At the time, however, I was just relieved that I'd told someone. It wasn't so bad. Who was next? The fertilizer rep came to the farm, so I told him. After that, I told everybody I saw–I couldn't keep quiet! I'm still telling everybody about Jesus."[69]

I have visited Angus' farm for a Mighty Men's Conference with 200,000 others. I have seen his amazingly loving life. He has become absolutely color blind to racial prejudice. Their farm has added an orphanage, a Christian School and other Christian ministries. The extended family continues to work the farm while Angus carries the message of reconciliation throughout the country and world.

The same Spirit of God that filled Paul and the Thessalonians can fill us today. But, you will not be filled by the Spirit to sit still. To be self-focused. You must desire to move out in step with Him. Even with a trembling faith. We don't fill our cars with gas, to keep them parked in the garage! Neither does God. He fills the believer to go somewhere and to do something. How good is the Good News to you? Is it this good:

"Or suppose a woman has ten silver coins and loses one. Does she not light a lamp, sweep the house and search carefully until she finds it? And when she finds it, she calls her friends and neighbors together and says, 'Rejoice with me; I have found my lost coin.' In the same way, I tell you, there is rejoicing in the presence of the angels of God over one sinner who repents" (Lk 15:8-10).

What we and the Thessalonians have found is much more valuable than a silver coin. Where's our celebration? Our joy? I think it is there, but it needs help getting out. Let the amazing Thessalonians help you. Paul needed their help later on and wrote, **"Finally, brothers, pray for us that the message of the Lord may spread rapidly and be honored, just as it was with you"** (2 Thes 3:1). Paul knew God had done a special work in and through the

[68]A Buchan, *Faith Like Potatoes* 2006, p 32.
[69]A Buchan, 2006, p 33.

amazing Thessalonians. But he did not think it was unique. Meant only for one church. He desired it to be seen everywhere. In all the churches he worked with and planted. Don't you want that, too?

For Reflection and Discussion

1. Have you ever seen the gospel "spread rapidly?" What was it that slowed it down in your opinion?

2. Recently there have been approximately 1 million Muslims becoming disciples of Jesus annually. Please read of these rapid expansions called Disciple Making Movements (DMMs). I recommend Jerry Trousdale's "Miraculous Movements: How hundreds of thousands of Muslims are falling in love with Jesus."

Chapter 27

Can love be pure today?

Our world is utterly confused about love. So was the Roman world. The Thessalonian church flourished in a culture of sexual looseness that makes ours look mild in comparison. The Lord Jesus calls his followers to live a life of holiness. Set apart for Him and for good. Let's first take a hard look at us, today, and then admire, once again, the power of pure love as it depicted the lives of the amazing Thessalonians.

Western Evangelicalism is not standing very successfully against the inroads of sexual immorality. Statistics concerning pornography are shocking to us, but a cause for mockery to modern pagans.[70] In a survey of over 500 Christian men at a retreat, over 90% admitted that they were feeling disconnected from God because lust, porn or fantasy had gained a foothold in their lives. Pastor Rick Warren's Pastors.com website conducted a survey on porn use of 1351 pastors in which 54% of the pastors had viewed Internet pornography within the last year, and 30% of these had visited within the last 30 days.

Sexual sin is not only a male issue. The results of a ChristiaNet poll reported by Marketwire.com record the following:

- 50% of all Christian men and 20% of all Christian women are addicted to pornography
- 60% of the women who answered the survey admitted to having struggles with lust
- 40% admitted involvement in sexual sin in the past year
- 20% of the church-going female participants struggle with looking at pornography on an ongoing basis.

Constant availability to porn via computers puts sexually illicit pictures and productions within the touch of a finger. For any man I know, including myself, there is an absolute need for a web safety filter that blocks all porn access. We are wired with sexual weakness. It is virtually every man's struggle. Part of our fallen, sinful condition. Guard against this monster that devours in secret. Behind closed doors. Where love goes to live but actually dies.

The ominous threat that illicit sexuality poses today demands Christian men be humble and honest about our need for accountability in this area. If you (as a man) or your husband are not a part of a Christian community of

---

[70]See The Daily Atheist website. Feb 14, 2008.

men that understand and deal with these issues, you are courting disaster. I highly recommend that you join or start a group like "The Men's Fraternity" in your area. This organization and its main leader, Dr Robert Lewis, have helped men all over the world with the issues of manhood, marriage, fatherhood and the workplace with incredible success.[71] My life, marriage and work in ministry have been greatly blessed by being a part of The Men's Fraternity.

Thessalonica was worse off than our culture, as bad as it is. What many still view as illicit sex was open, accepted and normal then. Religion was often combined with sex. "Pagan temples regularly doubled as brothels, and sexual practices of all sorts were at least tolerated if not actively encouraged within the society as a whole."[72] John Stott expands this point,

It is not surprising that the apostle begins with sex, not only because it is the most imperious of all human urges, but also because of the sexual laxity–even promiscuity–of the Graeco-Roman world. Besides, he was writing from Corinth to Thessalonica, and both cities were famed for their immorality. In Corinth Aphrodite, the Greek goddess of   sex and beauty, whom the Romans identified with Venus, sent her servants out as prostitutes to roam the streets by night. Thessalonica, on the other hand, was particularly associated with the worship of deities called the Cabiri, in whose rites 'gross immorality was promoted under the name of religion.' It may be doubted, however, whether Corinth and Thessalonica were any worse than other cities of that period in which it was widely accepted that men either could not or would not limit themselves to their wife as their only sexual partner"[73]

In that portion of his letter, where he reinforces what he had taught them in person, Paul boldly reminded his young converts,

"It is God's will that you should be sanctified: that you should avoid sexual immorality; that each of you should learn to control his own body in a way that is holy and honorable, not in passionate lust like the heathen, who do not know God...For God did not call us to be impure, but to live a holy life. Therefore, he who rejects this instruction does not reject man but God, who gives you his Holy Spirit" (1 Thes 4:3-8).

Paul taught his converts that to follow him was to follow Jesus (1 Thes

---

[71]Access The Men's Fraternity at www.mensfraternity.com Or phone 1-800-446-7228

[72]NT Wright, *Paul for Everyone: Galatians and Thessalonians* (Louisville, KY: Westminster John Knox Press, 2004), p 118.

[73]J Stott, *The Message of 1 & 2 Thessalonians* (Downers Grove, IL: InterVarsity Press 1991) p 81.

1:6; 1 Cor 11:1). So, when he wrote to the Thessalonians as being "**in God the Father**" (1:1) and immediately (1:4) and repeatedly (19 times) called them "**brothers**," it was clear: The role of being a true sibling in a spiritual family was to be embraced by all Christ-followers. Everywhere. Even if one's own natural family, ethnic, social or work groups would not do so. Is this still true today?

You might think that you been taught the truth of Christian brotherhood. But, have you been shown it? If you have not seen Christian people of various backgrounds living like biological brothers and sisters normally do–then you have not been taught this truth. To teach, in the biblical sense of the word, is not merely to have something explained intellectually. It is to fully reveal. To show. To model.

This is what Paul told Titus to teach when he was left on Crete "**to straighten out what was left unfinished**" (Titus 1:5a). Crete was a wild place, as we will see in later chapters. An island nation where the level of immorality had sunk to even deeper depths than most other places in the Roman Empire. Paul told Titus he would need to "**appoint elders in every town** (*polis* - city)" (Titus 1:5b). That was a huge job. To help him assess who was elder material, Paul listed qualifications. And the vast majority of those guidelines involved one's character, not merely his teaching ability (see Titus 1:6-9). Why did he insist on moral maturity? Paul explains, "**For there are many rebellious people, mere talkers**" (Titus 1:10a). Titus was to refute them, not only by sounder reasoning, but by his example. "**In everything set them an example by doing what is good...for the grace of God that brings salvation has appeared to all men. It teaches us to say 'No' to ungodliness and worldly passions, and to live self-controlled, upright and godly lives in this present age**" (Titus 2:7,11). Titus was to teach by deed as well as by word.

So, I return to our point. When you joined your church did you join a family? Or an organization? Jesus, Paul and the amazing Thessalonians described and depicted God's called-out ones (His *ekklesia*-church) as a substitute family. As fully functioning as the one they had been born into. Where today are the Evangelical Christians who are actually loving one another as brothers?

The Thessalonians would not have heard these words like some do today, who say, "Come on, Paul, loosen up a little. Don't be an old killjoy, throwing cold water over all our fun." These words come easily to today's Christians, but not to disciples like the Thessalonians. You see, the Thessalonians had been involved in the orgies. They knew that the fun was not, after all, fun for long. That unbridled sex had its consequences physically, socially and spiritually. Breeding disease, ruining marriages and demeaning the soul. Every woman hated being sexually used by a man. Just as they do today. Deep down in their hearts, both men and women felt dirty that their religion was stooping to that level in order to have some staying power in their lives.

115

They were ready for Paul's words about holiness and love. And so they welcomed his message as liberating. As Max Lucado so well portrays,

"In the 3rd century Saint Cyprian wrote to a friend named Donatus: 'This seems a cheerful world, Donatus, when I view it from this fair garden under the shadow of these vines. But if I climbed some great mountain and looked over the wide lands, you know very well what I would see: brigands on the high road, pirates on the seas, in amphitheaters men murdered to please the applauding crowds, under all roofs misery and selfishness. It really is a bad world, Donatus, an incredibly bad world. Yet in the midst of it, I have found a quiet and holy people. They have discovered a joy which is a thousand times better than any pleasure of this sinful life. They are despised and persecuted, but they care not. They have overcome the world. These people are Christians...and I am one of them.'

What a compliment! A quiet and holy people. Is there any phrase that captures the essence of the faith any better? A quiet and holy people. Quiet. Not obnoxious. Not boastful. Not demanding. Just quiet. Contagiously quiet...A quiet and holy people. That describes the church in Thessalonica. May that describe the church today."[74]

It was not as hard for the Thessalonians to be holy as it seems to be for many professing Christians today. That leads us to a crucial question. Which is your bigger struggle—To be holy or to be impure? To be good or evil? Put in another way, What is your default mode? The real **you** to which you naturally go when no pressure is on. Do you naturally pursue righteousness or unrighteousness? How you answer these related questions really reveals your spiritual condition. As Paul wrote to the Romans,

> **"Don't you know that when you offer yourselves to someone to obey him as slaves, you are slaves to the one whom you obey— whether you are slaves to sin, which leads to death, or to obedience, which leads to righteousness? But thanks be to God that, though you used to be slaves to sin, you wholeheartedly obeyed the form of teaching to which you had been entrusted. You have been set free from sin and have become slaves to righteousness"** (Rom 6:16-18).

Could the following phrases be seriously posted for today's Evangelical youth groups and Christian schools without being laughed at? "Avoid sexual immorality. Control your body. Love does not equal sex. Don't do porn. Love is always pure." Such words were welcomed by the amazing Thessalonians. Not seen as impossible to obey. The Holy Spirit had radically redirected their lives from lust to love. Have you welcomed him to do the same

---

[74]M Lucado, *1 & 2 Thessalonians* (Nashville, TN: Thomas Nelson , Inc 2007), vii.

for your life?

For Reflection and Discussion

1. How effectively do you start each day by being filled with the Spirit, so that you have the power to turn away from temptation and follow Jesus throughout the day?
2. How often do you think about the reality of Christ's presence with you?
3. You should get the little classic, The Practice of the Presence of God by Brother Lawrence. I repeat reading through it constantly with great blessing!

Chapter 28

All in the family?

L ove looks like a family. At its best. Listening and laughing and crying together. Helping one another. Giving hope. In Western social development, both the family and love have been losers. There are few areas of life where we differ more from 1st century Christians than with this subject of brotherly love. There are few areas in this book that deserve your reflection and thorough response more than this one. That is why I am devoting four chapters to it. And I can assure you, the Thessalonians are a safe model to follow here, too. **"Now about brotherly love, we do not need to write to you, for you yourselves have been taught by God to love each other"** (1 Thes 4:9). This is a monumental verse. We need to spend a lot of time thinking about it because the level of Christian love has sunk dangerously low. Unlike the Thessalonians, many of you need to be written to about brotherly love. That's why God moved me to write. And that is why you are reading this book. We have not done well with our brotherly relationships as **"members of God's household"** (Eph 2:19b). Things must change.

Remember, 1 Thessalonians is likely Paul's first letter preserved for us in the New Testament. There are only a couple problems he had to address at Thessalonica. Most of his words were spent reinforcing what had made them so amazingly fruitful. And encouraging them to keep up the good work. To just do it more and more (1 Thes 4:1, 10). The emphases he made in this letter were main points of his teaching and life. They would be further developed again and again in all his other writings. So his emphasis on brotherly love is significant.

Jews did not love Gentiles like brothers. Paul was a Jew. He was a follower of Jesus. And love had led Jesus to go through Samaria, even though Jews would walk around its borders (John 4:4ff). Samaria had a large population of Jews who had married Gentiles, so strict Jews would not contaminate themselves by setting foot on their soil. Paul, the converted Pharisee, was once a champion of such prejudice. But now he was turning heads by what he wrote to the Thessalonians.

In fact, few things that he wrote in this letter would have struck 1st century readers with more amazement than the way he used kinship family terms describing Christians' relationships with each other. And his making it absolutely clear that Christians were not only brothers and sisters in name. They were to commit themselves to functioning as one family throughout the world!

Joseph Hellerman concludes his well-referenced work, "The Ancient

Church as Family," with these words:

> "From first century Palestine to third-century Carthage, the social matrix most central to early Christian conceptions of community was the surrogate kinship group of siblings who understood themselves to be the sons and daughters of God. For the early Christians, the church was a family."[75]

His specific thoughts concerning Paul and the Thessalonians are helpful.

> "The outset of 1 Thessalonians reveals Paul's conception of community as he wished it to function among his converts...It is important to note at this point that already in 1 Thessalonians, probably the first extant letter of Paul's that we have, the kinship model is deeply embedded in the text. Nineteen occurrences of sibling terminology sprinkled throughout the epistle reflect a kinship metaphor that is in turn reinforced by the references to God as father of the community and by the expressions of family-like affective intimacy that are found elsewhere in the letter. We will discover that the ...social model reflected in Paul's first extant letter is not unique to 1 Thessalonians. Rather, the idea of the church as family is ubiquitous in Paul's writings and is, therefore, central to Paul' understanding of the manner in which interpersonal relationships are to function in the community to which he writes....
>
> For Paul, moreover, the family idea represents much more than terminology and conceptual structure. Paul expects his readers to live out the metaphor in their day-to-day relationships"[76]

So, what did this all look like to Paul and his readers? How did the Mediterranean family work? Was Paul "following Jesus" in demanding believers to view and treat each other as family? And if so, what effect would this have on the 1st century Roman world?

The family structure of that time and place was what cultural anthropologists term, a patrilineal kinship group (PKG). That is, the father (patri) is the determiner of the family line (lineal). The wife would leave her family and join his. He would usually pay a dowry to her father (male guardian) which would be kept in store for her in case something unfortunate were to happen and she were to have to return.

---

[75] Hellerman, *The Ancient Church as Family* (Minneapolis, MN:Fortress Press 2001) p 225.
[76] Hellerman 2001, pp92-93.

The Bible does not advocate all aspects of the PKG as the ideal family structure. It just was how the Mediterranean world structured the family. And depending on what sub-culture one was from, the way it looked varied. But there were some basic similarities throughout most PKG families. And some of those differed significantly from our Western family structures.

Then (thankfully not today) a wife's status was often determined by whether she provided the family with children, especially males. And the strongest, most basic, bond of the family was NOT husband and wife BUT strong sibling ties. This is why calling other believers "brothers" and "sisters" was (and is) such a big deal. The extended family was thought of and provided for by everyone related by blood to the male leader. To be able to, and not to provide for a brother or unmarried sister, was unthinkable. Today's more tightly defined family units do not usually regard the extended family as seriously and demand as much.[77]

Jesus did not shock His Jewish hearers by teaching that His followers constituted a family. That was commonly understood of the 1st century rabbi-disciple relationship. They operated as a surrogate or substitute family with duties equal to those of the original biological family! To associate with rabbis was to enter their "house." The house of Hillel, the house of Shammai, the house of Gamaliel, the house of Yeshua, etc. But reading many of His statements today would demand a total rethinking of church relationships and responsibilities by us.[78] This is seen by what Jesus said in the following scenario:

> **"While Jesus was still talking to the crowd, his mother and brothers stood outside, wanting to speak to him. Someone told him, "Your mother and brothers are standing outside, wanting to speak to you."" He replied to him, "Who is my mother, and who are my brothers?" Pointing to his disciples, he said, "Here are my mother and my brothers. For whoever does the will of my Father in heaven is my brother and sister and mother."** (Matt 12:46-50).

Hellerman captures the staggering implications,

> "Jesus of Nazareth publicly dissociates himself from his natural family, professes loyalty to a new surrogate family, and apparently expects his followers to do the same. It is this resocialization—at the kinship level—that marks early Christianity as distinct among the voluntary associations of the Greco-Roman antiquity. The social

---

[77]See Hellerman 2001 pp 27-91 for thorough discussion.
[78]See Matt 8:21-22; 23:8-12; Mk 1:14-20; 10:28-30; 13:12-13; Lk 14:26.

solidarity characteristic of the family model, in turn, goes a long way to explain both the intimacy and sense of community so often cited as unique to early Christianity; and the attractiveness of the early Christian movement to displaced and alienated urbanites in the Greco-Roman world."[79]

Paul taught his converts that to follow him was to follow Jesus (1 Thes 1:6; 1 Cor 11:1). So, when he wrote to the Thessalonians as being "**in God the Father**" (1:1) and immediately (1:4) and repeatedly (19 times) called them "**brothers**," it was clear: The role of being a true sibling in a spiritual family was to be embraced by all Christ-followers. Everywhere. Even if one's own natural family, ethnic, social or work groups would not do so. Is this still true today?

You might think that you been taught the truth of Christian brotherhood. But, have you been shown it? If you have not seen Christian people of various backgrounds living like biological brothers and sisters normally do—then you have not been taught this truth. To teach, in the biblical sense of the word, is not merely to have something explained intellectually. It is to fully reveal. To show. To model.

This is what Paul told Titus to teach when he was left on Crete "**to straighten out what was left unfinished**" (Titus 1:5a). Crete was a wild place, as we will see in later chapters. An island nation where the level of immorality had sunk to even deeper depths than most other places in the Roman Empire. Paul told Titus he would need to "**appoint elders in every town** (*polis* - city)" (Titus 1:5b). That was a huge job. To help him assess who was elder material, Paul listed qualifications. And the vast majority of those guidelines involved one's character, not merely his teaching ability (see Titus 1:6-9). Why did he insist on moral maturity? Paul explains, "**For there are many rebellious people, mere talkers**" (Titus 1:10a). Titus was to refute them, not only by sounder reasoning, but by his example. "**In everything set them an example by doing what is good…for the grace of God that brings salvation has appeared to all men. It teaches us to say 'No' to ungodliness and worldly passions, and to live self-controlled, upright and godly lives in this present age**" (Titus 2:7,11). Titus was to teach by deed as well as by word.

So, I return to our point. When you joined your church did you join a family? Or an organization? Jesus, Paul and the amazing Thessalonians described and depicted God's called-out ones (His *ekklesia*-church) as a substitute family. As fully functioning as the one they had been born into. Where today are the Evangelical Christians who are actually loving one another as brothers?

---

[79]Hellerman 2001, p 25.

For Reflection and Discussion

1. Think about the breakdown of human relationships in our society. What have you done to hinder your relationships from being eroded? What has been effective?

Chapter 29

"Chains shall He break, for the slave is our brother"

The call of Jesus to join His family was remarkable in two obvious ways. First, for those who might be excluded from the new family. One's physical relatives sometimes became his enemies.[80] The previously unequaled authority of one's birth father was replaced by Jesus and the heavenly Father's roles.[81] The new family was surprising, secondly, for those who may now be included. Men and women of different nationalities, economic statuses, social positions, vocations, political alliances and legal standing (former criminals, present prisoners and exiles) were now members of the same family! With a genuine, supernatural love bonding them even more permanently than the bond of biological birth! It is with the disciples of Jesus that we first see women and children followers of a Jewish rabbi or sage called "disciples" (see Acts 5:14; 6:1; 9:36; Matt 10:42).

The impact this family reconstruction would have had on each context would depend on how literally and thoroughly the local churches functioned as a family. Like so many of our churches in the West, this did not always happen.[82] But it was thriving at Thessalonica. Causing a "you won't believe what I just saw" attraction of the Christian congregation there. The level playing field Paul wanted for Galatia, **with neither Jew nor Greek, slave nor free, male nor female**" (Gal 3:28), was a fact in Thessalonica. The **"one new man"** that Paul wanted to see emerging at Ephesus (2:11-4:16) was alive and well in our central Macedonian city.

Just think of what this must have meant to those living at that time. Paul and his team modeled a life of such love that racism, sexism and economic class-ism were being virtually eliminated. Enemies were loved instead of hated! No one had ever seen anything like that before. Let's think of this remarkable change in regard to just one group--slaves. Imagine what Paul's gospel would mean to both slaves and to those who accepted the Roman assessment of a slave's status.

"Slaves, in Roman law, were classified as chattel (personal property), not persons, as a 'speaking tool' that could be bought or sold or punished at the will of the masters. Some imperial rulings gave limited recognition to their humanity...By the reign of Hadrian (AD117-138)... the master's right of life and death had been taken away."[83]

---

[80]See Matt 10:36 quoted from Micah 7:6.
[81]See Matt 23:9; Lk 12:53; 2 Cor 6:18; Mal 1:6
[82]See Corinthians, James and 1 John.
[83]P Garnsey & R Saller, *The Roman Empire* (Los Angeles: Univ of California Press 1987), p

We know that converted slaves composed a significant group in the Early Church. When Paul wrote to the Ephesians he addressed wives and husbands (5:22-33), children and parents (6:1-4), slaves and masters (6:5-9). In this latter grouping he gives three verses of admonition to slaves, while only one verse to masters. This is the same epistle in which all Christians' equality in Christ had been dealt with in new and amazing depth. To Titus, ministering on Crete, Paul wrote of groups of old men, old women, younger women, young men and slaves.

One of Paul's epistles was written to Philemon. He was a Colossian church leader and slave owner. However reprehensible to us, we must remember that slavery in this period did not involve man stealing (like the slaves later forced into labor from Africa to the West). Philemon's slave, Onesimus, apparently had stolen from him and run away. This was punishable by death. But Onesimus had become a disciple through Paul's ministry. And Paul was now sending him back to his master, not merely "**as a slave, but better than a slave, as a dear brother**" (Ph 16). One can only imagine the social pressure this placed on everyone involved. It was a test case for sure. Was the brotherhood a sham or a reality? By the way, God will send you and your church many such test cases. Are you passing or failing them? The door forward to more fruitfulness is by loving, accepting and helping all true believers God sends your way.

The estimated population of the city of Rome was 1 million. The slave population was 300,000 or 30% of the total. The entire Roman Empire encompassed approximately 50 million with a slave population of 15-20% or 7.5 - 10 million people. That is a massive amount of humans representing a complex social group. What would happen if converted slaves were given equal rights to converted senators? Just to give you a glimpse of the prejudice existing at this exact time, listen to...

> "...the abusive language employed by the normally mild-mannered Pliny, as he described   his reaction to an inscription honoring Claudius' freedman (freed slave) Pallas with [great honors].   Pliny said, 'Personally I have never thought much of these honors whose distribution depends on chance rather than on a reasoned decision, but this inscription more than anything makes me realize what a ridiculous farce it is when they can be **thrown away on such dirt and filth**....'"[84]

By the way, one Near East scholar noted, that Paul, "who conducted most of his missionary activities during the reign of Claudius, languished for two

---

116.

[84]Garnsey and Saller 1987, p 120.

years in prison at Caesarea when Felix, <u>brother of Pallas</u>, was procurator of Judea."[85] Felix's brother (Acts 24) was the emperor Claudius' freed slave. Small world.

A natural question then arising was, "Can a church flourish with no distinction being made between wealthy politicians and penniless slaves?" This happened in Corinth where Erastus, Corinth's wealthy director of public works (Rom 16:23) was in fellowship with the many Corinthian slaves mentioned in 1 Cor 7:21-23. How could the church of Corinth or Rome survive if they accepted Paul's policy? What would others in the community think? Of course this tested the faith of everyone. It challenged the pride of the higher positioned and the patience of the lower. How would you have responded? How are you responding now to such tensions in your present "fellowship"?

Don't answer too quickly. Let me ask you a few more questions. I do so as your friend and brother. How many believers do you treat as closely as you would your own siblings? How much would you be willing to sacrifice to help a brother or sister in Christ? In the Early Church, here are a few of the acts recorded of Christians for one another:

- individuals selling themselves into slavery to get money to help the community's poor and starving.
- using church money to buy slaves' freedom once they converted to Christ
- sing the deacons fund to care for daily needs of orphans, widows, bedridden adults, sickly, prisoners, shipwrecked sailors, workers in the mines, exiles
- visiting, washing and applying medicines to those suffering from contagious diseases—often contracting the sickness oneself
- paying for the burial of the poor
- even paying the ransom to bandits who kidnapped Christians and held them hostage[86]

In the beautiful Christmas hymn, *O Holy Night*, the following words are sung:

"Truly He taught us to love one another;
His law is love and His gospel is peace.
Chains shall He break, for the slave is our brother,
And in His name all oppression shall cease."[87]

How many chains has Jesus broken in your church? In your town or city?

---

[85]E Yamauchi, *The World of the First Christians* (England: Lion Publishing 1981), p 76.
[86]Hellerman, 2001, pp 221-222.
[87]J Dwight in *The Celebration Hymnal* , p 285

Chains are only broken by great strength. And when they are, it is always with great amazement. Have others been amazed by the love of Christ in your life? By the chains His love has broken through you?

In the next chapter we will explore more of the ramifications of the amazing Thessalonians' "brotherly love." But right now let me ask, How brotherly is your love? In what ways does it differ from the love shown by those who do not have the Spirit of God? How do we respond to the needs of others? With judgment, deaf ears or assistance? How many Christians that you know would gladly, quickly and sacrificially open their home and wallets to you if you needed it? Have you ever done that to a needy Christian? How did Jesus love? Are we and our churches really following Him as did the amazing Thessalonians?

For Reflection and Discussion

1. As you consider the tough questions I ask throughout this chapter, take time to repent of anything unloving that the Holy Spirit convicts you of.
2. I have found the short book "Going to Church in the First Century" by Paul Banks, to be an amazing reminder of what worship and life looked like when disciples of opposite classes united in following Jesus.

Chapter 30

Welcome to Philadelphia!

I live in the city of Philadelphia. The name in Greek means "brotherly love" and is used five times in the New Testament. Paul used it only twice, writing to the Thessalonians and to the Romans. To the disciples living at the center of the empire in the city of Caesar, he wrote, **"Be devoted to one another in brotherly love"** (Rom 13:10). Those words were probably written some 6 years after he wrote to the Thessalonians. After Claudius had been poisoned by Agrippina, mother of Nero. The young man who, at 17 then, became emperor and reigned from 54-68 AD. It is no wonder that these emperors took their supposed divinity seriously. Listen to what Nero was taught to reflect on by his teacher, Seneca:

> Have I of all mortals found favor with Heaven and been chosen to serve on earth as vicar of the gods? I am the arbiter of life and death for the nations; it rests in my power what each man's lot and state shall be; by my lips Fortune proclaims what gift she would bestow on each human being; from my utterance peoples and cities gather reasons for rejoicing; without my favor and grace no part of the wide world can prosper; all those many thousands of swords which my peace restrains will be drawn at my nod; what nations shall be utterly destroyed, which banished, which shall receive the gift of liberty, which have it taken from them, what kings shall become slaves and whose heads shall be crowned with royal honor, what cities shall fall and which shall rise—this it is mine to decree."[88]

This man became a monster, killing even friends and family. Not to mention Peter and Paul. Oh, yes, he did order the deaths of both Seneca and Agrippina, too. No one was safe. Many think it was Nero who had Rome set on fire (64AD) and then accused local Christians of the act. After which he unleashed the worst persecution then to date. Paul commanded the Christians living in Rome to love one another as brothers. Publicly. Personally. Sacrificially. Certainly, if such a love were optional, like so many of us take it to be, Paul would have eased up on those living under the suspicious eye of Nero. Even members of Nero's household would be among the converted! (Phil. 4:22). Paul did not expect Romans of their status to fellowship as brothers with the rest of the disciples, did he? It amazes us

---

[88]C Starr, *The Roman Empire* (Oxford: Oxford Univ Press 1982), p 51

that Paul did not ease up on them. But he couldn't. What he wrote, God inspired. God wanted it to be written and to be done. No matter the cost. Do we really get that point? Be honest. Many of you feel it and agree with me that we just don't get it.

Remarking on our text (1 Thes 4:9), Leon Morris noted,

> "Two things in particular marked off the early Christians of New Testament days from contemporary society: the purity of their lives and the love that they practiced so fully. Here Paul passes from the one to the other. *Brotherly love (philadelphia)* is not the same as *agape*, the love towards all that must characterize those who have experienced the *agape* of God. It is to be exercised by the Christian towards all people, irrespective of their merit or (response). But he should also exercise a special *brotherly love* to those united with him in the household of faith. Outside of the New Testament *philadelphia* almost invariably denotes the love that binds together the children of one father; in the New Testament, it is without exception used for the love uniting Christians to one another. James Denney thought that the importance of this 'is not sufficiently considered by most Christian people; who, if they looked into the matter, might find that few of their strongest affections were determined by their common faith. Is not love a strong and peculiar word to describe the feeling you cherish toward some members of the Church, brethren to you in Christ Jesus? Yet love to the brethren is the very token of our right to a place in the Church for ourselves.' These words are not yet out of date."[89]

It is a shameful fact. Many of us Western Christians do not take the commands of brotherly love seriously. The amazing Thessalonians did. In his other use of philadelphia-love, Paul wrote, **"And in fact, you do love <u>all the brothers throughout Macedonia</u>."** (1 Thes 4:10). What did that really mean? Who were **"all the brothers in Macedonia"?** Let's look first at the ones in and around Thessalonica. We will look at the broader region in the next chapter.

What do we know of these early Christians? Several statements and hints from Scripture and non-biblical writings can help us develop a kind of general demography of the Thessalonian and other Greek churches. Remember, Philippi (Acts 16:11-40), Thessalonica (Acts 17:1-10a), Berea (Acts 17:10b-15), Corinth (Acts 18:1-18) and Cenchrea (Rom 16:1) were places in Greece where churches are definitely said to have been planted. Paul was in Athens, saw some converted, but there is no mention of a church

---

[89]L Morris, *1 & 2 Thessalonians* (Downers Grove, IL: InterVarsity Press 1984) pp 85-86.

being formed there (Acts 17:16-34). Greece was then composed of two Roman provinces: Macedonia in the north and Achaia in the south. Athens, Corinth and Cenchrea were in Achaia. The other three cities were in Macedonia.

Luke mentioned that among the Thessalonian converts there were some Jews, a large number of God-fearing Greeks and not a few prominent women (Acts 17:4). He named three men: Jason (Acts 17:16), Aristarchus and Secundus (Acts 20:4). We don't have time to look into all the significant details. But one fact must be noted. There is a command that scholars see pointing to illiteracy among many of the Thessalonians: "**I charge you before the Lord to have this letter read to all the brothers**" (1 Thes 5:27). This we want to investigate.

The presence of poverty and low educational attainments among the believers at Thessalonica should not surprise us. Such is assumed throughout New Testament churches. To Christians living in the highly-cultured Roman colony of Corinth, Paul wrote,

> "**Not many of you were wise by human standards; not many were influential; not many were of noble birth. But God chose the foolish things...weak things...lowly things of this world and the despised things—and the things that are not—to nullify the things that are. So that no one may boast before him**" (1 Cor 1:26-29; cf James 2:5-7).

Paul, encouraging the Corinthians to give more generously to his Judean fund, mentioned their Macedonian neighbors as living in "**extreme poverty.**" Yet they still showed "**rich generosity**" (2 Cor 8:2). How would the Corinthians respond?

They weren't all wealthy, even though their city was one of the most thriving seaports on the Mediterranean. Some of the Corinthians had been "thieves" (1 Cor 6:10) prior to their conversion to Christ. Normally it was the poor who were tempted to steal. In fact one of the criticisms of pagans against Christianity in its time before Constantine was that it was a religion of women, children, slaves and paupers. So, let's think of what it would have looked like to be a brother to all Christians indiscriminately. We have considered slaves. Now let's turn our attention to what would have been a significant segment of the congregation--the hundreds of disciples living in poverty. Gibbon, in his classic work, depicted the general poverty then in these words:

> " Such is the constitution of civil society, that whilst a few persons are distinguished by riches...the body of the people is condemned to obscurity, ignorance and poverty. The Christian religion, which

addressed itself to the whole human race, must consequently collect a far greater number of proselytes from the lower than from the superior ranks of life.... The new sect of Christianity was almost entirely composed of the dregs of the populace, of peasants and mechanics, of boys and women, of beggars and   slaves...."[90]

Though he thought Christianity's enemies exaggerated its membership's low achievements, Gibbon recognized that Christian apologists did not deny these claims. The Church of Jesus was largely a poor and under-educated group.

Few of us know of poverty at the levels of the 1st century poor throughout the Roman Empire. Consider that there was no governmental welfare system for those outside of Rome. And even there it consisted mainly of guaranteed supplies of only wheat and water. If a natural disaster occurred, like a famine (one plagued Greece around 51AD), only wealthier patrons could be called on to assist the poor. And this extended almost entirely to those living in cities. Not to the poor in rural areas. What was the living standard of the poor in good times?

The Roman Empire barely produced enough to provide sufficiently for its 300,000 soldiers and for its capital's population of one million. It was chiefly an agrarian (farming) empire that lived "at or near subsistence level."[91] The vast majority of the population was just barely existing. One artisan is recorded as owning "only a stool and a bed." One scholar summarizes, "the life of the peasants must have been grim, short, and abysmally poverty-stricken."[92] The poor of the city were bad off. The rural poor were hopelessly scraping to make ends meet.

"Roman civilization was an urban phenomenon, built on the agricultural surplus from the countryside. Not only did the cities exploit the countryside to feed and clothe their residents, but the urban dwellers, a small minority of the whole population, were also contemptuous of the masses as 'rustics', who were unacquainted with the sophisticated culture of urban life and often literally spoke a different language"[93]

Try to imagine how a believer would respond when he heard of a fellow Christian starving or struggling in the countryside. The physician/philosopher Galen, when describing how diseases spread in the countryside during a famine, wrote. "The country people...had to fall back on unhealthy foods...; they ate twigs and shoots of trees and bushes, and bulbs

[90]E Gibbon, *The History of the Decline and Fall of the Roman Empire* London: Penguin Books 2000), p 184.
[91]Peter Garnsey & Richard Saller, *The Roman Empire* (Los Angeles:Univ of California Press 1987), p 43
[92]C Starr, 1982, p 94
[93]Garnsey & Saller, 1987, p 119

and roots of indigestible plants; they filled themselves with wild herbs, and cooked fresh grass"[94]

Yet the Thessalonians showed brotherly love "**to all the brothers throughout Macedonia**." To those living in the city and outside of it. Later, Governor Pliny wrote to Emperor Trajan complaining against the spread of Christianity as follows: "Many of all ages, of all ranks, of both sexes, are being brought into danger (of conversion), and will continue to be brought. The blight of this superstition has not been confined to towns and villages (cities); it has even spread to the country."[95]

Can you now read those verses about the amazing Thessalonians without appreciating the search and sacrifice they would have made for their suffering fellow-Christians? And this was not from a position of great wealth for most of them. They constantly gave to others needier than themselves. In the name of Christ. With joy. Women and children, prominent patrons and their clients, teachers and students, masters and slaves were all becoming "**one new man in Christ**." And love was bonding them together. As our old friend, HL Hastings noted when commenting on Paul's declaration, "**We ought always to thank God for you, brothers, and rightly so, because ... the love every one of you has for each other is increasing**" (2 Thes 1:3):

> "The deep affection which Paul felt for the Thessalonians had borne its fruit in the rich development of Christian love in the church...The love which they bore was not the love pertaining to class or caste. It was not merely the rich loving the wealthy, nor the wise loving the intelligent, nor the fashionable people loving the refined, but the love of every one of them all abounded toward each other. It was a universal feeling–an all-pervading power that controlled and molded every heart and every mind. It was not the result of resolves and compacts and agreements; it was 'the love of God shed abroad in their hearts by the Holy Ghost.'"[96]

What impact would this have had on the onlookers? What attraction it must have drawn to Jesus and to the life He alone can give! This was loving one's neighbor as oneself. It was literally following Jesus's command to do what the Good Samaritan had done for the dying stranger who lay in his path (Lk 10:25-37). This is one of the reasons Paul would have seen no longer any

---

[94]In Garnsey & Saller 1987, p 97.
[95]In H Mattingly, *Christianity in the Roman Empire* (New York: WW Norton & Co., 1967), p 37.
[96]H Hastings, *Thessalonica: Or The Model Church* (New York: Rudd & Carlton 1861), p 71.

need for his team to evangelize in their region (1 Thes 1:8-9). And imagine, he had labored there for only about three months! The love of the gospel makes headway where all other efforts prove fruitless. Relentless acts of amazing love were reaching their entire region with amazing results. Let yourself imagine what would happen if we were to love our neighbors today in this way. With rich and poor, educated and uneducated, white collar and blue collar, of all races, just loving like brothers and sisters! Let your hearts soar to dream what it would be like if we were to adopt the loving lifestyle of the amazing Thessalonians!

For Reflection and Discussion

1. Can you name some "type" of people that it is just hard for you to naturally love? What's the problem do you think?
2. Why would it be hard for you to have your daughter or son marry into that group? Are your concerns biblical?

Chapter 31

Loving beyond our local church

I hope that reading these chapters do for you what they did for me in writing them. They made my heart gasp. When I consider the price the Thessalonians paid for their love of the brethren. The real cost in terms of time, money, effort, social stigmatization. The depths of their sacrifice and suffering. As I reflected on how easily I turn my head and walk away from a brother's need. I was ashamed. These chapters have led me to a deeper repentance and its ever-present partner: faith! Faith is looking to Jesus and being relieved that He did for me what I cannot do for myself. He died for my sins and gave me righteousness before the Father. His perfect brotherly love was what the Thessalonians and all disciples looked to when they failed!

Let's go a couple steps farther in examining what it meant for the Thessalonians to love **"all the brothers throughout Macedonia"** (1 Thes 4:10). We have looked in some detail at the cost of love in terms of brothers being slaves, rural dwellers and the poor. Of the difficulties, there must have been in loving them evenly. Yet this is just a sampling of the diversity that would have composed the churches throughout Macedonia.

Regional prejudices abounded in their day, just as they do throughout the world today. As Starr noted,

> "Men in the more solidly urbanized areas had long been jealously attached to their communities; even in the Empire this loyalty produced fierce rivalries between neighboring cities for titles of honor or possession of border lands. This mutual hostility was shared by all classes in the cities...Neither in the countryside nor in the city streets was the 'Roman peace' easily maintained; not far below the surface lurked all manner of violence"[97].

Yet the Thessalonian believers were willing to lay aside these deep-seated provincial prejudices in embracing all fellow disciples as brothers and sisters. As this was not easily done, the love that fueled this gracious spirit would have been noted with genuine awe. And it would have attracted multitudes toward the Church. Everyone down deep in their hearts wants to be so loved!

Cities back then would also try to outdo each other in courting the patronage of Rome and its emperor. The emperors certainly were among the

---

[97] C Starr, *The Roman Empire* (Oxford, England: Oxford Univ Press 1982) p 100.

wealthiest men in the empire. And they often gave away millions of sesterces, especially in times of need.[98] So, in a region that was repeatedly plagued by food crises and shortages, each city had a jealous regard for its patrons. Yet, because the Lord Jesus was their one true Ruler, these fierce rivalries between Thessalonica, Philippi and Berea were dropped. For some reason the Corinthians had a much harder struggle with their unity, opting rather to split and side together in smaller factions (cf. 1 Cor 1:10-17). Not so the amazing Thessalonians. The rivalry between Thessalonica and Philippi was huge. Both thrived as major cities on the famous trade route, the Via Egnatia, which linked Rome with the East and the North. Though Thessalonica had grown larger, with a population of about 200,000, it was Philippi that had a strategic advantage. It was a Roman colony. Luke mentioned this as a significant point in Acts 16:12. A colony "was essentially an extension of Rome. It was a community of Roman citizens established with a standard form of constitution modeled after that of Rome. Outside Italy colonies tended to be settlements of retired soldiers...."[99] This distinction, likely, was in Paul's mind when he wrote to the Philippians and said, "**Their mind is on earthly things. But _our citizenship_ is in heaven. And we eagerly await a Savior from there, the Lord Jesus Christ**" (Phil. 3:19b-20).

When you factor retired Roman soldiers into the area and, then, into the church, you have now included an infamously cruel and loyal group. Retirement occurred after 20 years (for army legionnaires), 25 years (for auxiliary infantry and cavalry), 26 years (for sailors). Retirement often was accompanied with money and/or land gifts. The military was Caesar's special supporters. And he took care of them. Roman senators were, next to the emperor, the highest officials in Rome and often the ruler's chief rivals. In a veiled threat, the Caesars would begin their official communications to senators with the words, "If you and your children are in health it is well; I and the legions are in health"[100] Starr further noted,

> "Above all, the soldiers were spiritually bound to their emperor. On enlistment they swore an oath of obedience 'to perform with enthusiasm whatever the Emperor commands, never to desert, and not to shrink from death on behalf of the Roman state'"[101]

It would have been a challenge for any self-respecting Thessalonian to treat a Philippian as a brother. But they did. And, with a large number of

---

[98]G Botsford, _The Roman Assemblies_ (New York: The MacMillan Co., 1909), p 8- (a sestercius was worth 5 cents, a denarius was worth 20 cents).
[99]P Garnsey & R Saller, _The Roman Empire_ LosAngeles:Univ of California Press 1987) p 27.
[100]C Starr, 1987, p 109.
[101]C Starr, 1982, p 111.

134

Philippians being retired Roman soldiers, with their deep sense of loyalty to the emperor, it is no wonder that suffering marked the Philippian church from the beginning. Paul wrote, to them from prison and reminded them, **"For it has been granted to you on behalf of Christ, not only to believe on him, but also to suffer for him"** (Phil 1:29). Rough, retired soldiers would almost see it as sport to persecute any Philippian daring to swear allegiance to another Lord than Caesar. Or to outsiders coming to their relief. Nevertheless, the Thessalonians were willing to do so. They showed love to all the brothers throughout Macedonia. And that included the Philippians.

So as not to carry on beyond the limited scope of this work, we will finally note that "Roman society was obsessed with status and rank; a Roman's place in the social hierarchy was advertised in the clothes he wore, the seat he occupied at public entertainments, the number and social position of his clients and followers, and his private expenditures on slaves, housing and banquets"[102] It would have been very difficult for anyone wanting to ascend the ladder of status in the Roman Empire to disregard the outward distinctions that kept each class in its place. But the first disciples were forbidden to do this. Jesus and Paul were rabid in their defense of the equality of the poor believer with every other believer. In fact, Paul often went beyond equality and made the poor more vital to the Kingdom! So the amazing Thessalonians rejected honor and promotion. Instead they lovingly embraced one another as equals. They would have certainly left their unique mark of love wherever they went.

In closing it is good to ask, where is the regional love of Christ today? How many Christians find it difficult to love even their own local church members as brothers? Much less those of another church or denomination! Yet we should transcend these local bounds and do so to all believers in our region–and beyond. How many churches languish because they have no conception of belonging to a Body larger than their independent congregation? Or denomination?

Too often today, if leadership and gifts for service are needed for any task, they must be found within the four walls of the local church or not found at all! If our church members are in need, they will simply have to suffer unless someone in their local congregation has the heart to help them. Vision dies because few dare see the Body of Christ as the regional church. Instead of our little independent enclaves. Suffering continues unnecessarily because leaders cannot and usually will not go outside their own group to help their needy parishioners. Our small-minded parochialism is not worthy of the same name as what Paul and the Thessalonians exhibited!

What we are doing in our rigid and relentless city-wide divisions in the Body is not biblical. When Paul wrote to the Thessalonians, he wrote "**to**

---

[102]Garnsey & Saller, 1987, p 199.

the church of the Thessalonians" (1:1). They were all one church. Though they, like the rest of New Testament believers, met in separate "house churches".[103] So the whole group of one entire city was written to as a single church (1 Cor 1:2). Luke wrote of "the church in Jerusalem" even though it met in separate places and groups as, for instance, Grecian and Hebraic groups.[104] We recognize that Evangelical churches have complex distinctions involving both tradition and truth. But should not those who are born again followers of Christ be doing more together, laying the secondary things aside for unity? Are we not also expected to "**make every effort to keep the unity of the Spirit in the bond of peace**" (Eph. 4:3)?

What would happen if a Presbyterian church began taking up an offering for a Pentecostal family? A Baptist pastor asking a successful Methodist church planter to come and lead a seminar on evangelism? But he's not one of us. Be careful now. How dare we think that way any longer! If God the Father calls him a son and Christ calls him a brother, how can I exclude him from at least some degree of fellowship? How much more could be done if today's Christian leaders were to embrace one another as colleagues and peers rather than competitors? If we encouraged all true believers to view one another as brothers and begin treating each other as such? If we lived as the first believers did and if we had the love of the amazing Thessalonians?

For Reflection and Discussion

1. Try to list several of the negative outcomes of local churches NOT working together for the advancement of Christ's Kingdom.
2. Would your church leaders be in favor of taking actions for a greater missional unity in your community? There's only one way to find out!

---

[103]See Acts 2:46; 5:42; Rom 16:5; 1 Cor 16:19.
[104]See Acts 8:1; 15:4; 6:1.

Chapter 32

The School of God

One of the greatest gospel promises in the Old Testament is found in the New Covenant. Those encouraging words from God include: "I will put my law in their minds...No longer will a man teach his neighbor, or a man his brother, saying, '**Know the Lord,' because they will all know me, from the least of them to the greatest**" (Jer 31:33-34).

The Holy Spirit is the best Teacher. To be taught by God is to be truly educated. It is to learn and be deeply impressed by the lesson God has implanted in the soul. What has God taught you? How many lessons from God have you so learned that they have become your way of thinking? Your practice?

This is what God taught the Thessalonians: "**Now about brotherly love, we do not need to write you, for you yourselves have been taught by God to love each other**" (1 Thes 4:9). Love is the fulfillment or goal of the Law. So, to be taught by God to love, then, is to be taught by God life's most practical lesson. To be taught the most important thing by the best Teacher. Wow! Now that is an education. And the Thessalonians were declared by God not only to be students—but graduates, in a sense. They had been taught. Lesson completed. God's love had been learned.

A Greek Orthodox commentator saw this point and wrote,

> "Here again the Apostle states that the Thessalonians are doing very well in showing love toward all the brethren—i.e., all the Christians— in the province of Macedonia. Therefore, he does not see the need for further comment. And the reason, he says, is that the Thessalonians have been taught by God and have learned from Him. Now this idea is taken from Jeremiah's famous prophecy about the new covenant...This is a clear indication that this prophecy was realized, according to Paul, in the community of the brethren where God's law was written upon their hearts...."[105]

It is important to realize that Paul used a word here that is nowhere else used in the New Testament. Emphasis is usually the point when unique words are used by Scripture writers. The special word Paul used was "Theo-didaktoi" or God-taught.[106]

---

[105]P Tarazi, *1 Thessalonians* (New York: St Vladimir's Seminary Press 1982) 142-143.
[106]See also Isa 54:13; Matt 16:17.

It is important what school one graduates from. To have an Ivy League education often advances a person further than graduating from a local community college. I did not graduate from Harvard or Cornell, etc., so I am not being elitist. Please don't be offended, just follow the point. Graduation with honors from the Wharton School of Business marks one with a certain prestige. And usually carries with it promise of significant employment and financial benefits. What school have you attended? What degree have you secured? What's hanging on your wall? What academic honors matter most to you?

The Thessalonians had been taught by God. By Jesus, whose words echo in Paul's, **"It is written in the Prophets: 'They will all be taught by God.' Everyone who listens to the Father and learns from him comes to me"** (John 6:45). The Thessalonians left the classes of the Cabiri, the rabbis and everyone else to attend the school of God. They became eager Freshmen. Front-row-seaters in the school of Jesus. The School of Love. How many Western Evangelicals have gone to this school? Have we really been taught brotherly love? For several semesters? First in its introductory and then in its advanced levels? It doesn't appear that many of us have.

But we will argue about which college is best. We will get our license plates emblazoned as alumni of certain universities. We will cheer for our college as long as we live. Who is cheering for Brotherly Love University? Who is leaving endowments to the deacons for the work of mercy ministry to help impoverished believers near us and around the world? Thank God there are still some who wear those colors. But it has lost its Ivy League status in our thinking. We have forgotten what an honor it is to sit at the feet of Jesus and learn from His life and words of love. Maybe it is because after attending his class no one gets a diploma. Or special recognition. Just the words, **"Go and do likewise"** (Lk 10:37; see 10:25-37).

I know that you likely study the Bible and love to read it. That you might even consider yourself an "armchair theologian." What I think needs to be said is, that unless you love others, the God (theo) you have studied (logian) does not appear to be the Jesus of the New Testament. Or perhaps you have mastered much **about** Him without really being taught **by** Him. Maybe we have become accustomed to opening our Bibles without thinking of Him being present and speaking its words personally to us. Is it possible that we study our Bibles far away from Jesus? A kind of distance learning that doesn't hear the Word speaking through the words of holy Scripture? I think many do. Maybe most of us.

The Thessalonians were the one group of Christians who were declared by an inspired apostle to be "taught by God" how to love. And as lovers, Jesus said, they became true theologians. Hear the last words of the great prayer of the Teacher, himself. **"I have made you known to them (theology), and will continue to make you known (teach theology), in**

138

order that the love you have for me may be in them and that I myself may be in them" (John 17:26).

Jesus still teaches theology. But not primarily to make us smarter. He teaches us about God so that His love will grow and develop in us. And the true love of God, according to this prayer, is the love that the Father has for the Son. Whenever we teach or preach about God–if love for Jesus is not the outcome, we have missed the point. We have failed the class. No matter how much we might have pleased others with our intellect or insights.

So, it's time to re-enroll. Class is in session. This is no boring course that you must take because someone else thinks it is important. It is the core of God's curriculum. And we are to be life-long learners. Don't be tempted to drop out of the class. Sure it's hard and sometimes drudgery. Love Works! Don't flunk out. Complete your assignments. Love Works! Even the amazing Thessalonians were warned by Paul never to leave the School of Brotherly Love. "**Yet we urge you, brothers, to do so more and more**" (1 Thes 4:10).

Who knows more than God? No lesson is more relevant and needed to learn than the one God teaches. There are so many temptations to just move on and leave love behind. Especially when others are begging you to go with them. "**You do not want to leave too, do you? Jesus asked the Twelve. Simon Peter answered him, 'Lord, to whom shall we go? You have the words of eternal life**" (Jn 6:67-68). Wise choice, Peter! Even though it wasn't popular.

When you walk with Jesus, He shows you God's love everywhere. "**The earth is filled with your love, O Lord. Teach me your decrees**" (Ps 119:64). If you have eyes to see and ears to hear, He will instruct you. By the still small voice of His Spirit. And through your Christian brothers and sisters. Let them all be your teachers. Their kind words. Helping hands. Warm hearts. Biblical admonitions. Wherever love is shown in Jesus' name, take it in. Study and admire it. Encourage it. Emulate it. Go and do likewise. Can you hear it? The bell is ringing. Take your seat again, with the amazing Thessalonians, at the feet of Jesus in the School of God's Love.

For Reflection and Discussion

1. Who in your church would be the best person to lead a class on "the school of God?" Why do you find him/her qualified to do so?
2. In what ways may "knowledge is power" be wrong?

Chapter 33

A huge disconnect

What comes to your mind when I say, "good works"? I am afraid that for many of us Evangelicals it is, actually, a negative concept. Good works are something that you are **not** saved by. Or something that legalistic churches have overemphasized. Maybe so. On both counts. But, if something special does **not** come rushing into your mind when you hear "good works"– you have been disconnected from a power that could both enrich you and everyone around you. I hope this chapter plugs you back in.

Another word to think about. Famine. Now that is a word most Western Evangelicals do not understand. Because, thankfully, we have never experienced it. Famine means hunger. Leading often to a slow, agonizing death. However grateful to God we might be that many of us have never been forced to "go to bed hungry," that is a liability to us when we read 1 & 2 Thessalonians. And most other biblical books. Because famine was a real and dreaded threat in those days. Like radical terrorists are today. It was something on the back of their minds. A threat they could not simply ignore. Something likely enough to happen that they had to prepare for it. Always looming around the corner.

One scholar who will help us several times in our next chapters, Bruce Winter, wrote, "There was famine in Greece in the forties and fifties and one that can be dated to AD 51. Tacitus declared that AD 51 was an 'ominous' year."[107] Remember that many have dated the writing of 1 Thessalonians at 51 AD. So, try to factor in famine, hunger, growing paranoia and desperation into the context as you read Paul's letter. This will help you grasp the powerful attraction linked with the Thessalonians' expressions of love. It will also help prepare you to understand what "good works" often meant in New Testament times.

It will be hard, but try to remove from your mind our shopping malls. And today's numberless products that are mass produced by factories from all over the world. Theirs was an agrarian culture, with the vast majority of people having very little extra money. Electricity. Lights. Engines. Vacuum cleaners and air conditioners were all non-existent. Think of it. No cars, stoves, microwaves and refrigerators. When it was dark, you went to sleep. Unless you had to finish a job by candlelight. When it was light, you worked. Or had someone work for you. You scraped to make ends meet. You ate the

---

[107]B Winter *Seek the Welfare of the City: Christians as Benefactors and Citizens* (Grand Rapids, MI: Wm B Eerdmans Pub Co, 1994), p 53.

same food day after day–if you were fortunate. Sure, there were a few wealthy people. But there was no large middle class like today. The options were essentially two: rich or poor. Depending on the ones to whom you were born, because there was very little chance for upward mobility. Until a new type of love came rushing into the world through Jesus and His followers.

Good works back then did not mean helping an elderly woman cross the street. Like a good boy scout. Or replacing your neighbors garbage cans back beside their house after the city's department of sanitation workers hauled the trash away. There was no trash because there were no disposable containers. No plastic. And, in fact, there was little garbage. Little waste. What humans did not consume, animals or birds did. Oh, yeah–not many were fat, either. Things were very different in those days.

Now think of the two words separately. Good. Works. What was good? And what was work? When put together in Scripture they usually meant doing something generous that really cost something. Something obviously needed (good) that took real effort (work). The words usually implied helping someone out of a very tight fix. Often financially. Or with food, shelter, clothing, a job--one of life's necessities. It certainly did not mean just being nice. Like opening the door for your wife. Which is a good thing–but not a good "work." Unless you are crippled and have a hard time moving. Then it might qualify because of the effort or sacrifice that the act demands.

In a culture like ours that idolizes personal comfort and possessions, the background needed to appreciate the stuff that makes "good works" is often absent. Like deep sacrifice and simplicity. The New Testament concept of good works is really hard for many of us even to relate to! So much today is so easy compared to the 1st century. Our "minimum wage" and our "poverty level" allow for a standard of living that the vast majority of Macedonians would have died for. Many of those we regard as "poor" today are truly rich in comparison to back then. Now you can better understand how the following Scriptures would have been first understood:

> **"In the same way, let your light shine before men, that they may see your *good deeds* and praise your Father in heaven" (Matt 5:16).**

> **"Each man should *give*.... And God is able to make all grace abound to you, so that in all things at all times, having all that you *need*, you will abound in *every good work*. As it is written: He has scattered abroad his *gifts to the poor*, his righteousness endures forever" (2 Cor 9:7-9).**

> **"Therefore, as we have opportunity, let us *do good* to *all***

people, especially to those who belong to the *family of believers*" (Gal 6:10).

"And let us *consider* how we may *spur* one another on toward *love* and *good deeds....* "And do not forget to *do good* and to *share* with others, for with such sacrifices God is well pleased" (Heb 10:24; 13:16).

"What good is it, my brothers, if a man claims to have faith but has no *deeds?* Can such faith save him? Suppose a brother or sister is *without clothes* and *daily food.* If one of you says to him, 'Go, I wish you well; keep warm and well fed,' but does nothing about his physical needs, what *good* is it? In the same way, faith by itself, if it is not accompanied by *action,* is dead" (James 2:14-17).

"Live such *good* lives among the pagans that, though they accuse you of doing wrong, they may *see* your *good deeds* and glorify God on the day he visits us...For it is God's will that *by doing good* you should silence the ignorant talk of foolish men" (1 Pet 2:12,15).

These quotes are from a wide range of New Testament books. Written over decades. My point is–they all agree that good works were costly acts to help someone in serious need. And when they were performed in Jesus' name, a powerful witness of the new life in Christ was revealed. Power that helped normal people show they believed that it was better to give than to receive. The power of this new life of love was truly atomic.

We are saved by faith in Christ alone. But what I am affirming is that true faith cannot live in total isolation. Closed up in one's mind. Faith that does not work, is not alive. This is clearly shown by Paul's famous statement:

"For *by* grace you have been saved, *through* faith; and that not of yourselves, it is the gift of God; *not* as a result *of* works, that no one should boast. For we are His workmanship, created in Christ Jesus *for* good works, which God prepared beforehand, that we should walk in them" (Eph. 2:8-9- NASB).

Not *of* works, but *for* good works. So we can say, Faith Works! And, understanding what "good works" are, we can affirm that true faith is willing to work hard for others. At a personal cost. That is what "good works" meant when written in the New Testament.

The Thessalonians saw good at work in Paul. His faith worked. His

142

love for them was apparent. He spent late hours as a leatherworker, maybe making tents for soldiers (1 Thes 2:9). Showing the Thessalonians how Christ-love sweated for others. And he also delighted doing the little acts of love that were not so costly. The smile. Paying attention when any of the others spoke. Holding the little child's hand. Saying, thank you. The Thessalonians knew that if they showed this same fully formed Jesus-empowered love to those around them, it would keep producing an amazing harvest! And it did. I hope you will believe that for yourself, too. Christ is risen, and is still working in this world through believers like you. Every good work will matter. "Your *labor* in the Lord is not in vain" (1 Cor 15:58). As NT Wright again so powerfully states,

> "What you do in the Lord *is not in vain.* You are not oiling the wheels of a machine that's about to roll over a cliff. You are not restoring a great painting that's shortly going to be thrown on the fire. You are not planting roses in a garden that's about to be dug up for a building site. You are – strange though it may seem...– accomplishing something that will become in due course part of God's new world. Every act of love, gratitude, and kindness; every work of art or music inspired by the love of God and delight in the beauty of his creation; every minute spent teaching a severely handicapped child to read or to walk; every act of care and nurture, of comfort and support, for one's fellow human beings...; and, of course every prayer, all Spirit-led teaching, every deed that spreads the gospel, builds up the church, embraces and embodies holiness rather than corruption, and makes the name of Jesus honored in the world–all of this will find its way, through the resurrecting power of God, into the new creation that God one day will make. That is the logic of the mission of God. God's re-creation of his wonderful world, which began with the resurrection of Jesus and continues mysteriously as God's people live in the risen Christ and in the power of his Spirit, means that what we do in Christ and by the Spirit in the present is not wasted."[108]

This is his promise: "**God is not unjust; he will not forget your work and the love you have showed** *him* **as you have helped** *his people* **and continue to help them**" (Heb. 6:10). You show him love every time you help a believer. The living Christ is always looking. He really does take it personally whenever we take in Christian strangers, clothe the naked, tend to the sick and visit those imprisoned for his name. He said so. "The King will reply, **"I tell you the truth, whatever you did for one of the least of these brothers of mine, you did for me**" (Matt. 25:40-43). He delights in such

---

[108]NT Wright *Surprised by Hope* (New York: HarperCollins, 2008), pp 208-209.

acts of love. Especially when they are inconvenient and costly. When we expect nothing in return. As truly good works. Pause with me and repent of your lack of love for others. Ask God to re-plant in you the desire and discipline to do works that are good. For that to happen, you have to have the time and resources to assist those in need. Let's see how the amazing Thessalonians found enough time and money to help huge numbers of needy neighbors. Even in the midst of famine and persecution.

For Reflection and Discussion

1. Again, think of someone in your church who would be fit to teach a class on "good works." Why did you choose her/him?
2. Do you think it is likely that a person is truly saved whose life is devoid of good works? How much devotion to doing good works would you think is "a safe amount" for a believer to have?

Chapter 34

Doing missions through a quiet, working love

I am zealously missional. My life has been focused on winning souls and making them disciples who "**obey everything Jesus has commanded us**" (Matt 28:20). For many years, my first concern was with mainly speaking the Word. Sharing the gospel verbally with sinners. The sooner the better. Turning the conversation to Jesus and then pressing the point of personal faith in Him. I still do that. But I have learned from the Thessalonians a better way to witness. And they had learned it from Paul. Who, as we have seen, had learned this way from Jesus. It is the way of peace rather than pressure. A way that is incredibly fruitful while being patient, prayerful and guided by love. Love does not force itself on the beloved. It asks questions and listens, going only as far as the other is ready to go. A truly quietly effective way of witnessing.

The Thessalonians had witnessed so effectively that Paul wrote, "**the Lord's message rang out from you not only in Macedonia and Achaia- your faith in God has become known everywhere. Therefore we do not have to say anything about it**" (1 Thes 1:8-9). That is an incredible report. All of Greece (the Roman provinces of Macedonia and Achaia) had been touched with their story. And "everywhere" else. Leon Morris helps us understand what Paul might have meant by "everywhere," when he wrote in the NIV Study Bible note, "1:8 - *everywhere*. In every place they visited or knew about. The news spread because Thessalonica was on the important Egnatian Way; it was a busy seaport and the capital of the Roman province of Macedonia."[109]

The text does not say through what form the gospel message spread. The rest of the epistle helps by describing it. What is surprising, is that Paul chose to describe their witness like a bell being rung. A bell rings when it is moved by an outside force. A bell does not ring itself. The form of the verb is in the passive not active voice. The Thessalonians, like a bell, were being moved to ring. And what a beautiful noise they made! The Lord's message was being heard.

One thing we know, the Thessalonians did not all leave the city to go on missionary journeys. Some might have. But Paul had taught them as a church to reach the lost differently. By making disciples through selfless love inspiring amazing works and words. In that order. First prove your love and

---

[109]L Morris, *In NIV Study Bible* (Grand Rapids, MI: Zondervan Publishing House 1995), p 1823.

then talk about it. Or as he would pray, "**May our Lord Jesus Christ and God our Father...encourage your hearts and strengthen you <u>in every good deed and word</u>**" (2 Thes 3:16-17). Good works lead to opportunities to share good words. This resembles the explicit commands that Jesus gave to the 72 when He sent them out. Listen carefully, for thousands today are following this Luke 10 model with tremendous fruitfulness:

> **"When you enter a town and are welcomed, eat what is set before you. Heal the sick who are there and tell them, the kingdom of God is near."** (Luke 10:8-9)

Healing precedes speaking. The gift of the gospel sounds better wrapped in the package of good deeds. And now we know that good deeds are costly acts that meet basic needs. Paul's prayer noted that God would encourage and strengthen them to do what otherwise was impossible. To love others with His love. The need may be health related or financial or domestic or ...? We have to get close enough to see or sense the need, so we can respond when the Spirit fills us with wisdom and love. And flows through us to free the captives He has sent us to.

Although it is placed in our Bibles after his other church letters, I have already shared with you that 1 Thessalonians was likely Paul's first biblical letter. If it was written before the others, it arguably deserves special prominence. Certainly more than it has been given. In it he has one prayer. And this is his first request in it: "**Now may the Lord make your love increase and overflow for each other and for everyone else, just as ours does for you**" (1 Thes 3:12). The agape love of God filled Paul. He wanted it to absolutely fill them to overflowing. And he prayed that the love would first flow to each other (fellow Christians) and then "everyone else."

Think of it. Everyone else. That, my friends, is the disciple's lifetime job. Letting God's love pour through us all the time. But is it really our goal today? Or is something else filling our hearts? After all our plans, is there any room left for Jesus? For good works? To overflow with love means there is no room left for anything else. Or to have all that we do or say flavored and energized by the love of Jesus flowing through us. What would happen if we prayed Paul's Thessalonian prayer incessantly for one another today? Would God be pleased to replace our ho-hum love with the amazing love of His Son? I am sure that He would. And then we would begin to see Thessalonian fruit. Even while we are "on the job."

The Thessalonians were living so differently from before, that everyone was talking about it (1Thes 1:9). Part of the marvel was their new approach to work. We have seen how Paul worked. He labored strategically, "**...We worked night and day, laboring and toiling so that we would not be a burden to any of you. We did this...in order to make ourselves a**

146

model for you to follow" (2 Thes 3:8-9). Similarly he told the Ephesian elders,

> "**I have not coveted anyone's silver or gold or clothing. You yourselves know that   these hands of mine have supplied my own needs and the needs of my companions. In everything I did, I showed you that by this kind of hard work we must help the weak, remembering the words the Lord Jesus himself said, 'It is more blessed to give than to receive.'**" (Acts 20:33-35).

Paul worked as a tent maker to model for His disciples the necessity of working. So that they could help others both physically and spiritually. How can you help others in dire need without resources? How can you have resources without working? A few of the Thessalonians thought they had a better system. But the majority of the Thessalonians got this message.

So, the love for which he prayed in his first request (3:12) was already flowing. The Thessalonians, unlike many believers today, began immediately to follow Jesus in a life of true discipleship. And, as Jesus promised the disciples in the Upper Room, they began bearing **"fruit that remains"** (John 15:16). Remember, Paul wrote the following after having been with them only a few months. **"Finally brothers, we instructed you how to live in order to please God, as in fact you are living. Now we urge you to do this more and more"** (1 Thes 4:1; cf. 4:10; 5:11). Why does it take so much longer today? What's gone wrong?

Paul was highlighting their implementation of his work/witness model when he wrote,

> "**Now about brotherly love we do not need to write to you...in fact, you do love all the brothers throughout Macedonia. Yet we urge you, brothers, to do so more and more. Make it your ambition to lead a quiet life, to mind your own business and to work with your hands, just as we told you, so that your daily life may win the respect of outsiders and so that you will not be dependent on anybody**" (1 Thes 4:9-12).

We will continue to dissect this passage. But first, a summary,

> "The Thessalonians, to Paul's delight, were already living this life of practical love, taking care of one another financially. What's more, they seem to have extended this outreach of giving and support further afield, to the other churches of Macedonia and quite possibly other places as well). This implies that the Thessalonian church was both larger and perhaps wealthier than others in the area. Paul wants

147

them to build on this work and increase it. Let it overflow, he says."[110]

First, please note that this text (4:9-12) is one short paragraph. One unified context. Verse 11 carries on the thoughts introduced in 9 and 10. In fact v. 11 is continuing the same sentence started in v. 10. So the NIV (different from NASV) was not helpful in breaking its linguistic unity and cutting up the text into two paragraphs. Paul's point about the brotherly love they were to show (v 10) is directly connected to his command to do manual labor as a way of opening the hearts of outsiders (vv 11-12). It could be represented like this:

Brotherly love + Manual labor = Open doors for the gospel

You can be sure, first, that when God fills us with His love and we do the work He gives us to do, amazing and unexpected doors open up. NT Wright captures this implication and states,

> "I don't care too much for money,' sang the Beatles... 'Money can't buy me love.' Now that is of course true. But 'love' is a strange word in most languages, and there are connections between love and money which surprise us. And the point of this little paragraph is that money can *express* love, and, indeed, that if the love is genuine it will find an outlet in financial generosity....

> "...The paragraph makes it clear, as do similar passages elsewhere in the New Testament that this 'love' is expected to issue in practical support within the Christian community, and also, as far as possible, in the world outside. God's own expression of his love resulted in his total self-giving in the person and death of his son. Christian expression of the same love must have the same self-giving quality, and money is an inescapable part of that."[111]

This is not how most churches approach evangelism. Or how most missionaries plan and fulfill their mission. But it is how the model church evangelized. So we should consider it as sound missional strategy that has led to great missional success. Of course it will need some modification in each context. But, to share the gospel without sharing oneself in needed expressions of love, is to "miss the boat" and choose to swim. You may

---

[110]NT Wright, *Paul for Everyone: Galatians and Thessalonians* (Louisville, KY" Westminster John Knox Press 2004), pp 121-122.
[111]NT Wright, 2004, pp 120-121.

eventually get to your destination. But it will take you much longer and be much harder. Try the boat of love. Paul said, **"We loved you so much that we were delighted to share with you not only the gospel of God but our lives as well"** (1 Thes 2:8a). The gospel works. But the gospel shared through a life of love really works!

Secondly, Paul wanted their lavish love for **"all the brothers throughout Macedonia"** to continue **"more and more."** How many of us, having done something BIG for a Christian or non-Christian, then think: "Whew! Check that off the list. That's a job well done. Time to move on or, better, time to relax." We have been programed to be project-minded rather than people-minded. Churches like to accomplish projects. But it is far harder and less glitzy to develop lasting relationships with people in need. Paul would reprove us and say, "just keep helping others with your good works in Jesus' name." Sure, we need to be wise and not wear ourselves out. But, just being honest with you, my tendency after completing a well-planned project, for many years was to think, "enough already." Rather than Paul's thinking-- let's "do it more and more." Why? Because I loved little. Love gives a capacity, an energy, a perseverance that no other fuel can supply.

Thirdly, how does Paul recommend his readers to continue showing brotherly love? The text seems so strange saying: 1. Be ambitious about being quiet. Let your work do your talking. Think twice before speaking. At one time in my life, I would have considered that cowardice rather than sound missional strategy. 2. Focus on your own life and work (business). We will look at this important statement next chapter. 3. Work with your own hands. John Stott helps us understand why this would have been such a marvel and spectacle, writing,

> "It was the Greeks who despised manual work as degrading to free men and fit only for slaves. Christianity came into direct collision with this view. Paul the tentmaker reinforced the example of Jesus the carpenter and gave dignity to all honest human labor."[112]

I am not saying we *must* work occupationally in missions. But that my training did not appreciate the place and power of tentmaking (vocational) strategy as a general model for use everywhere in missions. And not just for restricted cultures. What was the result of this strange devotion to hard work as a way to be able to show love to your brothers? Paul promises that doing this day in and day out would **"win the respect of outsiders."**

"Outsiders, looking at a new movement that made striking claims

---

112J Stott, *The Message of 1 & 2 Thessalonians* (Downers Grove, IL: InterVarsity Press 1991), p 90.

about Jesus as Lord of the world, would be interested to see what effect it had on the behavior of the members. Financial behavior, like sexual behavior, is one telling indicator of the health and integrity of the movement. And within the fellowship, those in need should be provided for. This was why the place of widows, women left without a breadwinner, so quickly became important in the early church (Acts 6:1; 1 Tim 5:3-16). These are not side issues, away from the real theological heart of the Christian gospel. If God has created a new family in Christ, and if that family is based on and characterized by nothing less than self-giving love, these things are vital. Happy the church, today, that discovers what love in practice looks and feels like."[113]

Amen! Isn't that a major point of evangelism and missions? To earn the right to speak? To open doors that allow us to address intimate spiritual issues? Of course it is. But who would think that giving sacrificial support for mainly Christians (it is *brotherly* love) would deeply impact non-Christians? Jesus thought that. And He said so, **"By this *all men* will know that you are my disciples, if you love *one another*."** (John 13:35). That is why Paul thought it, too. And so did the amazing Thessalonians. Dare we think it? I hope so!

For Reflection and Discussion

1. What is your church's evangelistic strategy? Is it effective?
2. What would happen if the outreach strategy of your church followed Paul's directives mentioned in this chapter?

---

[113]NT Wright, 2004, p 122.

Chapter 35

Would you say, No! to the easy money?

There was a problem in Thessalonica. And it did not involve, as many have wrongly inferred, some of the Thessalonians selling their property and waiting for Jesus to come. The problem involved a relatively small number who were tempted with easy money and comfort. So, what's so bad about that, you might ask? Wouldn't focusing on that issue be making a mountain out of a mole hill? Let's see what Paul thought. That might make us re-think a few more things about how we who are from the USA have chosen to live our lives in the wealthiest nation in human history.

So that you appreciate the pressure they faced, let's make this personal. Would you work if you did not have to? If you were able to strike a sweet deal that would allow you to live comfortably just by being a loyal and active supporter of some benefactor? Be honest. If you could live off the wealth of a friend who just became a sports star. Would you? Well, a somewhat similar opportunity existed in Thessalonica and other cities across the Empire.

The agreement was called patronage. The parties involved were the patron (or benefactor) and the client. If you had a patron, you were pretty much on easy street. You did not have to stoop to do manual labor. You and your family had the money, clothing, food and shelter to live comfortably. You could leave the hard work to the slaves and less fortunate.

> "Clients of patrons were not drawn from the bottom of the social scale. They were recruited by a patron from the ranks of those who were of a slightly lower status....'The 'have nots' did not belong to a household.... They were society's insecure members. They lacked the safety net which a master or a patron afforded in times of uncertainty or adversity such as famines or strife caused by political machinations. On the other hand, 'the haves' may not have been materially wealthy...but they did have a household which guaranteed them protection."[114]

As Winter elsewhere states,

> "Rich citizens were expected to be civic benefactors.... The parasitic client relationship with a patron...would have been the one reason

---

[114]B Winter, *Seek the Welfare of the City* (Grand Rapids, MI: Wm Eerdmans 1994), p 203

why some citizens apart from the rich in Thessalonica, or any other city in the empire, did not have to work."[115]

There were strings attached to the assistance a client would receive. This is how it often worked. In exchange for a patron's support, the client would visit his villa every morning to pay respects. The benefactor would appear and be fawned over by his entourage "in return for food, money, clothing and other favors."[116] The more crowded the house, the higher the status to both patron and clients. These things were noticed and reported throughout the city. A large gathering greatly impacted the patron's public reputation. "Clients could contribute to their patron's social status... by accompanying him on his rounds of public business during the day and applauding his speeches in court. In return, they could expect handouts of food or small sums of money and sometimes an invitation to dinner."[117] Clients were of different levels. And their superiority would determine in what order they actually stood and when they were allowed to speak. It was pretty humiliating at times. But it beat being poor. The patron's arrogance towards his clients would often take debasing forms. But the upside of the relationship made the bootlicking bearable.

And having a patron really was valuable when it came to the frequent times of calamity. Try to imagine a society without insurance. The Roman Empire did not have a system of government-sponsored aid relief during calamities. There was no FEMA or Red Cross to help victims following a natural disaster. No Salvation Army to come alongside of you after a devastating fire or destructive drought.

So, how did people cope during times of great need? Apart from one's extended family, who would always do what they could, you needed a wealthy patron. Without a patron or benefactor, people simply suffered. If you think the proverb, "It's who you know that counts" is true today–it was much more so in 1st century Roman cities. One scholar noted, "It would not be an exaggeration to say that the prosperity of the cities rested in large part on the generosity of their leading citizens."[118] The wealthy would try to help their city during a calamity by offering public gifts. For this help, they were often memorialized on monuments built outside the city. Hundreds of such have been unearthed.

All such evidence helps us understand the situation that Paul was addressing in his letters to the Thessalonians. The patron-client connection

---

[115]B Winter, 1994, p. 42.

[116]P Garnsey & R Saller, *The Roman Empire* (Los Angeles: Univ of California Press 1987), p 122.

[117]Garnsey & Saller 1987, p 151.

[118]CP Jones *The Roman World of Dio Chrysostom* (in B Winter, "Seek the Welfare of the City, Grand Rapids, MI:Wm B Eerdmans Publishing Co, 1994), p 29.

threatened the unity and family structure of the young church. Before we examine the specific Thessalonian texts related to this, it is good to consider Paul's shocking aim:

> "Paul set out to change the established convention of (patronage). In doing this he was initiating in Gentile regions a radical social ethic which he regarded as binding on Christians. The client must now become a private Christian benefactor. When this social change was introduced into new Christian communities, it must have been the most distinctive public feature of this newly emerging religion in the Roman East."[119]

In the passage previously examined (1 Thes 4:9-12), Paul commands, **"Make it your ambition to lead a quiet life, to mind your own business and to work with your hands...so that your daily life may win the respect of outsiders and so that you will not be dependent on anybody"** (vv 11-12). After giving examples from other relevant sources, Winter rightly notes,

> "It therefore makes sense to see this comment concerning 'minding one's own affairs' in 1 Thes 4:11 as taken from a popular description of public and private life. It was clearly the opposite to being concerned about the public activities of one's patron. The patron's very purpose in establishing a financial relationship with a client was that the (client) would not need to attend primarily to his own affairs. He was being supported by his   patron in order to give attention to the (patron's) concern in the public domain."[120]

Paul was clearly forbidding those who were "in Christ" from choosing or continuing in a connection as a client. They are to mind their own business, not the patron's. They are to be quiet, not busy making public shows of support for their benefactors. They are not to be in anyone's hip pocket. Not to be financially dependent on anyone.

Think of the command to work with their own hands. This would have several positive outcomes. Instead of disturbing the patron, it would actually ease his financial burden. Disciples of Jesus would have left the patronage system with no hard feelings. To become a new type of benefactor. And that would certainly win the respect of some of the city's most prominent leaders. Christianity was creating a whole new group of givers!

Not to mention the respect and admiration of the majority of Thessalonians who were not connected to patrons and had to work with their

---

[119]B Winter, 1994, p 42.
[120]B Winter, 1994, pp 49-50.

own hands. Joining the artisans in their business would mean that believers leaving the patronage system would be choosing a lower social status. Willingly moving socially downward, like Jesus. And living like brothers with those who were poorer. What was happening with most in Thessalonica, was also desired by Paul when writing to the Ephesians: "He who has been stealing must steal no longer, but must work, doing something useful with his own hands, that he may have something to share with those in need" (Eph. 4:28). We can hardly imagine, in their limited economic environment, what massive respect from outsiders and open doors for the gospel such a lifestyle would produce!

> "In his day, Paul determined to see the abolition of the patronage system in the Christian community. One of the tasks of Christians was to go beyond their own needs to the needs of others. It constituted the most visible signal to the society of its day of a new community in which the function of all able-bodied members...was to do good.... They did good because good needed to be done, and did so without expectations of reciprocity or repay- ment."[121]

This is why Paul clearly challenged those few Thessalonians who hesitated to renounce patronage. It threatened the viability of the church's unity, family structure and testimony. In his first letter, he wrote, **"And we urge you, brothers, warn those who are idle"** (1 Thes 5:14a). The problem with not working, then, was not because they thought Jesus was coming soon. And they wanted to be rid of material things. Quite differently, there were some who just were finding it hard to break ties with their patrons. In his next letter, written some months later, he was much more insistent.

> **"In the name of the Lord Jesus Christ, we command you, brothers, to keep away from every brother who is idle and does not live according to the teaching you received from us. For you yourselves know how you ought to follow our example.**
>
> **We were not idle when we were with you, nor did we eat anyone's food without paying for it. On the contrary, we worked night and day, laboring and toiling so that we would not be a burden to any of you. We did this, not because we do not have the right to such help, but in order to make ourselves a model for you to follow. For even when we were with you, we gave you this rule: 'If a man will not work, he shall not eat.' We hear that some among you are idle. They are not busy; they are busybodies. Such people we command and urge in the**

---

[121]B Winter, 1984, p 60.

Lord Jesus Christ to settle down and earn the bread they eat. And as for you, brothers, never tire of doing what is right. If anyone does not obey our instruction in this letter, take special note of him. Do not associate with him, in order that he may feel ashamed. Yet do not regard him as an enemy, but warn him as a brother" (2 Thes 3:6-15).

The strength of this admonition is astonishing! Especially granted the closeness of Paul to the Thessalonians. We can only conclude that Paul, and the Spirit that led him, believed the patronage system that favored a few and despised the poor, was a potentially lethal compromise of true Christianity. It had to go. And be replaced by a radically different lifestyle. One of becoming a willing patron to all who are in need. Yes, every disciple a patron! Or as Winter states,

> "It expanded the definition of benefactor to encompass all those in the Christian community who had the capacity to meet the needs of others from self-generated resources. It required all to be the doers of good. This involved the renunciation of the client's full-time role in (public life) forcing Christians to withdraw from an unproductive existence where they were part of the paid retinue of a patron."[122]

Paul's rules for believers living in a secular society were clear:

- These were commands to be received as if from Jesus
- Paul's example of sacrificial self-support was given as a model for all in the new Christian community
- Clients were to leave unnecessary, dependent connections
- If capable of working and unwilling to work, they were not to be fed or given other favors by wealthy believers or the church's mercy ministry
- Church discipline was to occur for any refusing to renounce an unnecessary dependence on the patronage system
- Never to regard or treat an erring brother as an enemy
- Never tire of doing good (i.e., being Christian benefactors)

Those were days of unbelievable pressure. But love never fails. It wins. "The Christian social ethic can only be described as an unprecedented social revolution of the ancient benefaction tradition. All able-bodied members of

---

[122]B Winter, 1984, p 201.

the Christian community were to seek the welfare of others...."[123]

So, I return to the question. Would you say NO to the handouts fostered by patronage? Would you choose to love and help those in need, at great personal cost, like the vast majority of the amazing Thessalonians did? Sure you would—with Jesus' help.

For Reflection and Discussion

1. Now that you better understand why some of the Thessalonians were "not working," what do you think about Paul's command that they should give up the life of patronage and work with their own hands?
2. How would this "standard" or demand be received in your church?

---

[123]B Winter, 1984, p 209

Chapter 36

The amazing Thessalonian women

When Paul first spoke of Christ in Thessalonica "**not a few prominent women**" (Acts 17:4) were converted. Who were they? This "may mean that they belonged to the upper class in the town (or were) wives of the leading men."[124] Either way, they would likely have been connected with the system of patronage. Which would have meant they were proud of their social position. And not likely to give it up easily. Like us. Women needing to hear what Paul later wrote to their brothers and sisters in the capital, "**Do not be proud, but be willing to associate with people of low position**" (Rom 12:16b). Humility is the only soil out of which healthy Christianity can grow.

Wealthy male and female Christians were not discouraged by Paul from continuing to act as patrons. But, they had to go about it differently. They had to humble themselves more socially. Secular patrons would not reach too far below their own status in choosing clients. However, Christian patrons were no longer to think in terms of social class. They had become members of a classless society! "**From now on we regard no one from a worldly point of view**" (2 Cor 5:16a). What could Christian patrons require in return for their good works? In fact, they were not to demand a payback. Paul had taught them what the Master had taught everyone, "**I showed you that by this kind of hard work we must help the weak, remembering the words the Lord Jesus himself said: It is more blessed to give than to receive**" (Acts 20:35-36).

Wealthy Christian women would have found their new spiritual family structure extremely challenging in many ways. Think of their non-Christian husband's political and social aspirations. How could he let his wife associate publicly with those he and his peers viewed as "trash"? No wonder many such men would not be willing to stay married (see 1 Cor 7:10ff).

I am sure this will not come as a major revelation. But, women are generally more sensitive to scent than are men. We don't usually buy our buddy's birthday gifts from Bed, Bath and Beyond. Women of means could afford perfumes and other aesthetics unknown to poorer Christians. You, then, might find it interesting that it wasn't until 50AD, that "Romans learned

---

[124]IH Marshall, *The Acts of the Apostles* (Grand Rapids, MI: Wm B Eerdmans Pub Co 1980), p 277.

the use of soap from the Gauls."[125] Having fellowship with poorer sisters and brothers would have challenged one's preferences of smell, taste and sight. And that usually matters a lot to women. But the Thessalonian sisters died to such cultural preferences.

Each "prominent" woman who became a disciple had to decide quickly whether her new faith was worth the price she might have to pay. If she divorced her husband, she could take much of her dowry with her as she returned to her father's household. But not much else. Her husband owned the property. The power of the male head was immense in Roman law. Most women are concerned with support, security, family and the future. These were heightened concerns back then. The facts were these:

> "Roman fathers continued until the late fourth century to exercise the power of life and death in choosing whether their newborn children were to be exposed or raised. If a father decided to bring up a child, he had considerable legal control over it until his death. For instance, his consent was required for the legitimate marriage of a son or daughter, and only in the second and third centuries was his power to break up his children's marriages restricted.

> The power that would seem to have been most awkward and oppressive from day to day was the father's (her husband's) sole right to own property in his familia (family). Sons could be given an allowance..., but according to the legal rules the paterfamilias (male head of the family) had the rights of formal ownership over all this property, including any accruing to his children through labor, gifts or bequests.... The paterfamilias also had a good deal of latitude in disposing of the family property upon his death."[126]

Those prominent Christian women would have been faced with the difficult issue—will I trust Jesus for everything or not? They understood that with this new Way, there were not two ways: one for the rich and one for the poor. It was one new family in Christ. Imagine how you would respond under similar pressure.

What about those women who were not wealthy? Surely the poorer ones would be given a break from Paul's general rule of good works. Unless doing good works was absolutely vital for them, too. Unless true Christianity cannot be preserved in anyone apart from showing love to others through good deeds.

---

[125]B Grun, *The Timetables of History* (New York: Simon and Schuster 1991), p 25.
[126]P Garnsey & R Saller, *The Roman Empire* (Los Angeles: Univ of California Press 1987), pp 136-137.

Paul everywhere championed the theme of Christian unity. In our position as adopted heirs of God, "**there is neither...male nor female, for you are all one in Christ**" (Gal 3:28). We are united in all that salvation produces in the areas of both belief and behavior. And this includes everyone's doing good instead of evil. Even the poor. So, all the general commands to do good works would apply to everyone. "**Make sure that no one pays back wrong for wrong, but always try to be kind to each other and to everyone else**" (1 Thes 5:15).[127] Surely his prayer included every man and woman in Thessalonica when he prayed: "**May our Lord Jesus Christ himself and God our Father...encourage your hearts and strengthen you in every good deed and word**" (2 Th 2:16-17).

So how important to the life and health of the church were women and the good works they did? Consider Dorcas (or Tabitha), a woman, "**always doing good and helping the poor**" (Acts 9:36). She was a disciple so valuable to her church that, when she suddenly died, they sent for Peter, himself. "**And when he arrived he was taken upstairs to the room. All the widows stood around him, crying and showing him the robes and other clothing that Dorcas had made while she was still with them**" (9:39). Amazingly, Peter prayed and was then led to command her to rise. In a very tender way, "**He took her by the hand and helped her to her feet**" (9:41). "**This became known all over Joppa and many people believed in the Lord**" (9:42).

This was one good woman. She was indispensable to the fellowship because of her tender acts of love. So, God empowered Peter to raise her from the dead! And many believed. No one knows what their good works will lead to. No woman who bakes a loaf of bread as a gift, calls a friend to encourage her on the phone, visits a widow and cleans her bathroom or does something more prominent for another can estimate how precious that act is. When fueled by love. But this is sure—others will "believe in the Lord" more deeply through it. Because when His love flows constantly through our hearts it is an unmistakable proof of His supernatural presence.

In his many remarks to young Timothy, left in Ephesus to help the church through some difficulties, Paul wrote briefly of women. "**I also want women to dress modestly, with decency and propriety, not with braided hair or gold or pearls or expensive clothes, but with good deeds, appropriate for women who profess to worship God**" (1 Tim 2:9-10). It would not have been the poorer women whom he advised not to dress expensively. They could not afford to. It was the wealthy women. Like the sisters at Thessalonica. Prominent women. What's to be their dress? Their normal day-to-day attire? Good deeds. How radical! When others look at you, what do they see? What sticks out about you?

---

[127]See also Rom 2:10; 2 Cor 9:8; Eph 2:10.

In that great commercial city of Ephesus, Timothy was told,

"Command those who are rich in this present world not to be arrogant nor to put their hope in wealth.... Command them to do good, to be rich in good deeds, and to be generous and willing to share. In this way they will lay up treasure for themselves as a firm foundation for the coming age, so they may take hold of the life that is truly life" (1 Tim 5:17-19).

It is not easy for a young minister to command the rich to do anything. Much less when it involves their money. What was Paul thinking? Was he angry with Timothy? Putting him into such a difficult spot? No! The command he was to deliver concerning money was vital to the state of Christianity in Ephesus. As it is in America today. Those who have much more than they need (the truly wealthy) are commanded to be rich in doing good deeds.

Doing good will not impoverish you. It will enrich you. And it will really be a good insurance policy because it prepares for the coming age. Something that mere money cannot do. Here's a hard question. Would you welcome a young man like Timothy coming into your church and commanding such things in the name of Christ? Telling you what to do with your money?

As if we needed more proof that good works applies to all men and women, Paul removes all doubt by applying the rule of good works even to widows! He wrote,

"No widow may be put on the list of widows unless she is over sixty, has been faithful to her husband, and is well known for her good deeds, such as bringing up children, showing hospitality, washing the feet of the saints, helping those in trouble and devoting herself to all kinds of good deeds" (1 Timothy 5:9-10).

The Early Church did not indiscriminately shower money on everyone. There was just too much real need to waste anything on those who could and should be helping themselves. So they made lists. The **"list of widows"** would have been kept by Church officials. It was the women who were **"widows really in need"** (1 Tim 5:3). They are described as **"left all alone"** (5:5), or those without any extended family assistance. Roman Law and practice carefully stipulated how the elderly were to be cared for. That is why a Christian who did not take care of his family, was considered **"worse than an unbeliever"** (5:8). As actually having **"denied the faith"** (5:8). Wow! So, good works and the true nature of Christianity are vitally linked.

Even for how widows were to live.

Twice in the inspired requirements we just read (5:9-10) Paul mentions a widow as doing "good deeds." Humble, sacrificial works of love. Winter notes,

> "The concept of benefactions is central to our understanding of this passage and furthers our investigation of social ethics in the early church.... The godly widow's conduct is described in terms of benefactions. It is important for our enquiry to note that the hallmark of the Christian widow who qualified for support by the church was a life which had been given to benefactions...5:9-10....
>
> In concluding...it should be noted that the honoring of the benefactor/widow who is the 'true' Christian widow further substantiates...that benefactions were obligatory not   just for the Christians who were wealthy, but for all Christians capable of earning money or undertaking good works such as widows were meant to do. The move 'downwards' on the social scale of those who were to seek the welfare of the city as its benefactors would have given the Christian message its most distinctive social ethic and indeed its unique characteristic in (public life)."[128]

Whether prominent, poor or widowed– the women of the Early Church would have been known for good deeds. Wherever they were located and under whatever conditions they lived. Because they were filled with the same Spirit of love. The story that follows, though occurring at a later time and place in the empire, well captures the love that bound the amazing Thessalonian women together. The love that your region needs to see flowing from you to every other sister in Christ.

Perpetua, a 22-year-old daughter of a pagan nobleman, became a Christian. Her slave, Felicity, also was converted. They were arrested and imprisoned. Felicity was eight months pregnant and Perpetua had recently given birth to an infant son. Her father tried to get her to retract her faith in Jesus, even bringing her son to the trial. Nothing availed. The two women, though worlds apart in status, were sisters and friends. They encouraged one another in prison as they waited the day of execution with several men.

"On the day of the execution the prisoners were brought to the arena, where, according to Roman custom, the men were to be taken

---

[128]B Winter, *Seek the Welfare of the City* (Grand Rapids, MI: Wm B Erdmans Pub Co. 1994), pp 76-78.

first to be tortured for the entertainment of the crowd before their execution. Saturus [deacon and teacher of the women] stopped at the gate for one last word with Pudens, the prison governor, who later turned to Christ and became a martyr himself. The men then were sent into the arena with a bear, a leopard and a wild boar. Saturus was so mangled and bloody that spectators ridiculed him, shouting, 'He is well baptized!'" Perpetua and Felicitas (who had given birth to her baby in prison) were stripped and sent into the arena to face a 'mad heifer.' [When Felicitas was once knocked down, Perpetua approached her friend, helped her up and they faced the bull holding hands together]. The gory torture soon became too much for the crowd and the people began shouting, 'Enough!'

"When this preliminary exhibition was ended, the young women were brought to the executioner, at which time Perpetua called out to some grieving Christian friends: 'Give out the Word to the brothers and sisters; stand fast in the faith, love one another, and don't let our suffering become a stumbling block to you.' She was then taken to the gladiator to be beheaded."[129]

For Reflection and Discussion

1. How many women do you know whose lives would parallel the Thessalonian women? What has most struck you about them?
2. What can you do to better raise your daughters and granddaughters to be like these amazing women?

[129]R Tucker, *From Jerusalem to Irian Jaya: A Biographical History of Christian Missions* (Grand Rapids, MI: Zondervan Publishing House, 1983), pp 34-35.

Chapter 37

A wild assignment

Timothy, son of Greek and Jewish parents, was Paul's very young assistant when the apostolic missionary team first visited Thessalonica. He traveled extensively with Paul and was singled out as a unique helper (Phil 2:19-22). Paul co-sent with Timothy six of the letters included in the Scriptures. He sent him on crucial missions. To Thessalonica when Paul was forbidden to return (1 Thes 3:1-3). And, as we saw, to Ephesus. To help deal with some problems including come very difficult money-related issues.

Titus, a Gentile, was also one of Paul's "true" sons in the faith. Like Timothy, he joined Paul for many years, being mentioned more than a dozen times in his writings. Paul calls him his partner and fellow worker (2 Cor 8:23). He did not have an unlimited number of trusted helpers. So when he sent them on a mission, it was a priority placed on his soul by the Spirit of God. And he left Titus in Crete to "**straighten out what was left unfinished and (to) appoint elders in every town**" (Titus 1:5). His time spent with Paul in Macedonia prepared him well for what he was about to face.

Although this takes us away from Thessalonica, I need to tell you what he faced on Crete because Americans cannot hear too often that money matters. What we do with it often defines the health of our faith. And the impact our witness will have. Most of us struggle with money. Some of the Thessalonians did, being tempted to ride the gravy train of patronage.

The Cretans' temptation was different. But it was still with money. And with all its life killing partners: greed, covetousness, deceit and selfishness. So, whether to Thessalonica, Ephesus, Corinth or Crete, Paul was ready to dispatch his most trusted sons when the cause of Christ urgently demanded it. And financial problems were urgent problems that needed to be addressed. They are not small or secondary issues to God. Are they to you?

You have probably never been anywhere remotely like Crete. D. Edmond Hiebert writes, "The fourth largest island of the Mediterranean, Crete lies directly south of the Aegean Sea. In NT times life in Crete had sunk to a deplorable moral level. The dishonesty, gluttony and laziness of its inhabitants were proverbial."[130] Just how bad were the Cretans? Paul quotes a Cretan poet, Epimenides, as accurately describing them: "**Cretans are always liars, evil brutes, lazy gluttons**" (Titus 1:12). Ouch! And this view

---

[130]DE Hiebert, *In the NIV Study Bible* (Grand Rapids, MI: Zondervan Publishing House, 1995), p 1849.

is verified by others. The facts are:

- The Greek word, "cretanize" meant to lie or to cheat
- Few cultures had a worse reputation than Crete's. In the ancient world the three most evil C's were

Cretans   Cilicians   Cappadocians

- The Greek historian Polybius recorded, "Money is so highly valued among them, that its possession is not only thought to be necessary, but in the highest degree creditable. And in fact greed and avarice are so native to the soil in Crete, that they are the only people in the world among whom no stigma attaches to any sort of gain whatever."[131] Getting money was the issue to most Cretans. Not how they got it.
- So the judicial system's judgments against many serious crimes took the form of fines rather than imprisonment. This hit the Cretans where it hurt the most.
- Paul's description of Cretans as **"evil brutes"** (or beasts) used strong and unusual words. They are the opposite of "good" and "human." Perhaps he was alluding to the mythology about the minotaurs (half bull/ half man) that supposedly originated on Crete. His words portray men with a bestial nature. Living like dangerous monsters.
- Cretans were described not only as gluttons, but lazy gluttons, using the Greek word "non-working" as lazy. It denotes a people hating to work and loving to eat.

But God's love for the world included the Cretans. So the gospel must go to them. But in what form? By word only? Or in the combination so successfully taught by Paul and modeled in Thessalonica– **"in every good deed and word"** (2 Thes 2:17)? A model that Titus would have been amazed by in Macedonia, before he left to take Paul's letter to Corinth.[132]

Paul wrote strongly to Titus. Saying he was to **"silence"** men who are **"mere talkers and deceivers"** (Titus 1:10-11). People **"who claim to know God, but by their actions they deny them. They are detestable, disobedient and unfit for doing anything good"** (Titus 1:16). There are always people who sound good. But their lives simply do not measure up. It's not in them to do good for long. Unless they repent, their influence is cancerous.

In his introduction to the book of Titus, Hiebert notes, "Especially

---

[131]Polybius, Histories Book 6, trans. Evelyn Shuckburgh (Cambridge, Ontario: in parentheses Publishing 2002), p 378.

[132]See 2 Cor 7:5-6; 8:6, 17.

significant considering the nature of the Cretan heresy, are the repeated emphases on '**doing what is good**' (1:16; 2:7,14; 3:1,8,14)...."[133] The content of Paul's counsel to Titus reminds of what he had much earlier written to the Thessalonians in passages we have already considered. He said,

- "In everything set them an example by <u>doing what is good</u>" (Titus 2:7).

- "(Jesus Christ) who gave himself for us to redeem us from all wickedness and to purify for himself a people that are his very own, eager to <u>do what is good</u>" (Ti 2:14).

- "Remind the people to be subject to rulers and authorities, to be obedient, <u>to be ready to do whatever is good</u>" (Titus 3:1).

- "...I want you to stress these things so that those who have trusted in God may be careful to devote themselves to <u>doing what is good</u>. These things are excellent and <u>profitable</u> for everyone" (Titus 3:8).

Titus was to be a model in doing what is good. Paul used the same word (tupos - 2:7) he earlier used in describing what the Thessalonians had become (1 Thes 1:7). I would expect that Titus worked hard with his own hands, like Paul had shown him. By being the opposite of lazy. The followers of Jesus were redeemed to be eager to do good works. And Paul used the word for personal profit (3:8) when speaking of the <u>benefits</u> of doing good works. Like us, the Cretans were always interested in profit. But they needed to be shown the strange truth of God. The fact that real, personal advancement comes by giving not taking. Imagine what a radical thing this would have looked like on the island of Crete! Instead of brilliantly scamming others through deception, disciples would deliver compassion! They weren't only to be "ready" to do good works, but actually "**devoted**" to them.

Well, Titus had his work cut out for him. But he and Paul had seen how a fledgling congregation of only a few months old had lived such a life of love that it became the big news along the Via Egnatia rivaling news from Rome! And they knew that the Spirit that had energized the amazing Thessalonians could do the same in the Cretans! And dare we believe can also do likewise today among evangelical Americans!

In concluding his letter to Titus, Paul was led to once more express the pivotal point that the gospel cannot exist without good works flowing from it. But he did so in a rare way. He would throw aside his usual literary custom in forming his conclusion (3:12-15). In the midst of his normal final

---

[133]Hiebert 1995, p 1850.

remarks, with its housecleaning details, greetings and benedictory blessing, he would passionately interject one more fiery ultimatum:

"Our people must learn to devote themselves to doing what is good, in order that they may provide for daily necessities and not live unproductive lives" (Titus 3:14).

Paul just simply could not resist saying it one more time. Just as he did earlier in the letter Titus carried from Macedonia to Corinth. There he also interrupted his conclusion to the wayward Corinthians with this warning, **"If anyone does not love the Lord—a curse be on him. Come, O Lord!"** (1 Cor 16:22).

Titus knew Paul deeply loved him. Like a son. Paul wasn't just throwing him to the wolves with this wild assignment to Crete. It was too urgent and vital to be ignored. He understood that unless their lifestyle of selfishness was replaced with one of love, Crete would never truly be Christianized. Titus was to focus on "appointing elders in every town" who, with other virtues, would be **"hospitable, ones who <u>love what is good</u>"** (Ti 1:5,8). The gospel had to be both preached and personified. For without leaders modeling lives of amazing love, the new believers would too soon morph into the mediocrity of those **"having a form of godliness but denying its power"** (2 Tim 3:5). Many of us today need to re-examine our hearts and our commitment to love in light of our commitment to money. **"For the love of money is a root of all kinds of evil. Some people, eager for money, have wandered from the faith and pierced themselves with many griefs"** (1 Tim 6:10). This was true in Thessalonica and Crete. And it still is true today.

For Reflection and Discussion

1. What changes need to take place in our seminary training of future pastors to ensure that they emerge more like Timothy?

Chapter 38

Blown away by love

We have covered a lot of ground in our examination of the love of the amazing Thessalonians as it related to good works. I could call everything up to this point as "cake." Now comes the icing. If the cake has been delicious–wait 'til you try the icing! It's found in a text that utterly astounds us. Words that simply are hard to comprehend because they portray a level of love and giving that few of us have ever seen. Words that reveal a love that is supernatural not natural. The very love of Jesus returning to earth in His children. And all this in a time of famine and suffering. What would happen if that love settled upon American Christians today? In our time of far greater prosperity? How many doors and hearts would be blown away by its irresistible force?

The reign of Claudius Caesar (41-54AD) saw several serious famines occur. In fact,

> "When he came to power in January, 41 he had an immediate chance to show how seriously he valued the support of the people (of Rome). It was during a grain shortage in which it was claimed that only eight days' supply remained: the shipping season ended in October and would not begin again until March. This was countered by emergency   measures: insurance money would be paid by the Emperor himself to persons who took the risk of bringing in winter supplies and lost their vessel...."[134]

At another time, "A shortage at Rome in 51 led to a riot from which Claudius was lucky to escape into the Palace."[135] Famine struck throughout the Empire, including Judea. The church, being a family, quickly responded to their siblings' suffering. In Acts we read,

> **"During this time some prophets came down from Jerusalem to Antioch. One of them, named Agabus, stood up and through the Spirit predicted that a severe famine would spread over the entire Roman world. (This happened during the reign of Claudius.) The disciples, each according to his ability, decided to provide help for the brothers living in Judea. This they did, sending their gift to the elders by Barnabas and Saul"** (Acts 11:27-30).

---

[134]B Levick, *Claudius* (New Haven, CT: Yale Univ Press 1990), p 109.
[135]B Levick, 1990, p 109.

The famine mentioned here is estimated to have occurred around 46 AD. Before Paul's first missionary journey.[136] The gift given by the Christians in Antioch no doubt helped the believers in Judea to survive. But the poverty of Judean believers continued. And Paul was led by God to help again, in a greater way, some 10 years later towards the end of his 3rd missionary journey. It is significant to our study to see how the churches throughout Macedonia are said to have responded to this, because the Thessalonian church was one of them (with Philippi and Berea). Before leaving for Jerusalem, Paul wrote concerning this mission:

> **"Now, however, I am on my way to Jerusalem in the service of the saints there. For Macedonia and Achaia were pleased to make a contribution for the poor among the saints in Jerusalem. They were pleased to do it, and indeed they owe it to them. For if the Gentiles have shared in the Jews' spiritual blessings, they owe it to the Jews to share with them their material blessings. So after I have completed this task and have made sure that they have received this fruit, I will go to Spain and visit you on the way"** (Rom 15:25-28).

Paul did not fully explain to the Romans the lengthy and difficult process involved in this ministry of mercy. Remember, it went from largely Gentile churches to Jewish Christians. He had to share the need. Motivate towards giving to it. And collect the gifts from the various churches. He also wanted representatives from many of the churches to accompany him with the gift. It was a huge ordeal and produced a large entourage. It would have been a spectacular display of true Christian unity. But Satan was opposing it on many fronts, as NT Wright explains,

> **"When God's work is going ahead, dark forces will do their best to thwart or undermine it, as he admits at the next stage of the project (...at Romans 16:31 he asks the Roman church to pray that the collection will be 'acceptable' to the Jerusalem church, since he knows they may well be inclined to turn up their noses at money coming from non-Jewish sources). So he knows that at every stage the project is a tricky one...."[137]**

Which brings us to the icing. To one of the most amazing texts concerning Christian life in the Early Church. And to an amazing display of

---

[136]See FF Bruce, *The Book of Acts* (Grand Rapids, MI: Wm B Eerdmans Pub Co., 1954), pp 243-244 for a good discussion.

[137]NT Wright, *Paul for Everyone 2 Corinthians* (Louisville, KY: Westminster John Knox Press, 2003), p 85.

the power of the Holy Spirit enabling normal Christians to do extraordinary deeds. The Corinthians had promised to help their poor Judean brothers. But, for some reason, were slow in completing the task. Paul, to further inspire their giving, reminded them of how their northern brothers and sisters had responded to the need,

> "**And now, brothers, we want you to know about the grace that God has given the Macedonian churches. Out of the most severe trial, their overflowing joy and their extreme poverty welled up in rich generosity. For I testify that they gave as much as they were able, and even beyond their ability. Entirely on their own, they urgently pleaded with us for the privilege of sharing in this service to the saints. And they did not do as we expected, but they gave themselves first to the Lord and then to us in keeping with God's will**" (2 Cor 8:1-5).

Let's try to break this down a bit. If you ever needed the help of the Holy Spirit to understand and appreciate the Word, it is here. So pray. Maybe the Lord will bless you with "eyes to see." Before continuing, please read the last passage again slowly and prayerfully. Taking in each amazing phrase.

Paul begins with God, even though he is highlighting the hearts and deeds of humans. They can only give because of "**the grace that God has given the Macedonian churches.**" All such amazing love from Christians has its true beginning in the amazing grace of God! We should never be too quick to pass over God and praise man. Christianity is a religion of grace from beginning to end. You and I can do no good apart from Christ.

Next, Paul uses a strange equation. It looks like this:

most severe trial + overflowing joy + extreme poverty = rich generosity

This is not reality as most of us know it. But it is reality. It is what we have seen in Thessalonica. And now it has spread throughout the whole province. Trials normally make us more conservative. Spending less. Severe trials usually cause people to stop giving altogether. During them, they are thinking of survival. Not so with these Macedonians. The greatest trials (those which involve death, family break-up, etc.) normally would not produce overflowing joy. Joy that could not be contained. Irrepressible delight. But it did in Macedonia. Add to this pot the ingredient of poverty. No. Extreme poverty. The kind which we associate with unlivable conditions. Little to no rain for crops. Few jobs. Totally inadequate income. Yet the joy remains. Does this sound impossible to you yet? There's more to come.

The new math of Jesus adds up these elements and tells us the sum. My math would state the sum as: "what next, Lord?" Or as, "give me a gun

169

so I can shoot myself." But the math of the new creation yields this sum: <u>rich</u> <u>generosity</u>! We are beyond logic here. We have entered another realm of reality. The realm of God's love. In that place anything is possible. I am sure that you, as a believer, have had moments there. But they have probably been too few and far between. Like mine.

Paul testified solemnly that the Thessalonians and their provincial neighbors gave more than they were able to give. Somehow. By faith. By love. Looking at another bottom line than what accountants focus on. Have you ever found yourself doing more than what you could imagine yourself doing? I am sure that you have. When you were walking in the Spirit. It is one thing for an athlete to nonchalantly say, "I give 110% all the time." It is quite another thing to see the memorable few times when some pro actually does that. But they are doing it in their wealth. During a game. Not the Thessalonians and their Christian neighbors. They gave 110% just because they literally loved to give 'til it hurt.

We must pause at another place. Where Paul wrote, **"they urgently pleaded with us for the privilege of sharing."** Paul was reluctant to let them give as much as they wanted to. In fact, the urgent pleading was more like begging, as the NASB translates, **"begging us with much entreaty for the favor of participation in the support of the saints."** Most people beg for themselves. Or for a child perishing in a house fire. But to beg for the opportunity to give out of poverty and while in deep persecution? That is the work of God, not man. That is unforgettably powerful. And it was by that spirit of amazing love that the Thessalonians had reached their region and become such a renowned church.

The Thessalonians and others did not need to be coaxed. They did it **"entirely on their own."** All they needed was need. That's it. They heard of need and moved into action. Beyond all of Paul's expectations. How could they? Paul then explained, to help the Corinthians and us understand their incredible response.

"They gave themselves first to the Lord." But weren't they already saved? Sure. This was something different. It must have been a kind of perpetual rededication. With every trial came a new recommitment. A renewal. That's what it sounds like to me. I know what it is to be renewed by the Spirit many times a day. By reconnecting with Jesus. But to beg for the opportunity to make this kind of financial commitment to others. That is a depth and height to which I can only pray that God will take me. And you. After committing themselves to the Lord, they had the grace He alone can give to commit themselves to Paul. And to his mission of mercy. This "meant that under an impulse that came from God himself, they gave money with almost reckless generosity."[138]

This amazing example encouraged and emboldened Paul, no doubt, to

---

[138]NT Wright, 2003, p 86.

push the Corinthians.

"We might have thought that he was pushing his luck, trying to carry on with this project after all that has passed between him and Corinth; but he will not be deterred. He is desperately concerned for the unity of the whole Christian family, and he has glimpsed, as part of his missionary vocation, the possibility of doing something so striking, so remarkable, so practical that it will establish a benchmark for generations to come, a sign that Jewish Christians and Gentile Christians really do belong together."[139]

I hope that the love of the amazing Thessalonians, that had spread throughout all of Macedonia, will affect you. And that you will now do three things:

- **Pray** for grace truly to desire to enter more fully into the new creation of Christ. Where love is the language and joy is the spirit. A joy to love. A joy to give.
- **Pray** for grace to give up the old way. The way of self first. The love of money and what it can buy for you. And ponder what His love could produce through you. What open doors and open hearts and praise of Jesus could break forth. Let your renewed heart desire it. Long for it.
- **Pray** that God will fill you with the desire to "**do the good works which he has prepared in advance for you to do**" (Eph 2:10). The opportunities are coming. Are you willing? Are you ready?

Will you be empowered to live like the amazing Thessalonians and their Macedonian colleagues? Will you dare to pray for it?

For Reflection and Discussion

1. If the Thessalonians are the model church and they, themselves model disciples, how do you and your church stack up in comparison?
2. What patterns does the Spirit convict you of that needs to be changed?
3. Are you willing for Him to change them? How will that happen?

---

[139]NT Wright, 2003, p 85.

Chapter 39

Suffering Love

How can I portray pain as productive? That's the challenge facing me in this chapter. And beyond that–I want us to study suffering in such a way that we will come to welcome it as one of the great signs of God's love to us! Because that is what He said suffering is when we are involved. Please pray that we will see this as a biblical reality because without suffering we cannot become what the amazing Thessalonians became. They were disciples of Jesus. And Jesus promised that His disciples would suffer. **"If anyone would come after me, he must deny himself and <u>take up his cross daily</u>, and follow me'** (Luke 9:23).

The writer of Hebrews stated the obvious when he wrote, **"No discipline seems pleasant at the time, but painful"** (Heb 12:11a). Suffering hurts, whatever form it takes. And our natural tendency is to avoid that which hurts us. But the writer then adds what is far less obvious, **"Later on, however, it produces a harvest of righteousness and peace for those who have been trained by it"** (Heb 12:11b). Suffering has a purpose. It is part of the plan of a good and loving Father. Therefore, suffering is necessary or it would not happen. God is not malevolent, inflicting pain unnecessarily. No, the problem that requires pain is our problem. Our hearts must be so fearful of being exposed that nothing but suffering can really open them up. We must believe that either our own or another's heart will always be touched through our suffering. Do we? The Thessalonians surely believed that. They had to, because suffering was a promised part of their embracing the Way of Jesus from the outset. Note how often Paul brought up the painful subject to them and some conclusions that flow from his teaching:

"You became imitators of us and of the Lord; in spite of <u>severe suffering</u>, you welcomed the message with the joy given by the Holy Spirit. And so you became a   model to all the believers in Macedonia and Achaia" (1 Thes 1:6).

- Jesus walked with the Father, yet suffered
- Paul lived for Jesus and others, yet suffered

· Since all Christians must suffer, the Thessalonians became the model of how to do it - with joy empowered by the Spirit. Are they your model in suffering?

"You suffered from your own countrymen" (1 Thes 2:14).

> · Hatred of the name and cause of Jesus is greater than the natural ties of flesh and blood

"So that no one would be unsettled by these trials. You know quite well that we were destined for them. In fact, when we were with you, we kept telling you that we would be persecuted. And it turned out that way, as you well know" (1 Thes 3:3-4).

> · Suffering can be unsettling when considered apart from God's wise and loving plan
> · Christian teachers should not deceive their hearers by holding back from teaching them the certainty of suffering in the Christian's life
> · Love strengthens us in times of suffering. As one noted long ago,

"What gives me some ease and sweetens the feelings I have for your griefs is that they are proofs of God's love toward you. See them in that view and you will bear them more easily....Ask of God, not deliverance from your pains, but strength to bear resolutely, for the love of Him, all that He should please, and as long as He shall please.

> Such prayers, indeed, are a little hard for our nature, but most acceptable to God, and sweet to those who love Him. Love sweetens pains; and when one loves God, one suffers for His sake with joy and courage.... Comfort yourself with Him, who is the only Physician of all our maladies. He is the Father of the afflicted, always ready to help us. He loves us infinitely more than we imagine. Love Him, then, and seek no consolation elsewhere."[140]

"For God did not appoint us to suffer wrath but to receive salvation through our Lord Jesus Christ" (1 Thes 5:9).

---

[140]Brother Lawrence, *The Practice of the Presence of God* Grand Rapids, MI: Spire   Books, 1967), pp 56-57.

· There is suffering as sons being disciplined by our Father. And there is suffering as a legal consequence of our sins by our Judge. All believers are appointed to the former;[141] no believer, to the latter.[142] Jesus has died in our place and taken our hit. Again listen to Brother Lawrence, who in the last week of his life wrote,

"God knows best what is needful for us; and all that He does is for our good. If we knew how much He loved us, we should always be ready to receive equally and with indifference from His hand the sweet and the bitter. All would please that came from Him. The sorest afflictions never appear intolerable, except when we see them in the   wrong light. When we see them as dispensed by the hand of God, when we know that it is our loving Father who abases and distresses us, our sufferings will lose their bitterness and become even matter of consolation."[143]

· The difference between the believer's suffering and that of the unbeliever can well be seen in the way that Paul spoke of death to the Thessalonians. In 1 Thes 4:13-15, a disciple's death is called a "**sleep**" three times. Like closing one's eyes and entering into rest. But not so the description of the death of Jesus, our Substitute, in that same passage. His was not a sleep. It was a dying in all its horror. A full death. He became sin for us. He was abandoned by God for us. **"We believe that Jesus died and rose again so we believe that God will bring with Jesus those who have fallen asleep in him"** (1 Thes 4:14). He died so that we could, as it were, sleep rather than die. With sleep there is a future. An awakening.

"Therefore among God's churches we boast about your perseverance and faith in all the persecutions and trials you are enduring" (2 Thes 1:4).

· Suffering is so difficult, that when one does it well, he becomes a source of real thanks. Even boasting. Suffering tests the quality of one's character.

---

[141]See Acts 14:22; Phil 1:29; 2 Tim 3:12.
[142]See 1 Thes 1:10; Jn 3:36; Rom 5:9.
[143]Brother Lawrence, 1967, p. 59.

174

· It is especially our faith that is assaulted by sufferings. At first glance, it is hard to believe that a loving Father would put us through such pain. We simply do not realize how much good it will produce. Suffering reveals hearts and turns us to Jesus. His half-brother, James, chose to start his letter dealing with the problem of Christian suffering. **"Consider it pure joy, my brothers, whenever you face trials of many kinds, because you know that the testing of your faith develops perseverance. Perseverance must finish its work so that you may be mature and complete, not lacking anything"** (James 1:2-4). There's another amazing equation:

Suffering (faith testing) + perseverance = maturity (lacking nothing vital)

I guess we would **"consider it pure joy"** if we really believed God was wisely advancing us through all we suffer. May your faith rest in that reality.

"All this is evidence that God's judgment is right, and as a result you will be counted worthy of the kingdom of God, for which you are <u>suffering</u>. God is just: He will pay back trouble to those who <u>trouble you</u> and give relief to you who are <u>troubled,</u> and to us as well. This will happen when the Lord Jesus is revealed from heaven in blazing fire with his powerful angels. He will punish those who did not know God and do not obey the gospel of our Lord Jesus. They will be punished with everlasting destruction and shut out from the presence of the Lord and from the majesty of his power on the day he comes to be glorified in his holy people and to be marveled at among all those who have believed. This includes you, because you believed our testimony to you" (2 Thes 1:5-10).

· God reigns. He has a kingdom. All those who love Him and His people, will find themselves opposed, sometimes viciously, by those who hating Jesus' kingdom.

· Unimaginable judgment is ahead for those who persist in their opposition of God and His people. And, likewise, inexpressible joy for those who believe and keep holding on to Jesus. This hope was a staggering sight to behold then, just as it is today. Donfried notes,

"The Stoics understand affliction as part of accepting fate; for Paul, suffering is part of the cosmic struggle which is leading to God's triumphant victory.... For Paul, God is the one who through Christ has inaugurated the imminent redemption of the created order"[144]

· Few things convict the unbeliever more of his sin and coming judgment than the believer who suffers with love and patience (see Phil 1:27-28).

So, why are disciples "**destined for trials?**" (3:3). It is not merely because our sealed hearts are forced open by the pressure of suffering. Giving Jesus access into parts of us that earlier we had been unwilling to open up to Him. It is also because others' hearts are touched when we suffer well. The evangelistic impact of suffering is incalculable. Paul knew this and, so, was willing to be badly beaten when he did not have to be. Suffering takes us to places we would never choose to go ourselves. It opens doors to needy people we would never have otherwise met. Peter powerfully alluded to this when he wrote,

> "**Live such good lives among the pagans that, though they accuse you of doing wrong, they may see your good deeds and glorify God on the day he visits us....For it is commendable if a man bears up under the <u>pain of unjust suffering</u> because he is conscious of God....To this you were called, because Christ suffered for you, leaving you <u>an example that you should follow in his steps</u>....But even if you should <u>suffer   for   what   is right,</u> you are blessed. Do not fear what they fear; do not be frightened. But in your hearts set apart Christ as Lord. Always be prepared to give an answer to everyone who asks you to give the reason for the hope that you have. But do this with gentleness and respect, keeping a clear conscience, so that those who speak maliciously against your good behavior in Christ may be ashamed of their slander. It is better, if it is God's will, <u>to suffer</u> for doing good than for doing evil.... So then,   those who <u>suffer</u> according to God's will should commit themselves to their faithful Creator and continue to do good**" (1 Pet 2:12, 19-21;3:14-16; 4:19).

We have marveled at the mature love of the Thessalonians, though they were new converts to Christ. Perhaps this is a main reason WHY their

---

[144]K Donfried, *Paul, Thessalonica and Early Christianity* (Grand Rapids, MI: Wm B   Eerdmnans Pub Co., 2002) pp 124-125.

love was so amazing. Through suffering it was challenged early and often. Unlike many of us, they had no time to grow fat and comfortable. They had to believe in the risen Jesus or absolutely give up. There was no room for compromise. Their faith was immediately put to a severe and enduring test. And do we dare question the love or wisdom of God in permitting this to happen? Paul's epistle would have never been written as it was and they would not likely have become the model for us all, had they not suffered so. In them we see the promise of Jesus fulfilled, "**every branch that does bear fruit he prunes so that it will be even more fruitful**" (John 15:2b). Do we really believe that suffering is far better than comfort and painlessness in this life?

Could it be that when we ask to be drawn closer to Christ and made more fruitful, we are unknowingly asking for something that can only come through a good strong dose of suffering? Do we have enough faith in His love and power, to trust Him and pray, "If suffering alone can open my heart and the hearts of others to you, dear Lord, bring it to me for Your glory and our good." When that prayer forms on your lips, you are closer to looking like the amazing Thessalonians than you think!

For Reflection and Discussion

1. Why are Christians today so averse to suffering?
2. I would strongly suggest that you get a copy of my recent book, Disciples Obey and read the closing chapter on the suffering of the first apostles and the model that they were in establishing what it looked like "to follow Jesus" in the 1st century.

Chapter 40

Dying Love

It might not be all that helpful simply to say that Christians in the Early Church were willing to die for their faith. The fact was, in their minds, they had already died as a result of their faith. Before persecution ever struck them. They had died with Christ. Not in word only, like so many today. But in reality. That is why severe persecution could not stop them. You can't kill a dead man. You can't offend someone who has no capability of offense. He does not feel resentment and anger as he once did. He does not feel for himself first, selfishly. He has become dead to that. He has been quickened and risen with Christ. Paul taught this to all believers as part of their faith and confession.[145]

Of course, some struggled more than others with this biblical truth that faith can win over feelings. That disciples are called to **"live by faith, not by sight"** (2 Cor 5:7). The Thessalonians were graced to grasp their death to sin. And their life in Christ. Not perfectly of course. But well enough to be promoted as **"imitators of ... the Lord in spite of severe suffering"** (1 Thes 1:6).

The Thessalonians actually lived a new life. In Christ they had been ushered into a new reality. A new Kingdom. This had no parallel among the religions, guilds and clubs that Romans voluntarily joined. As one scholar notes,

> "...The Christian groups were exclusive and totalistic in a way that no club nor even pagan cultic association was.... To be 'baptized into Christ Jesus' nevertheless signaled for Pauline converts an extraordinarily thoroughgoing re-socialization, in which the sect was intended to become virtually the primary group for its members, supplanting all other loyalties."[146]

Christianity was a new order of Jesus-love that existed alongside the old order

---

[145]See Rom 6:4; 12:1; 1 Cor 15:31; 2 Cor 5:14; Gal 2:20; Eph 2:5; Phil 2:5,8; Col. 2:20,3:3; 2 Tim 2:11.

[146]W Meeks, *The First Urban Christians* (New Haven, CT: Yale Univ Press 2003), p 78.

of self-love. The kingdom of life and light vs. the kingdom of death and darkness. Paul warned them that the old order would not be easily replaced. It had been defeated already in Christ. The change had started. The old has gone, the new has come![147] What finite power can defeat the power of the infinite God? None, of course! This they ardently believed.

Though optimistic, the Thessalonians were realists. They saw the stripes on Paul's back. They knew the emperor's threats were not inconsequential. Sure, there would be suffering and losses in the battle. Some would die physically. But that only brought them more quickly to their goal. Their leader boldly taught that to die was a gain not a loss (Phil 1:21). So death was no obstacle to those who had already died in Christ. He was stung for them and death's stinger had been removed from threatening them (1 Cor 15:54-55). Jesus had killed death. What could its threat do any longer to them? It was like a fangless cobra. It looked intimidating but was really harmless. The Thessalonians had chosen to live in Jesus by faith. And they could hardly wait to see Him. Paul's letters to the Thessalonians were full of this message of hope. A hope in Christ that drained all the dread from death. What those words did for the Thessalonians, they should do for us, too. For we are one in Christ with them.

Just how did their hope impact their view of death? Let's reflect on the verses where Paul speaks of the return of Jesus in his first letter. Every chapter of 1 Thessalonians in our Bibles ends with at least a mention of that event. We have seen just how different Christ's coming will be as compared to those royal visits of the Roman emperors. Many a city was impoverished when trying to impress and entertain royalty as it passed through. Wanting to make an impression that would bring some significant royal patronage to the city down the road. Many of the Thessalonians were then impoverished. Few would have wanted a visit from Claudius. None could afford it. But all the Christians wanted the coming of the Christ! He would on that day exchange their poverty for his wealth! No Caesar would or could do that.

It would be a coming of such great glory that nothing in between that future Day and their present circumstances mattered all that much to them. His Second Coming was the event to prepare for. To live in the light of. It would change everything! No suffering endured would matter any longer. Not even death. Loved ones lost. Families split up. All social embarrassment and public humiliation paled in the light of the glorious life that was to be given to all His followers. Unless the glory of His appearing grips your soul as it did the Thessalonians, you will never become like them

---

[147]See Jn 12:31; 2 Cor 5:7; Eph 1:20-21; Col 1:13; 1 Jn 5:4.

in this world. Suffering will always cause you to go weak in the knees. Until you join them in actually living with the certainty of Christ's coming ever in your mind.

It is unfortunate that evangelical disagreement over the details of Christ's Second Coming have caused the blessed hope to become little more than a point of debate among Christians. This has also been a reason why Paul's letters to the Thessalonians have been often overlooked and underappreciated. There's just too much Eschatology in them. Don't read the following verses looking for details that prove your position. Read them marveling at how they transformed the Thessalonians from superstitious pagans to spiritual Philadelphians! Messengers of love, willing to face death and die rather than abandon their faith. Paul wrote to the Thessalonians:

> **"They tell how you turned to God from idols to serve the living and true God, and to wait for his Son from heaven, whom he raised from the dead—Jesus, who rescues us from the coming wrath"** (1 Thes 1:9b-10).

Christian conversion includes turning away from our enslavements. And then turning, in a willing enslavement, to the true God. That is what "to serve" means. One way we serve the Father is by <u>waiting for</u> his Son, Jesus, in a very specific way, as this is the only time that Greek word is used in the NT. Hendriksen noted,

> "The force of this verb *to await* must not be lost sight of. It means *to look forward to with patience and confidence*. This *awaiting* means far more than merely *saying*, 'I believe in Jesus Christ, who ascended into heaven and from thence he shall come to judge the living and the dead.' It implies *being ready* for his return. When you *await* a visitor, you have prepared everything for his coming...and all this in such a manner that the visitor will feel perfectly at home. So, also, awaiting the very *Son of God* who is coming out of heaven implies the sanctified heart and life."[148]

There is a time of colossal wrath coming. And it sounds like those who will be saved from it are those who are waiting with great expectation for Jesus. Are you waiting for Him or are you completely focused on and totally engrossed in the here and now? Are you like so many who are waiting for "your ship to come in" or for "retirement?" Are you waiting for "things"

---

[148]W Hendriksen, *1 & 2 Thessalonians* (Grand Rapids, MI: Baker Book House, 1955), p. 57.

or for the Son of God who is coming? Don't be caught looking for things when the main Man in the universe is about to appear. To be unready is fatal, as it betrays an idolatrous heart.[149]

> **"For what is our hope, our joy, or the crown in which we will glory in the presence of our Lord Jesus when he comes? Is it not you? Indeed, you are our glory and joy"** (2:19-20).

How special Paul made the Thessalonians feel! Even when the Lord Jesus returns, Paul will not forget them, being so personally absorbed into the moment of seeing Jesus that they become a dim memory. Jesus would not want that! His love is to be shared. It is to be simultaneously given to God and to our neighbor. This is a special verse in the whole NT. "This is the first occurrence of *parousia* in Christian literature. It means basically 'presence' but it came to be used as a technical expression for a royal visit. In the NT it became the accepted term for the second coming of the Lord...."[150] Do we conceive of Christ's return in terms of a great gathering of all believers who have been significant in our lives? Like Paul did the Thessalonians? Or more as a personal pleasure? Of individual deliverance and glory? I think most of us American Evangelicals probably impoverish ourselves by taking the individual rather than corporate view.

> **"May he strengthen your hearts so that you will be blameless and holy in the presence of our God and Father when our Lord Jesus comes with all his holy ones"** (3:13).

The heart is what matters. Not outward show. Or even Christian service. How strong is your heart? What makes it faint with fear? What discourages it? You must share that with someone. Let others know your weakness. You will be surprised to find that we all need our hearts to be encouraged or strengthened. And nothing accomplishes that as much as simple faith in the gospel!

> **"Brothers, we do not want you to be ignorant about those who fall asleep, or to grieve like the rest of men, who have no hope. We believe that Jesus died and rose again and so we believe that God will bring with Jesus those who have fallen asleep in him. According to the Lord's own word, we tell you that we who are**

---

[149]See Matt 21:33-41; 22:1-14; 24:36-51; 25:1-13, 14-30, 31-46.
[150]L Morris, *1 & 2 Thessalonians* (Downers Grove, IL: InterVarsity Press, 1954), p 68.

still alive, who are left till the coming of the Lord, will certainly not precede those who have fallen asleep. For the Lord himself will come down from heaven, with a loud command, with the voice of the archangel and with the trumpet call of God, and the dead in Christ will rise first. After that, we who are still alive and are left will be caught up together with them in the clouds to meet the Lord in the air. And so we will be with the Lord forever. Therefore encourage each other with these words. Now, brothers, about times and dates we do not need to write to you, for you know very well that the day of the Lord will come like a thief in the night. (1 Thes. 4:13-5:2).

Persecution had likely taken its ultimate toll in Thessalonica. Some had already died for their faith. The cause of concern among the Thessalonians was simply this: Will those who died miss out on the glory of Christ's Coming? They had all so anticipated the event, that the thought of loved ones not being present for it brought deep grief to their souls. Paul did more than soften the suffering of their souls. He turned their grief to joy by the facts which the Spirit gave to him concerning the Day of the Lord. Not only would the dead in Christ be there. They would rise first! They would be the first to resurrect and greet the King in the clouds. Then we, with them, would accompany Him back for His glorious reign. Whether millennial or not, I will let you keep arguing about that. There are good arguments on each side. Don't let the debate rob you of the hope. That Day is worth all the temporal suffering that Satan is allowed by Jesus to throw our way!

"May God himself, the God of peace, sanctify you through and through. May your whole spirit, soul and body be kept blameless at the coming of our Lord Jesus Christ. The one who calls you is faithful and he will do it" (1 Thes 5:23).

Three times in one verse Paul noted God's part in the perseverance of the Thessalonians. Otherwise it would have been impossible. That's true everywhere. We need God to give us inward peace. We need His help "through and through," which is another Greek word used only here in the NT. It means everywhere and in every way. We need to be set apart to God all the time. And we just don't have the nerve and focus for that. Good thing that the One who initiated our salvation by a sovereign summons (call) will also see it through to the end. The task is too great for us.

182

Death is a very human experience. It can absolutely seize our minds and control our lives if we let it. We all long for the day when there will be no more pain, suffering and death. Which brings to mind a comment we can all sympathize with,

> "Have you ever wondered what that 'loud command' of 4:16 will be? It will be the first audible message most have heard from God. It will be the word which closes one age and opens a new one. I could very well be wrong, but I think the command which puts an end to the sorrows of earth and initiates the joys of heaven for the people of God will be two words: 'No more.' Perhaps the King of kings will raise his pierced hand and proclaim, 'No more.' No more loneliness. No more tears. No more death. No more sadness. No more crying. No more pain. Jesus promised that 'the end will come' (Matt 24:14). For those who live for this world, that's bad news. But for those who live for the world to come, it's an encouraging promise."[151]

Yes, and a promise well worth dying for. Since Jesus took death's terrors away, we no longer hate it, but rather love it. Death has been transformed from a scary shaft leading who knows where, to a golden door that leads into life. Jesus has taken all the darkness away. Death becomes to us just another moment during which we walk with Jesus. A moment of love. A moment of security in which we are assured of His love and presence. The amazing Thessalonians were filled with a love that was not afraid to die at any moment. Are you?

For Reflection and Discussion

1. Are you afraid to die?
2. Are you ready to die? Why or why not?
3. What do you think would happen if severe persecution met every young person going to college and every worker at work in the USA?

---

[151]M Lucado, *1 & 2 Thessalonians* (Nashville, TN: Thomas Nelson, 2007), p 59.

Chapter 41

Praying Love

As we conclude looking at the Thessalonians, we must not omit their practice of prayer. Prayer was their constant companion. As it had been that of their mentor. Paul was a praying man. And not just occasionally. He obviously viewed prayer as a big part of his ministry for others. He begins his letter, **"We always thank God for all of you, mentioning you in our prayers"** (1 Thes 1:2). In his two letters to the Thessalonians, he mentions prayer no fewer than eight times. Three times it refers to his prayers for the Thessalonians.[152] Three times he requests prayer from them for him and his team.[153] And he gives one extraordinary command concerning prayer, **"Pray continually!"** (1 Thes 5:17).

Paul and his missionary team practiced what he preached. **"Night and day we pray"** (1 Th 3:10). **"...We constantly pray for you"** (2 Th 1:11). You could not have been a true follower of Paul without being committed to prayer. Before going further with this point, let me ask a few questions. I will offer some answers later.

- Why is prayer such a problem for most Western Christians?
- Why do pastors rank prayer as their #1 difficulty?
- What does it mean to "pray continually?"
- Is anybody really praying for you?
- Are you really praying for anyone?
- What happens when we do not pray amply?

When Paul wrote his letters, he included prayers in them. He wanted his readers to know what he was praying for. And why. Before we look at how he prayed for the Thessalonians and consider how he might pray for us, let's simply note how he prayed for another great church. The church at Ephesus.

As our focus is on love, pay close attention to what Paul prays about love for the Ephesians. He wrote, **"I pray that you being rooted and established in love, may have power, together with all the saints, to grasp how wide and long and high and deep is the love of Christ, and**

---

[152]See 1 Thes 1:2; 3:10; 2 Thes 1:11-12.
[153]See 1 Thes 5:25; 2 Thes 3:1-2.

to know this love that surpasses knowledge—that you may be filled to the measure of all the fullness of God" (Eph 3:17b-19). What Paul prayed for them, he prayed for all believers everywhere. He was concerned for their love. He wanted the love of the Ephesians to be overtaken or replaced by the love of Christ. Because it is the truest and best love. The widest, longest, highest and deepest love. Imagine it! Jesus' love can be known by us. It can be experienced by us. It can fill us. And, if it does, we will be as filled up with all the fullness of God as we finite and fallible disciples can possibly be. But only if we seek this by prayer.

I hope you will seek for yourself (and all others) what Paul sought for the believers of his day. Pray to be filled with the love of Jesus! And emptied of your own love. Do you realize that to have the love of Jesus working through you is greater than to have knowledge about Jesus in you? Look at Paul's prayer for the Ephesians again. That is what he says. Love trumps knowledge. Knowledge about Jesus can puff us up with pride. But the love of Jesus will bend us down in service to all others. Only when that door of Jesus-love opens up to you, can you walk into the room of the fullness of God. The door of knowledge, alone, cannot upon up to you His fullness. You must move beyond knowing to loving. Make this your prayer. Learn to speak the language of love and you will communicate well with everyone. As NT Wright notes,

> "...The resurrection is not, as it were, a highly peculiar event within the *present* world (though it is as that well); it is, principally, the defining event of the *new* creation, the world that is being born with Jesus. If we are even to glimpse this new world, let alone enter it, we will need a different kind of knowing, ...an epistemology that draws out from us not just the cool appraisal of detached ... research but also that whole-person engagement and involvement for which the best shorthand is 'love'... (agape).

> "Love is the deepest mode... of knowing because it is love that ... affirms and celebrates that other-than-self reality. This is the point at which much modern epistemology breaks down. The sterile antithesis of 'objective' and 'subjective'...is overcome by the epistemology of love, which is called into being as the necessary mode of knowing of those who will live in the new public world, the world launched at Easter, the world in which Jesus is Lord and Caesar isn't."[154]

Bonhoeffer helpfully adds,

---

[154]NT Wright, *Surprised by Hope* (NY: HarperCollins 2008), pp 73-74.

"...Spiritual love does not desire but rather serves, it loves an enemy as a brother. It originates neither in the brother nor in the enemy but in Christ and his Word. Human love can never understand spiritual love, for spiritual love is from above; it is something completely strange, new, and incomprehensible to all earthly love."[155]

Paul's prayer for the Ephesians is interesting in the light of what Jesus later said of their love (Revelation 2:4-5). Maybe the Ephesians never saw God's love overtake their knowledge. As Paul had prayed. Perhaps, like many of us, their lives turned more cool and calculating than passionate and practical. Whatever happened, it impacted their love. Which affected everything.

When Paul prayed for the Thessalonians, his prayer about love was offered more as a benediction than as a prayer. He did not place the love of Christ as a goal for them yet to reach. But as something they already knew and of which they need only be constantly replenished. **"May the Lord make your love increase and overflow for each other and for everyone else, just as ours does for you"** (1 Thes 3:12).

Now to that verse that has challenged Christians down through the ages. **"Pray continually"** (1 Thes 5:17). I see this as a call to live in a ceaseless, conscious communion with God. As often as possible. To walk with God. Like Enoch and Noah.[156] How is this possible apart from loving God? We can discipline ourselves to do almost anything. But walking with God is not chiefly a matter of self-discipline. It is a matter of love. It is love that drives the heart to constant communion. Love for Jesus lets go of everything and everyone else. Because we simply do not love them as much as we love Him. Love wins the battle for our minds and wills that self-discipline can never win.

Having made prayer a life-long study, the most helpful book I have found, apart from Scripture, is Brother Lawrence's (1605-1691), "The Practice of the Presence of God." I keep a copy of it close by and often refer to it. It greatly helps remind me of the sweetness of ceaseless prayer. Listen to a few of his words,

> "He had no other care at first but faithfully to reject every other thought, that he might perform all his actions for the love of God....That the most excellent method he had found of going to God was that of doing our common business without any view of pleasing men, and (as far as we are capable) purely for the love of God....

---

[155]D Bonhoeffer, *Life Together* (NY: Harper & Row Publishers, 1954), p 35.
[156]See Gen 5:24; 6:9; Heb 11:5-6.

"That his prayer was nothing else but a sense of the presence of God, his soul being at that time insensible to everything but divine love.... That we ought not to tire of doing little things for the love of God, who regards not the greatness of the work, but the love with which it is performed....

"That when he began his business (in the kitchen where he worked), he said to God, with a son-like trust in him: 'O my God, since thou art with me, and I must now apply my mind to these outward things, I beseech Thee to grant me the grace to continue in Thy presence; and to this end do Thou prosper me with Thy assistance, receive all my works, and possess all my affections.'

"As he proceeded in his work he continued his familiar conversation with his Maker, imploring His grace, and offering to Him all his actions. When he had finished, he examined himself how he had discharged his duty; if he found well, he returned thanks to God; if otherwise, he asked pardon and, without being discouraged, he set his mind right again, and continued his exercise of the presence of God as if he had never deviated from it. 'Thus by rising after my falls,' he said, 'and by frequently renewed acts of faith and love, I am come to a state wherein it would be as difficult for me not to think of God as it was at first to accustom myself to it.'"[157]

Many books on prayer today are not usually that clear. You will all do well to buy one of his books, preferably a copy with his conversations, letters and spiritual maxims included. It will help you better understand the fusion of love and prayer. And to learn to **"pray continually"** like the amazing Thessalonians did.

I will now offer some brief answers to the questions posed at the beginning of this chapter. They are not meant as the final word. Or as a full answer, of course. I'm just offering some help as a struggling disciple to other Christ followers.

· Why is prayer such a problem for most Western Christians?

Since our love for God (and others) is so underdeveloped, we do not think about Him (or them). We lack the love needed to fuel and focus our prayers. We can't sustain prayer without love. So, we don't pray because we can't pray. We do not have the fuel (love) we need to take the whole trip.

---

[157]Brother Lawrence, *The Practice of the Presence of God* (Grand Rapids, MI: Fleming H Revell - a division of Baker 1967) pp 22-30.

- **Why do pastors rank prayer as their #1 difficulty?** *Because we do not know God in a way that has deeply humbled us. Prayer is the posture of humility. Also, most of us were poorly mentored and trained in prayer. And we are so busy with so many other duties. Prayer just does not seem to produce what we think we need quickly enough. We love getting the job done. Checking off the list is more fulfilling to many of us than praising and thanking God. And interceding for others. We have sadly switched the apostolic order of ministry, putting prayer last, rather than first:* **"And we will give our attention to prayer and the ministry of the word"** *(Acts 6:4)*

- **What does it mean to "pray continually?"** *To practice the presence of God everywhere and in everything, filled with faith, love and joy.*

- **Is anybody really praying for you?** *Maybe not like Paul: day and night. Constantly. Every time they think of you. Because they do not see prayer as the wisest, kindest and most helpful thing to do for others.*

- **Are you really praying for anyone?** *Not unless you love them. If you do, you know exactly what Brother Lawrence is talking about—at least for a few minutes a day.*

- **What happens when we do not pray amply?** *Just look around you. That is probably what happens!*

I am sometimes asked, "Ed, how often do you pray?" It's usually an innocent question by a younger pastor or Christian. Here's my answer, "I pray whenever I think about God." They want a number of hours or a time-of-day answer. But, that no longer works for me. And I bet it doesn't with you, either. You pray when you really think about God, too. Some days I think about him a lot. Nearly constantly. But most days I have sad gaps. But, thanks to Jesus' death, those gaps have been all paid for. And thanks to His life, He offers me a righteousness without gaps! So, I do not beat myself up. When I regain my senses, I resume walking with God. I just confess my sin, thank him for Jesus and let His love fill me and flow from me again.

The Thessalonians learned from Paul that love looks like prayer. Constant prayer for people in real need. Weeping prayers for heartbroken people. Rejoicing prayers for delighted people. Simple and powerful prayers for everyone. Not preachy prayers. Just pouring-your-soul-out-to-God prayers. A heart that constantly says to others, "Let's pray now. Let's pray about that. Would you mind if we just asked God to help us with that right now?" NOT, like so many of us, saying, "I will pray for that later." You know what happens with most of those promises. Join with me and ask the Spirit to help your prayer life. And He will. **"The Spirit helps us in our weakness"** (Rom 8:26a). Love is His fruit and He'll fill you up with it–if you want it. Like the amazing Thessalonians wanted it and were filled.

For Reflection and Discussion

1. Have you ever studied prayer and begin to pray more regularly? What happened when you tried?
2. If you have succeeded in being devoted to prayer, share what you think most helped you to persevere in its practice.

Part 4 – Love Working Today

Chapter 42

What does unworthy Christianity look like?

How is your heart feeling right now? I pray that you are filled with hope. That rubbing shoulders with your brothers and sisters from Thessalonica has allowed the contagion of their love to spread into you. And opened your eyes to what the same Spirit can do and is doing today. Through you just as He is flowing through others all over the world! The Thessalonians were just humble believers who were filled with the love of Jesus. An entire church which, in spite of deadly opposition, chose to obey Christ with joy. Normal people who lived with an abnormal hope. Looking not for the coming of Caesar, but of Christ. Who would soon enough come and finish His new creation, begun so recently in and around them. They were already seeing its first harvest and savoring its first fruits. Theirs was not a wait-until-later faith. It was being realized then and there. Everywhere, everyone was talking about their lives of love and faith. They were so fresh and different. The others did not know just what to make of it. Or of this crucified Jesus who, they claimed, had defeated death and Satan by rising from the dead. At least they were all talking about it. And in that God was taking center stage! He was being glorified.

That excited Paul so much that he decided to write to them his first biblical letter. To encourage them just to keep it up. He identified the Thessalonians as models for us all to follow. In this last brief section of the book, I want to encourage you all to do just that. Up to this point I have mainly challenged you with questions. But now we need to move forward. Together. Accepting from God what we have learned. And seeking His Spirit's transforming power to mold us so we fit his best model. The model of Christ. And of His love. Which filled Paul and his disciples in Thessalonica. Are you ready to seek a thorough change? To renounce selfishness. Self-love. And let the Spirit of love renew everything in and around you? For to let love rule your life is to change everything. It will touch every relationship. You will begin to glorify God in new, small ways. Bearing fruit in abundance as you join the Thessalonians in rejecting all that is not love.

First, and quite quickly, we must be done with unworthy Christianity. To honestly face the fact that the Bible uses **that** language in describing the way many of us have been living. There are lifestyles that are unworthy of being associated with Jesus. Some of us have subtly slipped into these by focusing exclusively on God's amazing grace in forgiving our sin. Sometimes we are so sure that He will pick us up that we do not mind falling! Those who have chosen that self-indulgent path forget that Scripture warns us that we can become unworthy of Jesus. Unworthy of His name. A disgrace to His Kingdom.

I am not saying that true Christians can lose their salvation. But any form of Christianity that allows a follower of Christ to stay in his sin is not worthy of the name of Christ. He came to **"save his people from their sins"** (Matt 1:21). Not to leave them enslaved to sin. And any Christianity that makes grace a cheap thing just because it is offered as a free gift, does not understand biblical grace. The chapter on "Costly Grace" by the German martyr, Dietrich Bonhoeffer, is must reading by all evangelicals today.[158]

Paul had the goal of a worthy Christianity in mind wherever he made disciples. He knew that it was possible for a Christian to embrace an unworthy Christianity. This is why he wrote to the Thessalonians, "...**urging [them] to live lives worthy of God, who calls [them] into his kingdom and glory**" (1 Thes 2:12). How often have you considered the worthiness of your personal brand of Christianity? Or have you just assumed that it must be okay?

I want you to look at your life, your family, your church. At the way Evangelical Christianity works together in your town or city. And ask, "Is it worthy?" Is it glorifying God or actually degrading His glory? Do not be too negative. God has been at work in and around you all! Evangelicalism encompasses a huge variety of Christians. Wherever we find worthy Christianity, we must be delighted. Our hearts should immediately praise God for His work in His people. And we should encourage the brother or sister to keep it up! Let them know how it blesses us to see them so clearly walking with Jesus. I thank God that love is alive in Western Evangelicalism. Sadly, it just isn't our hallmark. Love for one another and for our non-Christian neighbors is not what people first think of when they think of an American Christian. Though it was the first thought of many who observed the worthy Christianity of the amazing Thessalonians.

Whenever we repent, it is equivalent to saying, "Forgive me, Father. That was not worthy of Christ." If it is something within us or our "group," that is unworthy, we should identify it as such. Confess it as unworthy. And turn away from it. Walking in the newness of life offered to us by the Spirit of God. We can actually only control our own repentance. We can't force others to repent. So prayer and patience is needed for others to get it. You can help them by showing them love and speaking the truth in love to them. Kindly modeling love for them. Taking them, as it were, by the hand and helping them go forward in love. Discipling them humbly. Gently. As the Holy Spirit has done to you. Countless times.

---

[158]D Bonhoeffer, *The Cost of Discipleship* (NY: The MacMillan Co., 1963) pp 45-60. See also my *Are You a Christian or a Disciple?* for a full discussion of grace, faith, repentance, obedience and suffering as they are largely misunderstood by many Christians.

The Bible often calls us to analyze ourselves. So let's take a serious, critical look at "the Christian life" as many of us have known it. Wanting a major overhaul if we need it. Since Jesus is alive and building His Church, we must reject the lifestyles that have only minimally impacted our world. Such an unworthy Christianity has run its course. Its time has ended. Let it go. Determine today to follow Jesus, who warned, **"Anyone who loves his father or mother more than me is not <u>worthy</u> of me; anyone who loves his son or daughter more than me is not <u>worthy</u> of me; and anyone who does not take his cross and follow me is not <u>worthy</u> of me"** (Matt 10:37-38).

Notice that the issue of worth with Jesus is linked with love. Whom will you love? What will you love most? Unworthy Christianity is not known for its love. Are you? How can we interpret these verses as teaching that God is going somehow to accept those whom Jesus has declared to be unworthy? That we can be positionally justified and safe with the Father while not deeply loving His Beloved Son? Is it really possible to be saved without having love for God and neighbor? For most of our lifetime? No, it is not!

Love to Jesus is declared by Paul to be an indispensable evidence of true, saving faith. So he closed his letter to the Corinthians, which was full of warnings, saying, **"If anyone does not love the Lord–a curse be on him."** (1 Cor 16:22a). He concludes his letter to the Ephesians saying, **"Grace to all who love our Lord Jesus Christ with an undying love"** (Eph 6:14). The apostle could not conceive of any other type of Christian. Is it wise that we can?

Paul also spoke of worthy Christianity to the Ephesians. **"...I urge you to live a life <u>worthy</u> of the calling you have received. Be completely humble and gentle; be patient, bearing with one another in love."**[159] Completely humble. Pride may be our greatest enemy. A proud Christian is as unworthy as a loveless Christian. God resists the proud.

Be brave. Like one of my parishioners was. Get two copies of CJ Mahaney's "Humility: True Greatness," and slowly read one copy. Marking it up. Taking its message to heart will change your life forever. Its twelve chapters make a great adult Sunday School class or small group study. Then give the other copy to your pastor. Like my sister kindly did to me when I was her pastor. We pastors are all often tempted by pride. It is a deformity that is hard to see in ourselves but easy to see in others. An ugly Christianity is an unworthy Christianity. And pride is ugly. A gentle, patient love of one another, though, is a beautiful thing. Worthy of association with Jesus. The Beautiful One.

Returning to our focus on the Thessalonians, Paul was especially thrilled with the type of Christianity they were advancing. He wrote,

---

[159]Eph. 4:1; cf Phil 3:17; Col 1:10.

"We ought always to thank God for you, brothers, and rightly so, because your faith is growing more and more, and the love every one of you has for each other is increasing. Therefore, among God's churches we boast about your perseverance and faith in all the persecutions and trials you are enduring. All this is evidence that God's judgment is right, and as a result you will be counted worthy of the kingdom of God for which you are suffering" (2 Thes 1:3-5).

Paul made it clear that the Thessalonian brand of Christianity was not going to miss its mark. They were going to be declared by God as worthy representatives of His Son. Even though others despised and persecuted them, God would accept them. Will He count us worthy? Can He fairly own us in the same way He owns them if our love is hardly alive? Did you notice that Paul wrote to the entire church and specifically said that every one of them had love for the other? It was a church-wide trait. How wide is the trait of brotherly love in your church? And among our churches in the West? How famous are we for our love? You can start developing this trait right now!

Love cannot be renewed within us without repentance. We have seen how the church at Ephesus was warned by Jesus to repent of forsaking their first love or He would remove their church's testimony from the earth (Rev 2:4-5). He does so because such churches are unworthy of His name.

Jesus, however, sent a message to another church,

"Yet you have a few people in Sardis who have not soiled their clothes. They will walk with me in white, for they are worthy. He who overcomes will, like them, be dressed in white. I will never blot out his name from the book of life, but will acknowledge his name before my Father and his angels. He who has an ear, let him hear what the Spirit says to the churches" (Rev 3:4-6).

What does unworthy Christianity look like? Dare I say it? Just look around you. A forgetful, materialistic, self-absorbed Christian is one in name only. He cannot have a deep relationship with Jesus. Only a distant one, if any at all. And you must not forget that the first time the word Christian was used in the Bible, it was a depiction of the disciples of Jesus living in Antioch. "The disciples were first called Christians at Antioch" (Acts 11:26b). Disciples do not let distance grow between them and their Master. Many Christians do. A true discipleship relationship with Jesus is worthy Christianity. A relationship at a distance, on our terms is unworthy Christianity.

196

A Christian who gets more excited about football than worship is unworthy. And I am not knocking getting excited about sports! It is one of the few remnants of western culture that still brings and keeps people together. But what happens when the team loses? When the season ends? How depressed do you get? Remember, our team cannot lose. Our season never ends. Through Christ, the old has gone and the new has come! Join with me today in repenting of an unremarkable Christianity. Of our being pathetic and powerless shells of the original. Unexcited and passionless. Without either great love or courage. Of being that kind of unworthy Christian whom CS Lewis mildly scolded in his sermon in 1942.

> "Our Lord finds our desires, not too strong, but too weak. We are half-hearted creatures, fooling about with drink and sex and ambition when infinite joy is offered us, like an ignorant child who wants to go on making mud pies in a slum because he cannot imagine what is meant by the offer of a holiday at the sea. We are far too easily pleased."[160]

Say yes to the true and attractive Christianity that amazed the world of the 1st century Thessalonians. And can recapture the attention and heart of ours today.

For Reflection and Discussion

1. How did this chapter affect you?

---

[160]CS Lewis, *The Weight of Glory* (NY: HarperCollins 2001) p 26.

Chapter 43

An Equal Love

We must now confront a universal problem. I have seen it in every country I have visited. I have felt it in myself. I am speaking of our bias against those unlike us. And our desire to remain different and divided. Superior. Unlike the Thessalonians, who regarded every believer, regardless of position, education or ethnicity, as a brother or a sister in the Lord. And who treated with equal dignity the converted slave and the believing patrician. Who, as we have seen, loved each Christian with the true love of Jesus. And who practiced what James commanded, **"My brothers, as believers in our glorious Lord Jesus Christ, don't show favoritism."** (James 2:1). What must we do to regain true brotherly love? The kind of love that sees and treats all believers as family? How can believers become one in reality, ending all unbiblical inequality?

We must first deal with our hearts. Because prejudice has found a home in our hearts. Honestly answer this question: *"When you see a believer of another color or culture—do you see your brother?"* Can your heart immediately make the kind of connection it does with family? If what I first see is a man who is Black. Or a sister who is Asian. Then, I am not fully seeing the one who is there before me. And in that moment of blindness, I am actually missing the work of Christ. Something He came to the cross to do. The indestructible work of God which Paul described as follows:

> **"For [Christ] himself is our peace, who has made the two (Jew and Gentile) one, and has broken down the dividing wall of hostility...His purpose was to create in himself one new man out of the two, thus making peace, and in this one body to reconcile both of them to God through the cross, by which he put to death their hostility"** (Eph 3:14-16).

One goal in His work of redemption was to eliminate walls of hostility between humans. What right do we have to accept only part of His saving work and reject another aspect of it? Yet that is what we do when we allow the cross to smash the wall between us and God BUT do not allow the same cross to demolish all wrongful walls dividing us from other disciples. Like social standing, age, educational achievements or gender. The same death aims at accomplishing all of this. And forever uniting us.

Racism is an emotive word. Laced with undertones of political correctness and misunderstanding. When I see it in our hearts, I am not necessarily talking about overt racial hatred. I am referring to something often much more subtle. Our preferred distance and aloofness from certain "types" of Christians. I am addressing the kind of provincialism that will do almost anything for our own local church but next to nothing for the evangelical church down the street or across town. Do you deny the existence of that kind of prejudice within much of Evangelicalism? And within you? Prejudice cannot long coexist with the love of God in us.

We must realize that there is often both pride and prejudice behind our exclusions of other Christians. I err when someone's being Reformed or Charismatic or Baptist or Catholic, etc. means more to me than their being a true believer. I see such traditional barriers between Christians as often harmful. Not quite as innocent and inevitable as we might make them out to be. Denominational divisions can hinder the work of the Holy Spirit. Who is the great Uniter. But he is also the Spirit of truth. So, the Holy Spirit allows some level of disagreement to exist as a healthful way of maintaining important distinctives of conscience between us. Unity without strict uniformity. But He can be the Author of this only if those distinctives remain secondary rather than becoming primary. If the non-saving truths that distinguish us are not as important to us as the living faith that saves and unites us. You might not have experienced the beauty of biblical fellowship across denominational lines. I do every week. And it is sweet.

I recognize that racism and prejudice are deep issues. I am not trying to overly simplify the issue and easily solve a complex problem. The division will not just disappear. But whenever Jesus is allowed into the picture, a new reality occurs. To introduce Jesus is never to do something that is of little account. Or childish. Remember what it cost Him and heaven for us to be reconciled! I believe that whenever Jesus is really lifted up by faith, seemingly intractable problems can begin to be solved. Brilliant secular sociologists, cultural anthropologists and philosophers have written copiously on racism. Some have even ventured suggestions toward a solution of this problem. None, though, have won the day and settled this issue. I am not trying to match their academic brilliance. But I know One who surpasses it. Jesus is the elusive remedy they have sought. His power can do what all their conclusions cumulatively could not. Because He is God. And the unity of His children is His expressed desire.

Just open your heart to what God could do in and through you. His infinite power can accomplish what no summits, seminars, retreats or books have been able to accomplish. I know He can make us one because he made the Thessalonians one with all the believers in Macedonia. And that was one hugely diverse population. I believe He can change us all because He took a narrow, bigoted, Gentile-despising Jew, named Saul, changed his nature (and name) and put these words in his mouth: "**May the Lord make your love increase and overflow for each other and for everyone else, <u>just as ours</u>**

<u>does for you</u>" (1 Thes 3:12). The mainly Gentile Thessalonians felt the power of Paul's love. And it filled them, so that when he wanted to collect funds for Jewish Christians in Judea, they begged him for the privilege of giving. Even while impoverished, they found a way to give lavishly. They knew no prejudice. Love had destroyed it, if not perfectly, at least largely so.

Paul was not exaggerating when he spoke of the resurrection power of Christ in us believers in the following radical way,

> **"So from now on we regard no one from a worldly point of view. Though we once regarded Christ this way, we do so no longer. Therefore, if anyone is in Christ, he is a new creation; the old has gone, the new has come! All this is from God, who reconciled us to himself through Christ and gave us the ministry of reconciliation: that God was reconciling the world to himself in Christ, not counting men's sin's against them. And he has committed to us the message of reconciliation"** (2 Cor 5:16-19).

It is wrong for you who are united with the risen Christ to regard another human primarily from a worldly point of view. From the former ways of division. From a racial, economic, educational or medical point of view. From anything that makes a person despised or intimidated by others. Because we are now in Christ and see everything differently as a result. Old and young. Male and female. Black and white. Rich and poor. Diseased and healthy. Handsome and homely. To each of us God has committed a ministry of reconciliation. Now racism and reconciliation are incompatible. Favoritism that sees and treats believers differently is a disease. Do you really want to be cured of it? Or, God forbid, is that a sin that you can easily live with?

I think I should treat the sin of my separation from you as a brother in Christ similarly to how I have treated my separation from God. I must hate it. Reject it. Repent of it. Turn my back on it, by the power of the Holy Spirit, and begin to walk down a new and different path. When I confess my sin for my own salvation, I no longer believe that my sin is really there. As an obstacle between me and God. I believe it has been taken away. Then I start living out of my new faith and freedom. And I am strengthened by God to begin to act differently. And, amazingly, I really do experience a new life. If I do not live out my faith, though, I will not change.

Prejudice is not different. It is a sin deep within us all. **"What causes fights and quarrels among you? Don't they come from your desires that battle within you?"** (James 4:1). Every person loves his own tribe. And innately thinks it is superior. But it is not. **"From one man he made every nation of men"** (Acts 17:26). We all have a common forefather, Adam. We are equally human. And now we all have one Savior, Jesus. The second Adam. We must see every believer as equal in Christ. Equally His children. Equally justified. Equally one another's brothers.

We do not embrace that truth by a living faith, though, until we begin to see and treat our faith-brothers as true brothers. If the Father has called someone His son or daughter, then they are my brother or sister. If they have confessed Christ as their Lord and Savior, we are in the same family. And I must treat them so or I am rejecting the truth of who we are in Christ. I am in rebellion. I am in sin. And living in that sin, I am grieving the Holy Spirit. And, in that state, cannot be greatly blessed by Him.

We won't see color and cultural differences surmounted until we hate the unnecessary divisions they have caused. Until we reject a divided, separate Christianity as unworthy. As no longer an option. And this can be helped by prayer. By asking God to change you and change others you know. By praying fervently for the removal of racism's foundation within our hearts. Then its mighty walls can fall. Is anything too hard for God? This is exactly what happened in Thessalonica. And it amazed the world!

But there is something else that is needed beyond prayer. We must confess this ugly sin of embedded bias for what it is. We must tell our brothers that we have not only sinned against them, but we still at times struggle with that sin. Racial profiling arises from our hearts and tempts us to judge those who do not look, dress, speak and live like us. We must ask them to forgive our sin. To seek the assurance of God's pardon through them saying to us, "You are forgiven through Jesus. And I forgive you, too."

Dietrich Bonhoeffer was absolutely right. There is no real communion or fellowship where there is no mutual confession of sin. Openly. Humbly. To one another.[161] There cannot be any real repentance of racism and prejudice where there is not a desire to immediately walk in unity and equality. In true brotherhood. Repentance demands action. And the action demanded by racism is reconciliation. True Christian unity.

So, join me in standing with the risen Christ above all expressions of prejudice in Christ's Church. And begin to see others differently by the power of His Spirit who is in you. Do this personally. Right now. And then make a plan to break the barriers that have been separating you from other disciples of Jesus. Guess who's coming to dinner? That's right! Invite a believer from another tradition over to dinner. To talk, listen, pray and bond. That's a start. You will be amazed where one step will take you.

But there is something else you should do. Hold your spiritual leaders' feet to the fire. You are to follow them as they follow Christ. Don't

---

[161]D Bonhoeffer, *Life Together* (NY: Harper & Row Publishers 1954) ch 5: Confession and Communion pp 110-122. See also James 5:16; John 20:24; Matt 3:6; Acts 19:18; 1 Jn 1:7-9.

be too quick to follow them down all paths. Question those who have only good to say about your own denomination. And only bad about other true believers. Do this prayerfully, humbly and patiently. It is a sacred cow to many. But they need to offer it up to the Lord, themselves. Willingly. Pray that they will have the grace to let it go.

You must, first, pray that denominationalism will be displaced by Christ. And humbly ask your leaders why your church is not doing more with other truly Christian churches. Push for the kind of evangelical alliance that recognizes our unity without denying our differences. And if your minister or church needs help, contact me through the organization with which I am working.[162] Because that is exactly what I am spending a great deal of my time doing. I am constantly meeting ministers and bringing them together in the establishing of evangelical alliances.

Of course, such a church-wide work takes time. But it does not take as much time as you would think. It can start wherever two Christians (or ten) allow Christ to really be their life. That is the issue, as Bonhoeffer wrote,

> "Among men there is strife. 'He is our peace,' says Paul of Jesus Christ (Eph 2:14). Without Christ, there is discord between God and man and between man and man. Christ became the Mediator and made peace with God and among men...Now Christians can live with one another in peace; they can love and serve one another; they can become one. But they can continue to do so only by way of Jesus Christ. Only in Jesus Christ are we one, only through him are we bound together. To eternity he remains the one Mediator....

> "One is a brother to another only through Jesus Christ. I am a brother to another person through what Jesus Christ did for me and to me; the other person has become a brother to me through what Jesus Christ did for him. This fact that we are brethren only through Jesus Christ is of immeasurable significance.... Our community with one another consists solely in what Christ has done to both of us...The more genuine and the deeper our community becomes, the more will everything else between us recede, the more clearly and purely will Jesus Christ and his work become the one and only thing that is vital between us."[163]

I highly recommend that you slowly and prayerfully read his short book, "Life Together." It could help to change your life as it did mine. Though he was safe in the USA in 1939, he could not stay away from his needy countrymen.

---

[162]CityNet Ministries - PO Box 37 - Glenside, PA 19038
[163]D Bonhoeffer, 1954, pp 23-25.

He returned to assist the Confessing Church and the Resistance against Nazism. He went all over Germany speaking to clandestine groups while continuing his writing. Then in April 1943 he was arrested. But in prison he continued to bring comfort to everyone. Even being secretly taken by sympathetic guards from cell to cell to minister to despairing prisoners. Shortly before it was liberated by allied forces, by special orders from Heinrich Himmler, Dietrich Bonhoeffer was taken to be hanged by the Gestapo. The setting was described by a fellow prisoner as follows:

> "Bonhoeffer always seemed to me to spread an atmosphere of happiness and joy over the least incident, and profound gratitude for the mere fact that he was alive.... He was one of the very few persons I have ever met for whom God was real and always near.... On Sunday, April 8, 1945, Pastor Bonhoeffer conducted a little service of worship and spoke to us in a way that went to the heart of all of us.... He had hardly ended his last prayer when the door opened and two civilians entered. They said, 'Prisoner Bonhoeffer, come with us.' That had only one meaning for all prisoners–the gallows. We said good-bye to him. He took me aside (and said): 'This is the end, but for me it is the beginning of life.' The next day he was hanged in Flossenburg."[164]

May God help us join Bonhoeffer and the amazing Thessalonians in making **"every effort to keep the unity of the Spirit in the bond of peace"** (Eph. 4:3). Start reaching out today and begin to realize just how closely you are following the heart and will of Jesus who prayed, **"I have given them the glory that you gave me, that they may be one as we are one. I in them and you in me. May they be brought to complete unity to let the world know that you sent me and have loved them even as you have loved me"** (John 17:22-23).

For Reflection and Discussion

1. What steps can you take to help establish this kind of love in your life? In your family? In your church?

---

[164]D Bonhoeffer, 1954, p 13.

Chapter 44

A Giving Love

My dad was a dentist who gave up a lucrative practice to serve alongside of rural African pastors in an amazing ministry of mercy. I saw how he loved them. And they him. Luke was also a missionary. He was on Paul's team, joining it in Troas (Acts 16:7-10). But Luke, a Gentile believer, was also a doctor (Col 4:11-14). The only named physician in the New Testament. He, like my parents, was willing to give up enjoyment of things for love of others. And to obey the last command of our Savior.

Luke spent a long time in Philippi, so he would have seen, firsthand, the reach of the Thessalonians love into Philippi. He would have seen how they **"loved all the brothers throughout Macedonia"** (1 Thes 4:10). And he would have been amazed by it. When Paul came through Philippi on his way back to Jerusalem with the huge gift for the believers there, Luke went with him (Acts 20:5-21:18). When Paul was in custody in Caesarea, for some two years, Luke likely stayed near, because he later sailed with Paul from there to Rome (Acts 27:1-28:16). It is believed that it was during this two years while Paul was in Caesarea that Luke carefully gathered all the first-hand evidence he needed to write the gospel that bears his name (Luke 1:3-4) and the early part of Acts. When Paul appealed to Caesar and was sent to Rome, Luke was alongside of him. Which means that Luke was part of the shipwreck recorded in Acts 27! Think of that experience. Read its words closely. Luke was so full of love for Paul and the mission that even that ordeal did not turn him back!

Luke stayed with Paul when Paul was kept in house arrest for two years (Acts 28:30-31; Phile 24). He may have written Acts at the close of that period. When Paul was later imprisoned again, in Rome under Caesar Nero, he wrote his last letter (2 Timothy) and affectionately noted, **"Only Luke is with me"** (2 Tim 4:11a). Of course, Luke's life could have been threatened by the association. But the threat of death does not intimidate a brother filled with the love of God.

Luke understood love. He saw it energize Paul. And he was filled with it by the Holy Spirit. Throughout this book, we have seen how "love works." Love is not merely a feeling that stays within one's heart. Love acts. Luke lived a life of love. So, Paul called him **"my fellow worker"** (Phile 24). Luke would not have become one of the Apostle's most trusted friends and fellow workers without having the same love that filled Paul. It was never enough to Paul just to work for God. That work had to be driven by love.

Otherwise it was worth "nothing" (1 Cor 13:1-3).

To love, then, is to give. And most American Christians are simply not too good at giving. It is important to hear what our giving could accomplish, though these figures are a bit dated. In the December 2008 issue of Christianity Today, Rob Moll recorded the following facts:

- 36% (of American Evangelicals) report that they give away less than 2% of their income. Only about 27% tithe.

- American Christians—those who say their faith is very important to them and those who attend church at least twice a month—earn more than $2.5 trillion dollars every year!

- It is estimated that American Christians could realistically increase their giving by $85.5 billion each year.

- $10 billion would sponsor 20 million children for a year, and just $330 million would sponsor 150,000 indigenous missionaries in countries closed to religious workers. $2.2 billion would triple the current funding of Bible translation, printing, and distribution. $600 million would be enough to start eight Christian colleges in Eastern Europe and Southeast Asia.

Most of us live at a level of comfort and luxury that few in the history of the world have known. Yet most of us don't willingly share our possessions or give very much of our wealth away. It is hard enough for many to give more than a few bucks even during a worship service. At the one extended time during the week that many meditate on the One who gave heaven and His life away to save us! Even then it is hard to give. Why do so few tithe, even though Jesus recommended the practice (Matt 23:3, 23)? Because many are not His disciples. Disciples obey. Not perfectly, of course, but persistently more so than they disobey. They live out in their lives what Paul called **"the obedience that comes from faith"** (Rom 1:5b). Disciples obey God with a faith that constantly looks to Jesus and His righteousness.

The Thessalonians, unlike many of us, were famous givers. And they were renowned lovers as well. That's no coincidence. They loved and gave to believers and unbelievers alike. You see, great giving and great loving are connected. When God fills you with His love you will begin to give like only a child of God can give. Don't you want to be filled with the desire to give freely and lavishly? Rather than grabbing and holding on so tightly to your blessings. Let them go. If you don't, you will never enjoy the fruitfulness of Paul, Luke and the Thessalonians. You will never be filled with the love and power of Christ in this life.

Christ-like giving is a gift from God. The Thessalonians were among the Macedonians who possessed the **"grace of giving"** (2 Cor 8:7). Do you want God's grace? Be careful, now. Because one of its forms is giving. If you do not want to give, you really don't want the grace of God! Or at least the fullness of His grace. It's just not right to pick and choose which grace from God YOU want. Just open your soul to it all. Including the grace of giving.

I hope this next thought startles you. If you are not a sacrificial giver, you must not be filled with the Spirit. How do I know this? According to Dr. Luke, the Spirit is "the gift" of God.[165] How can one be filled with the greatest gift, the giving God himself – and not become a giver? If you are filled with something–that is what you are! A glass full of water is not a hamburger. So, I repeat. If you are not a giver, you are not filled with the Gift. The Spirit. And you are wasting the greatest resource you have! Paul used similar logic in his concluding benediction for the Thessalonians: "**Now may the Lord of peace himself give you peace at all times and in every way.**" (2 Thes 3:16). If God is peace, the person who is filled with God is filled with peace. The same is true of both love and giving. John said, "**Whoever does not love does not know God, because God is love**" (1 Jn 4:8). And, so, if you do not desire to give, you are not living under the controlling influence of the Giver.

When Paul wrote to Christians living across the Aegean Sea from Thessalonica, he said: "**Be imitators of God, therefore, as dearly loved children and live a life of love, just as Christ loved us and gave himself up for us as a fragrant offering and sacrifice to God**" (Eph 5:1-2). He commands us all to live a life that is consumed with love. Our love is to be "**just as Christ loved us.**" And how did He love? He "**gave himself up for us.**" True love gives. Gives itself away. Not just some money. Money is little more than a test. If you fail there, you haven't started living that life of love. The love that gives itself for another. Thessalonian love.

We saw how Paul, speaking of the Thessalonians and their neighbors said, "**And they did not do as we expected, but <u>they gave themselves first to the Lord and then to us</u> in keeping with God's will**" (2 Cor 8:5). Could YOU do that? Sure you could, if they did. You are believers, too. But, like them, you could not give sacrificially by your own power. You would need God's help. You get that <u>after</u> you give yourself sincerely and unreservedly to God. I am tired of today's evangelical experience to "give Jesus your heart," but doesn't seem willing to give Him much else. I don't think Paul or the Thessalonians could conceive of that possibility. To give Jesus your heart would be to give him your all. As I wrote elsewhere, there was no asking Jesus to be your Savior and then, later, making Him your Lord.[166]

It's time to give ourselves anew to Christ and to one another. To

---

[165]See Acts 1:4; 2:38; 8:20; 10:45; 15:8.
[166]See E Gross, *Christianity without a King: The Results of Abandoning Christ's Lordship* (Columbus, GA: Brentwood Christian Press 1992), 157pp.

start living a life of love. Of good works. Of giving. It should no longer be a question of whether you can afford to or not. You can't afford not to give! Here are some ideas I hope you find helpful:

- start with prayer, asking God to forgive your lack of love and giving–repenting for your church, too, if it struggles with loving others

- ask God to give you obvious opportunities to help others-TODAY

- determine to take some time that you would normally spend on yourself each week and devote it to doing good for others. Die a little to self and see how you begin to live

- give your ears in listening carefully to them

- give your heart in feeling sympathetically for their need

- give your hands in helping them physically

- give your lips in encouraging the needy with the gospel promises of abundant and joyful life **in Christ**

- plan to give a percentage of your disposable income into the work of the Lord. Beyond a tithe. Into mercy ministry. Boggle the minds of your pastor or the deacons by giving love gifts for them to use immediately

- or bake a pie, cookies or a meal and give them away. My mom would do that for families she read of in the local paper who just experienced some trauma. Several became believers. Love works.

Luke recorded Jesus' promise that still holds today, "**Give, and it will be given to you. A good measure, pressed down, shaken together and running over will be poured into your lap. For with the measure you use, it will be measured to you**" (Luke 6:38). This text should not be the sole property of our brothers emphasizing "prosperity theology." If we were filled with Christ's love, even while struggling with poverty, like the Macedonians were, we would find ourselves wanting to do good. And not mainly to get something in return. That is not remarkable. That is not grace. That is desperation. We are called to do unbelievable good. Giving heaping handfuls of good to others. Not expecting something in return. The type of good works that cause others to glorify God because they know such love and lavish giving could not come from any other source than God! Such giving in love opens the door for Kingdom progress and personal victory unlike any other strategy. "**Do not be overcome by evil, but overcome evil with good**" (Rom 12:21). Can you hear such teaching and not give yourself away? The amazing Thessalonians could not. They heard it from Paul and, by God's grace, did it throughout their region. Let's join them today!

For Reflection and Discussion

1. Ask the Spirit of God to show you what you can immediately give up for the Kingdom. And to whom or what you should donate its proceeds.

2. Now liquidate it, and surprise the receiver with your gift of love.

3. Remember how THAT made you and them feel.

Chapter 45

A Serving Love

As those who live in a democratic society, we do not take too kindly to the concept of being ruled by dictators, kings or even queens. To anyone who would limit our personal rights. As Americans, our nation's Bill of Rights includes:

- the rights of life, liberty and property
- the right of freedom of worship
- the right of free speech
- the right of freedom of the press
- the right of freedom of assembly
- the right to bear arms
- the right of jury by trial for serious crimes
- the rights of bail and protection from excessive punishment

So, we feel out of place when we read of early disciples yielding to Jesus an authority over them that limits or replaces any of these personal rights. To us as Americans, our Bill of Rights is sacred. To tamper with them creates a firestorm of opposition.

That would have surprised the Thessalonians. While deeply appreciating many of our freedoms, they would not have seen any problem with surrendering everything to King Jesus! Because that is exactly what they and other disciples regularly did.

This question will determine your life: Who is Jesus to you? How central to your life is He? Does it matter if you do not regard Him as your King? It surely does. I believe that issue is so central, that your identity and destiny are determined by your grasping and submitting to its truth. Dr. Charles Hodge was, perhaps, the most influential American seminary professor during the 19th century. For over fifty years, he taught thousands of students. Some of whom would become influential preachers, teachers, scientists and politicians. At his memorial service, a close friend and colleague said of him,

> "[No one I know] was more absorbed with the love of Christ. Around this central sun [of Jesus] ...his whole being revolved. Christ was not only the grounds of his hope, but the acknowledged sovereign of his intellect, the soul of his theology, the unfailing

[source] of his joy, the one all-pervading, all glorifying theme and end of his life....

If one were called upon to specify the most conspicuous feature of Dr Hodge's religious character, next to that pure love with which his whole nature was [filled], it would be his *humility*....Here was a man clothed with brilliant intellectual gifts...his utterances on all [church] and [theological] questions listened to by a great church with a deference [given] to no other living teacher, lauded by eminent theologians in Europe and America...and the constant object of undisguised and loving reverence to all around him, yet [he was ever as] modest and unassuming as a child–never asserting his [position]; never [forcing] his opinions; never courting a compliment; never saying or doing anything for effect; never [demanding] attention to himself *in any way*....To all eyes [except] his own he had approached as near to 'the stature of a perfect man in Christ Jesus' as any of those saints whose names the church has [preserved]. But so clear was his [grasp] of the spotless holiness of God, so transcendent his views of the love of Christ and the debt we owe Him, and so inwrought his sense of the [horrible nature] of sin, that he could only think of himself as a poor, miserable sinner saved by grace.... Therefore it was that our dear Professor was ever 'clothed with humility'–clothed--with it like 'a raiment'...covering all the powers of his mind, all the treasures of his learning, all the wealth of his [emotions], all that made him great and good, loving and beloved, all that moved us to look on him as one given to the church...to show how much a Christian may, even in this world, become like Christ."[167]

How different would we be today had our lives been touched by more men like Charles Hodge? People obviously filled with the love of Jesus. Of the countless quotations I could use to bless you with from his works, I will note just this one here. I hope it will whet your appetite to join me in reading from his many helpful books that are still in print:

"The Scriptures constantly speak of the Messiah as a king who was to set up a kingdom into which in the end all other kingdoms were to be merged. In addition, the Scriptures frequently designate Him as Lord, a term which, when used of God or Christ, means absolute [owner] and sovereign ruler....

In announcing to the Virgin Mary the approaching birth of the

---

[167]H Boardman in AA Hodge, *The Life of Charles Hodge* (New York: Charles Scribner's Sons, 1880), pp 606-608.

Messiah, the angel Gabriel said, 'Thou shalt conceive in thy womb, and bring forth a son...He shall be great, and shall be called the Son of the Highest: and the Lord shall give unto him the throne of his father David: and he shall reign over the house of Jacob forever; and of his kingdom there shall be no end' (Luke 1:31-33).... And our Lord Himself, when He entered upon His personal ministry, went everywhere 'preaching the gospel of the kingdom of God' (Mark 1:14). Much of His teaching was devoted to setting forth the nature of the kingdom which He came to establish. Nothing, therefore, is more certain, according to the Scriptures, than that Christ is a king....

Christ is the King of every believing soul. He translates it from the kingdom of darkness. He brings it into subjection to Himself. He rules in and reigns over it. Every believer recognizes Christ as his absolute sovereign, as Lord of his inward as well as of his outward life...

The special law of Christ's kingdom is that its members should love one another with brotherly love–a love which leads to the recognition of all Christians as brethren belonging to the same family and entitled to the same privileges and blessings, and a love which ministers to their necessities so that there be no lack. This law is laid down at length in 2 Cor 8. The law of the kingdom is that every man should labor to the extent of his ability to supply the wants of those dependent on him: 'Whoso hath this world's good, and seeth his brother have need, and shutteth up his bowels of compassion from him, how dwelleth the love of God in him?' (1 John 3:17)"[168]

When your soul truly submits to Jesus as Lord and King, no personal rights remain supreme. He reigns over our rights. So, whenever we wonder: What should I be thinking, saying or doing right now? The answer for us is simple: THE WILL OF KING JESUS! We should always be following Jesus. Applying His life and words to ourselves.

We have seen how slaves were esteemed in the Roman Empire. Yet, the same word used of a slave's relationship of submission to his master is used of our relationship to our Lord. Paul chose that word when he spoke of the Thessalonians' conversion: **"They tell how you turned to God from idols to serve the living and true God"** (1 Thes 1:9). As one New Testament scholar wrote, "The word rendered *serve* basically means serve as a slave and reminds us of the way Paul delighted to call himself a 'slave of

[168]C Hodge, *Systematic Theology abridged by Ed Gross* (Phillipsburg, NJ: P&R Publishing Co, 1997), pp 402-406.

Jesus Christ'. It underlines the whole-hearted nature of Christian service."[169] Do YOU get that? Christian service has certain parallels to slavery. If Morris is right, and he most certainly is, the nature of true Christian service must have certain elements. Aspects that parallel enslavement. Our service should be compelling, constant and complete. For every slave was compelled to do the will of his master constantly and completely. Or he would pay the consequences. Jesus spoke of discipleship as a parallel to slavery when He said, **"A disciple is not above his teacher, nor a slave above his master"** (Matt 10:24). Slaves often submitted out of abject fear. We serve our Rabbi and King Jesus out of love and joy. Because His way is better than ours. We are actually set free when we give up our own rule and submit to Jesus.[170]

The question that each of us as Americans should carefully consider is, "How do I respond if Jesus restricts my rights more than the Bill or Rights allows?" Do we as His disciples have complete freedom of speech? The right to say whatever we desire? Or to write or look at whatever we want? Or to use and dispose of our property however we want? The answer for all of these and similar questions is, No! Jesus is our King and His Word is our Law. We gladly submit to Him and to It. He is God and, therefore, greater than any human lawgiver. As Paul commanded, **"Carry each other's burdens, and in this way you will fulfill the law of Christ"** (Gal 6:2; also 1 Cor 9:21). Have you ever considered the teaching of the New Testament to be the laws of King Jesus?

All evangelicals would consider themselves devoted to the gospel. To the Great Commission of Jesus. Have you ever looked hard at what the Great Commission itself actually demands? **"Then Jesus came to them and said, 'All authority in heaven and on earth has been given to me. Therefore go and make disciples...teaching them to obey everything I have commanded you....'"** (Matt 28:18-20). You cannot understand the Great Commission rightly without seeing Christ's Kingship all through it. We "go" because He has authority over everyone in heaven and on earth. That means He is over you and me. And that includes our Bill of Rights. We are to teach all Christians to obey everything our King has commanded. That seems pretty clear. But, frankly, you and I know that most churches and ministries have lost that focus. So, the commitment of the Thessalonians seems strange. Who today is going to live and witness with the relentless, suffering love they showed, without a commitment to the Lordship of Christ? Without following Jesus as 21st century disciples?

We don't live like we belong to one Kingdom because many do not view Jesus as their King. No king, no kingdom. They stand and fall together. It reminds me of the last verse in Judges. **"In those days Israel had no**

---

[169]L Morris, *1 & 2 Thessalonians* (Downers Grove, IL: InterVarsity Press, 1984), p 47.
[170]See Ps 116:16; 119:32, 45; Isa 61:1; John 8:32,36; 2 Cor 3:17; Gal 5:1; James 1:25.

king; everyone did as he saw fit" (Judges 21:25). The Thessalonians would never have jeopardized their lives and families and futures as they did, unless salvation meant for them to bow at the feet of King Jesus. To how many evangelicals today does salvation really include that?[171]

Imagine the shame that higher placed Roman and Greek citizens would have felt when their family and friends called themselves, "the slaves of Jesus." To have their entire relationship to God depicted as that of a slave to his owner. But Paul described himself and wrote to them in those terms. And he would have been stupid to do so unless the true nature of our relationship to God and our service to Him demands the use of such language. Unless, in other words, he had to use the word "slave."

To whom do you belong? What governs your decisions on what you should do from one moment to the next? How often does Christ's will actually guide you? Does Paul's statement to the Corinthians seem excessive? **"We demolish arguments and every pretension that sets itself up against the knowledge of God, and we take captive every thought to make it obedient to Christ"** (2 Cor 10:5). Does Jesus really have the right to govern what we think? Paul obviously thought and taught so (Phil. 4:8). As Jesus had (Matt 5:28). That was because Paul was the disciple of Jesus and never left His "school."

Certainly we maintain the right of free speech, don't we? Paul commanded, **"Do not let any unwholesome talk come out of your mouths, but only what is helpful for building others up according to their needs, that it may benefit those who listen"** (Eph 4:29). The law of Jesus restricts our rights. His way is stricter than the Bill of Rights. In fact, in Scripture, it is the evil ones who say, **"We will triumph with our tongues; we own our lips—who is our master?"** (Ps 12:4).

I hope you are getting the point. Our rights are forfeited when we become the disciples of Christ. He owns our every thought, word and deed. In fact, the great commandment demands that even our inner feelings be submitted to the reign of love as well. He is to be loved with all our heart and soul. As well as all our mind. Whenever our feelings are other than love—we sin. We miss the point of life. We choose bondage rather than freedom.

Carefully consider what would happen if you were to ask your closest fellow Christians to describe your relationship to them. How long would it take for them to mention the word "servant"? I do not say this to shame you, but to encourage you to repent quickly of living like you belonged to yourself. Your family. Your church. Rather than to Christ and His Kingdom. We belong to one another. We are not going to see radical love transform our region until we submit wholeheartedly to the Lordship of Christ. Like the

---

[171]See E Gross in S Moreau, ed., *Evangelical Dictionary of World Missions* (Grand   Rapids, MI: Baker Books, 2000) article on "Salvation", pp 848-850.

amazing Thessalonians did.

For Reflection and Discussion

1. Reflect on the prediction Jesus made of the final judgment in Matthew 25:31-46. How do His words affect you? Why so?

Chapter 46

An Urgent Love

I write this final chapter with great optimism and hope! Because I know this book promotes the will of God for us all. And because I know that you want to do His will. One question is: how urgently is His love needed by those around you? And how serious are you about becoming a powerful channel of that love?

The world is crying for love. Just listen to their cries. They need it and want it URGENTLY. Before we look one final time at Paul's letter to the Thessalonians and feel how urgently he pressed them to continue loving, let's look at the same message from a few others. Outside of the Bible. It is truly amazing that over 100 different artists have recorded their own rendition of ONE song,

> "What the world needs NOW is love sweet love.
> It's the only thing that there's just too little of."

Let the words of Burt Bacharach's 1971 super hit sink in. Love is urgently desired everywhere. Many want it. But very few devote themselves to giving it. And no one perfectly. All of the time. That is where Jesus comes in, working in and through His Church. Pumping His love through you and me. We are the only Body of Christ on earth right now. As we close, reflect for a few minutes on some of the ways love's urgent need has been communicated. The ancient Athenian philosopher, Socrates (470-399BC), wrote,

> "One word frees us
> Of all the weight and pain in life,
> That word is Love."[172]

Not quite as famous a philosopher, Percy Sledge, "the Golden Voice of Soul," spoke the same truth about love even more effectively than did Socrates. Sledge topped both Pop and R & B Charts in 1966 singing, "When a Man Loves a Woman." In it he moans,

> "When a man loves a woman
> Can't keep his mind on nothing else

---

[172]From online source, Romantic Love Quotes

He'll trade the world
For the good thing he's found.
If she's bad he can't see it
She can do no wrong
Turn his back on his best friend
If he put her down.

"When a man loves a woman
Spend his very last dime
Tryin' to hold on to what he needs
He'd give up all his comfort
Sleep out in the rain
If she said that's the way it ought to be."

Politicians, when they are thinking right, do not disagree with this. Benjamin Disraeli (1804-1881), the only British Prime minister of Jewish heritage, converted to Christianity at age 13. He remained active in the Anglican church for the rest of his life. He saw no problem with being a cultural Jew while following Jesus. When a fellow British politician hurled an anti-Semitic remark his way, not rare in a day which also featured some awful anti-Jewish political cartoons, he replied, "Yes I am a Jew, and when the ancestors of the right honorable gentleman were brutal savages in an unknown island, mine were priests in the temple of Solomon." [173] This famous British politician, when speaking of love said,

"We are all born for love... it is [our] principle existence and [our] only end."[174]

Though they may not have chosen to hang out together, if fortunate enough to have lived in the same era, Bob Marley (1945-1981) agreed with Disraeli about the importance of love. The famous Jamaican singer-songwriter and musician helped propel reggae onto the world's stage. Marley, experienced much racial prejudice when young and when reflecting on racism later in life said,

"I don't have prejudice against meself. My father was a white and my mother was a black. Them call me half-caste or whatever. Me don't dip on nobody's side. Me don't dip on the black man's side nor the white man's side. Me dip on God' side, the one who create me and cause me to come from black and white."[175]

---

[173]From Wikipedia, Mar 3, 2009 article on Benjamin Disraeli.
[174]From online source, Romantic Love Quotes
[175]From Wikipedia, Mar 3 , 2009 article on Bob Marley

His consciousness about being mixed racially was certainly one factor in the production of his first recorded song, "Judge Not" in 1961. One of his most famous songs was entitled, "One Love, One Heart." In it he joins the longing of all others for,

> "One love, one heart
> Let's get together and feel all right
> Hear the children crying (One Love)
> Hear the children crying (One Heart)
> Sayin', 'Give thanks and praise to the Lord and I will feel all right.'
> Sayin', 'Let's get together and feel all right.'
> "One love, one heart Let's get together and feel all right
> As it was in the beginning (One Love)
> So shall it be in the end (One Heart)
> Alright, 'Give thanks and praise to the Lord and I will feel all right.'
> Let's get together and feel all right."

If you can get them out of their lab and off their computers long enough, even scientists would agree with the urgent need of love. Canadian born chemist Orlando A. Battista (b 1917), a prolific writer and the creator of 'quotoons" might not have condoned Marley's religious (Rastafarian) use of marijuana, but he did share his longings for love. Battista wrote,

> "The greatest weakness of most humans is their hesitancy to tell others how much they love them while they're alive."[176]

Cross the Atlantic and consider British composer Andrew Lloyd Weber (b1948), one of the most famous and successful songwriters of our day. Since Michael Ball and Sarah Brightman have sung his "Love Changes Everything," it has become one of the world's most famous love songs.

> "Love, love changes everything: Hands and faces, earth and sky,
> Love, love changes everything: How you live and how you die
> Love, can make the summer fly, Or a night seem like a lifetime.
> Yes love, love changes everything: Now I tremble at your name.
> Nothing in the world will ever be the same.
>
> "Love, love changes everything: Days are longer, words mean more.
> Love, love changes everything: Pain is deeper than before.
> Love will turn your world around, And that world will last forever.
> Yes love, love changes everything, Brings you glory, brings you shame.

---

[176]From online source, Romantic Love Quotes.

Nothing in the world will ever be the same.

"Off into the world we go, Planning futures, shaping years.
Love bursts in, and suddenly all our wisdom disappears.
Love makes fools of everyone: All the rules we made are broken.
Yes love, love changes everyone. Live or perish in its flame.
Love will never, never let you be the same
Love will never, never let you be the same."[177]

Weber's fellow countryman, John Keats (1795-1821), is recognized as one of the most influential poets of the English Romantic movement. He lived a very short life, but he grasped the power of love. Though he died of tuberculosis before marrying her, his love letter to Fanny Brawne has inspired millions.

"I have been astonished that men could die martyrs for their religion - I have shudder'd at it. I shudder no more. I could be martyr'd for my religion. Love is my religion And I could die for that. I could die for you."[178]

His words may not match the form of Keats' poetry and prose, but his words and music touch the heart, as well. His vocal sound is unique, and his awards are countless. Randy Travis (b 1959) has thrilled millions with this song declaring the lasting power of love:

Forever and Ever Amen (Travis)

You may think that I'm talking foolish
You've heard that I'm wild and I'm free
You may wonder how I can promise you now
This love that I feel for you always will be
But your not just time that I'm killing
I'm no longer one of those guys
As sure as I live, this love that I give
Is gonna be yours until the day that I die.

(Chorus)
Oh baby I'm gonna love you forever
Forever and ever amen
As long as old men sit & talk about the weather
As long as old women sit & talk about old men

---

[177]Lyrics by Charles Hart and Don Black.
[178]From online source, goodreads.

If you wonder how long I'll be faithful
I'll be happy to tell you again
I'm gonna love you forever and ever
Forever and ever amen..

They say time takes its toll on a body
Makes a young girls brown hair turn gray
Honey I don't care I ain't in love with your hair
No, if it all fell out well I'd love you anyway
They say time can play tricks on a memory
Make people forget things they knew
Well it's easy to see it's happenin to me
I've already forgotten every woman but you.

Oh darlin I'm gonna love you forever
Forever and ever amen
As long as old men sit & talk about the weather
As long as old women sit & talk about old men
If you wonder how long I'll be faithful
Just listen to how this song ends
I'm gonna love you forever and ever
Forever and ever amen
I'm gonna love you forever and ever
Forever and ever
Forever and ever
Forever and ever amen.

If asked to name one person in the 20th century whose life was personified by love, Mother Teresa (1910-1997) would be the choice of many. She truly believed everyone, even the poorest, the forgotten and the most despised in the world needed and deserved love. But hers was different than what the songs and quotes above speak about. The love she showed was more than human. It was the amazing love of Jesus. When she died, the Missionaries of Charity Order which she founded had over 4,000 sisters and over 100,000 lay volunteers, operating 610 missions in 123 countries. She simply said,

> "Love is a fruit in season at all times, and within the reach of every hand."[179]

---

[179]Quoted from online source, Romantic Love Quotes

The love of God has been the theme of many Christian hymns down through the ages. When we compare them to the songs of love sung by non-Christians, we see the huge difference. And our hearts ache for Christ's better love to be known by them all.

He was growing blind while preparing for the Christian ministry. His fiancée, unwilling to marry a blind man, broke off their engagement. George Matheson, later one of Scotland's great preachers, was heartbroken. "He consoled himself in thinking of God's love which is never limited, never conditional, never withdrawn, and never uncertain. Out of this experience it is said he wrote the hymn, O Love that Will Not Let Me Go on June 6, 1882."[180]

"O love that will not let me go,
I rest my weary soul in Thee.
I give Thee back the life I owe,
That in Thine ocean depths its flow,
May richer, fuller be."

One of the best expressions of God's love put to song was the hymn by Samuel Trevor Francis (1834-1925), O the Deep, Deep Love of Jesus. He wrote it as he remembered one lonely day when

"I was on my way home from work and had to cross Hungerford Bridge to the south on the Thames. During the winter's night of wind and rain and in the loneliness of that walk...I stayed for a moment to look at the dark waters flowing under the bridge, and the temptation was whispered to me: 'Make an end of all this misery." I drew back from the evil thought, and suddenly a message was borne into my very soul: 'You do believe in the Lord Jesus Christ?' I at once answered, 'I do believe,' and I put my whole trust in Him as my Savior."[181]

Remembering that fateful night, he wrote,

"O the deep, deep love of Jesus, vast, unmeasured, boundless, free!
Rolling as a mighty ocean in its fullness over me!
Underneath me, all around me, is the current of Thy love
Leading onward, leading homeward to Thy glorious rest above!

"O the deep, deep love of Jesus, spread His praise from shore to shore!

---

[180]R Morgan, *Then Sings My Soul* (Nashville,: Thomas Nelson Publishers 2003), p 206.
[181]R Morgan, 2003, p 197.

How He loveth, ever loveth, changeth never, nevermore!
How He watches o'er His loved ones, died to call them all His own;
How for them He intercedeth, watcheth o'er them from the throne!

"O the deep, deep love of Jesus, love of every love the best!
'Tis an ocean full of blessing, 'tis a haven giving rest!
O the deep, deep love of Jesus, 'tis a heaven of heavens to me;
And it lifts me up to glory, for it lifts me up to Thee!"

I have included all these quotations for one aim. To fan the flame of love. And not just the world's love. But the true love of Jesus. And to help you to desire it for yourself and all others. Urgently.

Paul loved the Thessalonians, yet he pushed them. Love at times is urgent. But it is also tender. Paul spoke urgently because he knew that when love is lost or displaced by something else–it is a horrible loss! However small and insignificant it may appear, love that is lost is a huge loss. However much the Thessalonians may have accomplished, if they moved on from love, they were moving on from Christ. And from the Spirit. So, notice how Paul urged the Thessalonians. Yet so gently. Carefully consider three texts.

> **"Finally, brothers, we instructed you how to live in order to please God, as in fact you are living. Now we ask you and <u>urge</u> you in the Lord Jesus to do this more and more"** (1 Thes 4:1).

> **"And in fact, you do love all the brothers throughout Macedonia. Yet we <u>urge</u> you, brothers, to do so more and more."** (1 Thes 4:10).

> **"And we <u>urge</u> you brothers, warn those who are idle, encourage the timid, help the weak, be patient with everyone"** (1 Thes 5:14).

The Greek word for "urge" means, literally, "to call alongside of." It is often used of one calling out for the aid of another. With tender, begging cries. Notice what Paul was earnestly urging the Thessalonians to do. Because God is urging you similarly:

- In 4:1 - to live always from <u>one motive</u> – to please God
- In 4:10 - to continue showing unexpected and lavish love to all believers in their entire region of Macedonia. Paul begged them just to do this more and more.

- In 5:14 - the idle urgently needed to be warned, while the timid urgently needed to be encouraged and the weak, to be helped. All required patience. We might want to admonish everyone BUT love knows how best to communicate. Some need sharp warning because they are playing with fire. Those clinging to the patronage system were wanting to receive rather than to give. Love needed to shake them up. But not so for the others. Love watches and listens. Love takes time to understand. If we admonish the timid or the weak, we might discourage them and actually harm them.

Paul had mentored them well in how love looked under different and often difficult circumstances. **"For you know we dealt with each of you as a father deals with his own children, encouraging, comforting and urging you to live lives worthy of God, who calls you into his kingdom and glory"** (1 Thes 2:12). He raised his spiritual children to trust and obey Jesus immediately. And that is what the Thessalonians did. Will you?

We are finished. It is now your turn. How will you respond to this book? Inflamed by the Spirit of Love to begin making a difference today? Or checking another Christian book off your list of "must reads" as you plod forward in your Christian life? Returning to a life lacking passion, excitement and fruitfulness.

No, I am sure God is at work in you. His own love filling your heart. By the power of his Spirit. I believe you will respond as you can and should respond. By opening your hearts to the fire of love! Just like the Amazing Thessalonians did. Who, when they later saw Paul again, had some urging of their own to do. Some earnest begging about love that astonished the apostle. He wrote, **"They urgently pleaded with us for the privilege of sharing in this service to the saints."** (2 Cor 8:4).

The urgent love in Paul sparked the same urgent love in others. And that amazing love that filled the Thessalonians so they could reach their region against all odds, can reach our world today. Because it is the love of God, himself. All powerful. Ever patient. Unstoppable. Victorious love. Flowing through you. Let everyone be amazed at the truth that has amazed us all: **"For God so loved the world that he gave his one and only Son"** (John 3:16a). God loved the world greatly and, therefore, gave a great gift for it. Jesus. Let him continue loving the world through you. Amen.

For Reflection and Discussion

1. Do you finish this chapter and book with some sense of urgency?
2. If so, what are your next steps in response to such an urgent situation?
3. Please feel free to email me at **ed.gross@comcast.net** and tell me what you have decided to do so I can pray for you and encourage you.

Appendix One
Are You a Christian or a Disciple?

Are you a Christian or a disciple? No, it is not a trick question. The two nouns are different words. Both biblical.[1] Both good. But both coming from very different origins. The Bible amply explains these words and gives us the background we need for rightly understanding and using them today. Please try to remember this: All true disciples are Christians. But not all Christians are true disciples. My goal is to help you see why this is a big deal. And the mess that has resulted from our confusing these words.

Here's a 21st century parable. Let's say Jesus wants to make an apple pie for the Father. So he tells you to go to the market and get him some nice tart Granny Smith apples. When you arrive, you become mesmerized by all the beautiful fruit you see. They are ripe and cheap. You begin to reason… if he likes one fruit, he will like these other types as well. If he can use Granny Smiths, think of the fruit salad he could make from all of these. So you go wild and begin to buy bananas, oranges, kiwi, grapes, pomegranates, mangos and pineapple. Oh yes, you also get some nice Granny Smith apples in case he still wants them when he sees all the other options. And then you return.

What would you think Jesus will say? Well done? Good job? I should have thought of that? This is what I think. Jesus would look at you and say, how can I make an apple pie from these other fruits? My Father loves apple pies and I want to please him. Yes, I know that an apple is a fruit. But not all fruits are apples. Yes, all fruits are good. But I asked you to go and buy apples—one specific kind of fruit—because only apples will produce the pie that my Father desires. You can do whatever you want with the other fruit. They are of no value to my plan. Give me those Granny Smith apples.

Jesus has given the Church a Great Commission. He has clearly told us what we are to do: "Go and make disciples." But, instead we focus on making Christians. What's the big deal, you might ask? Simply this—like the difference between apples and fruit--*all true disciples are Christians*. But *not all Christians are disciples*. He has a very specific goal in mind. The goal that the Father gave him to accomplish. The goal to make disciples. We have a much more general goal. To make Christians. Jesus has commanded us to follow him and make apple pies. We have gone out and chosen rather to make fruit salad.

---

[1] Christianos or Christian(s) is used 3 times in the NT. Matheteis or disciple(s) is used over 250 times.

9 781949 888317